Fallen Angels and Fallen Women

Fallen Angels and Fallen Women

The Mother of the Son of Man

ROBIN JARRELL

WIPF & STOCK · Eugene, Oregon

FALLEN ANGELS AND FALLEN WOMEN
The Mother of the Son of Man

Copyright © 2013 Robin Jarrell. All rights reserved. Except for brief quotations in critical publications or reviews, no part of this book may be reproduced in any manner without prior written permission from the publisher. Write: Permissions, Wipf and Stock Publishers, 199 W. 8th Ave., Suite 3, Eugene, OR 97401.

Wipf & Stock
An imprint of Wipf and Stock Publishers
199 W. 8th Ave., Suite 3
Eugene, OR 97401

www.wipfandstock.com

ISBN 13: 978-1-60899-405-2

Manufactured in the U.S.A.

For Kerry Walters
beati pacifici

Contents

Acknowledgments / ix

Chapter One / 1
Chapter Two / 49
Chapter Three / 86
Chapter Four / 114
Chapter Five / 142

Bibliography / 175
Index / 189

Acknowledgments

I GRATEFULLY ACKNOWLEDGE THE support of K. C. Hanson, whose mentorship guided my initial quest to understand Hagar's theophany in Genesis 16 and whose gift of Margaret Barker's *The Older Testament* continues to enlighten me. I owe a debt to Gregory C. Riley who taught me to trust my work.

I am grateful to the entire staff of Bertrand Library at Bucknell University, including James Van Fleet and Bud Hiller for their invaluable technical assistance. To Mary Neidig, Dan Heuer, Lona Sholly, and especially to Mary Jane Moser, librarian *par excellence*, who routinely went above and beyond the call of duty to assist me with this project.

Thank you to Stephanie Larson, Matthew Adams, and Mia Rikala for personally sharing their scholarship.

To my family who has always given me support: To June and Pod, Robert and Pat, Kelly and Gary, Gaffney and Amos who have lovingly put up with me. And to my "adopted" family whose gifts I cherish: To Sis, Kim, and Nancy.

To Chris Boyatzis, for his expert editorial assistance, and to Sedona, Janine, and Alan who waited patiently while I labored "upstairs" to write this book.

I am especially grateful to my colleague, mentor, and soul-friend Kerry, who continually inspires me with his loving devotion to his craft and who by his faith in action demonstrates that the vocation of writing is indeed a blessed path.

Chapter One

INTRODUCTION

In this chapter, we explore and analyze various myths from ancient Sumer, Ugarit, Egypt, and Greece in an attempt to bring to light those mythological antecedents that form the basis for the mythologies employed by the writers of noncanonical material of Qumran and the composers of the New Testament. We will briefly survey each geographical region in order to investigate those ancient cosmogonies, myths, and stories that function as the foundational background surrounding the highly complex and theologically significant interaction between "fallen" angels found in Genesis 6:4 and the "daughter(s) of men." The ultimate goal of this book is to understand the full significance of the term "daughter of man" (in the singular) and to illuminate more fully the concept that continues to intrigue biblical scholars and those interested in the person of Jesus of Nazareth and his connection to the epithet Son of Man.

Beginning with analysis of the myths of Sumeria, our aim in this chapter is to examine the structures that exist between the divine and human worlds as they are portrayed within the literary genres of both myth and epic. More specifically, we will concern our examination with how these worlds are gendered and how gender dictates the transversal of the boundaries between divine and human.[1] The way in which gendering and

---

1. The anthropologist Edmund Leach is helpful in establishing criteria for examining myths without discounting their religious significance. He also contends that "The central problem of religion is then to re-establish some kind of bridge between Man and God . . . the myth first discriminates between gods and men and then becomes preoccupied with the relations and intermediaries which link men and gods together . . . so too with sex relations . . ." (Leach, *Essential Edmund Leach*, 31). This is the purpose for the chapter.

sexual intercourse occurs (in most mythologies, but not in all) between both divine and human realms forms a trajectory that can be traced from the ancient myths of Sumer, Egypt, Greece, and finally, to the myths of Canaan and Israel. The ideological roots of the myths that include angelic beings, both "fallen" and heavenly, the origin of evil and its association with women, and the spiritual role of gender, are found within the literary mythologies that originate with Sumer.

The focus, therefore, must be on the various sexual aspects of the myths. Such sexual aspects will by necessity include some characteristics of mythologies that posit the preexistence or creation of water, air and breath; the separation of earth and sky; the creation of animals, etc. However, the major purpose of our analysis in this chapter will involve tracing the role of the (created) mortal human's involvement in the sexual "life of the gods." In the mythologies we survey, the concern is not exclusively on the reproductive attributes between human sexual encounters that flow from the original concepts of sexual relationships found in "the image and likeness" of the deity/deities. We are interested in the similarity between the ancient myths and cultures surveyed in establishing a connection between particular themes: (1) the human hope of the promise of immortality, (2) the attainment of (sexual) wisdom, and (3) the participation (either whole or in part) of the human mortal in the actual sexual life of the gods.

For the purposes of our study, a useful definition of myth is in order. Myth may be defined simply as the story (or stories) we tell ourselves about our relationship to all aspects of the divine. Bruce Lincoln has developed a helpful paradigm for classifying not only the genre and type of stories we will be examining but also the manner in which those stories are given power and authority. As he puts it, ". . . we would do better to classify narratives not by their content but by the claims that are made by their narrators and the way in which those claims are received by their audience(s)."[2] Lincoln classifies four narrative types: Fable, Legend, History, and finally Myth—and arranges them in the following taxonomy:

	Truth-claims	Credibility	Authority
Fable	-	-	-
Legend	+	-	-
History	+	+	-
Myth	+	+	+

2. Lincoln, *Discourse and the Construction of Society*, 24.

Lincoln makes the claim that of all the categories listed above, myth is the only classification type that "possesses both credibility and authority" and explains that "a narrative possessed of authority is one for which successful claims are made not only to the status of truth, but what is more, to the status of *paradigmatic* truth."[3]

THE MYTHS OF SUMER

There can be no doubt that the myths and literary stories of Sumer reflect actual correspondences to the civilization's social and economic history. But questions concerning the practical historical role of the mythmakers and their particular motivation in creating the King Lists, or arguments concerning the economic status of historical women and priestesses in Sumer, is not our main focus, although, certainly it will be occasionally helpful.[4] Neither are we concerned with the causal relationship between myth and history, insofar as it seeks to find in myth the source of certain religious practices based on gender, or seeks to find in the history of Sumer the source of myth. We are, instead, relying upon the definition of myth given by the mythmakers themselves and the acceptance of the authority of the myth adhered to by the readers of those myths—and the ultimate *paradigmatic truth* that the myth seeks to convey.

Gwendolyn Leick's interest in the erotic elements of the Sumerian myths permits her to observe that "unlike the Greeks, Mesopotamian writers did not describe some of their literary works as 'myths,' and they did not set out to compose 'cosmogonies,'" that is, those myths whose "concepts are worked into a coherent theory to account for the primary dynamics of the universe..."[5] Nevertheless, Leick understands that while the ancient Mesopotamians may not have assigned the appellation 'myth' to the story of the origins of the universe, modern scholarship does classify the various literary works of Mesopotamia into different genres.

---

3. Ibid. Emphasis in the original.

4. The kings of Sumer were known to have claimed "to have personal relations with the gods," but such claims come from documents not classified as literary myth but as inscriptions on literary stele. The ruler seeking legitimacy usually proclaims himself the "human offspring" of a god who is treated theologically as a "metaphorical parent" to the future king (Leick, *Sex and Eroticism*, 102). For an excellent treatment on historical women of Mesopotamia and gender, see (Bahrani, *Women of Babylon*) and also (Toorn, *From Her Cradle to Her Grave*).

5. Leick, *Sex and Eroticism*, 11.

Most modern scholars studying ancient Mesopotamia use a multidisciplinary approach (usually from the fields of anthropology, sociology, and biblical scholarship) to the interpretation of the myths of Sumer (and later variants found in Akkadian literature.) Bendt Alster is among the few Sumerologists who has expressly articulated an overarching "theory of myth," especially as it pertains to "myths of origins."[6] Avoiding questions pertaining to the "truth value" of the myths of Sumer, Alster points out that in Sumerian literary genres, there is a "categorical world order in which gods or men act as they do because they must."[7] The myths of Sumer present the reader with a vast range of metaphor and meaning—with the more sophisticated elements lost to us by due to the chasm of time and culture—that separates the modern reader from the ancient composer.

Using the popular Sumerian myth *Inanna's Descent to the Netherworld*, Alster points to the modern reader's quandary in comprehending the myth's "complete absence of motivation behind [the goddess] Inanna's decision to leave her cities for the underworld."[8] The impulse for the character development in various points of the Epic of Gilgamesh seems "literary rather than psychological."[9]

In Sumerian cosmological origin myths, creation begins—not ex nihilo—but from some *prima materia*.[10] Sexual reproduction is always the main focus of such stories. The creation of the world begins with a singular or unitary god (usually but not always female) who must be differentiated into a binary and gendered set of gods, both male and female, who reproduce in order to beget other deities, often taking take the form of the primal elements: earth, sky, water, etc.[11]

This binary paring is essential to the ordering of the Sumerian universe. The cosmological relationship between deity and created human,

---

6. Alster, "Enki and Ninhursag," 19ff. For an anthropological view, see "On Scholastic Nonsense: Myth and History" and "Holy Families: The Structure of Mythic Thought" in Leach, *Essential Edmund Leach*.

7. Alster, "Lugalbanda," 62.

8. Ibid. The myth has similarities to the Greek Homeric "Hymn to Demeter" which tells the story of Kore's (or Persephone's) abduction by Hades to the Underworld. For a translation of the myth, see Dalley, *Myths from Mesopotamia*, 154.

9. Mitchell, *Gilgamesh: A New English Version*, 26.

10. Leick, *Sex and Eroticism*, 12.

11. See Leick, *Sex and Eroticism*; Bendt, "Enki and Ninhursag"; Dickson, "Enki and Ninhursag."

Chapter One

however, is far less certain. Almost none of the scholarly literature focuses extensively on the transversal of the sacred and inviolate boundary between divine and human by means of sexual intercourse, both reproductive and nonreproductive.[12] We will examine the transversal of such divine/human boundaries in the case of certain demigods such as Lugalbanda and Gilgamesh. And we also discuss the boundary transversal process by which the gods bestow their imprimatur of kingship to their human servants, who are not of divine heritage but who are adopted by the gods for the very human purpose of ruling and administration.[13]

Sumerian myths of origin reveal an overarching focus on combat (where the world comes into existence through the divine's ability to vanquish chaos).[14] But there are other typologies that exist in Sumerian cosmogonies. Creation of the world may extend from the activities of the deity who inundates the earth with water (the chthonic myth).[15] The water used by Sumerian god Enki (who is the god of water and one of the creator gods in the Sumerian pantheon) in *Enki and Ninhursaga* may allude to a third type of creation myth—the marriage typology.[16]

In the earliest forms of Sumerian creation typologies, the unitary creator exists in a timeless and sexless state. The unitary becomes binary and sex occurs between the binary pair for the purposes of reproduction. With one rare exception, "the gods do not speak of love or emotion . . . the texts instead emphasize that male orgasm is an act of creation."[17] This

---

12. Dickson discusses "boundary crossings" of the god Enki (in the myth of Enki and Ninhursaga) solely in the divine realm and not as it pertains to humans. See Dickson, "Enki and Ninhursag."

13. The adoption of humans by the Deity for the purpose of kingship occurs also in Israel, for example, in Psalm 2:7.

14. See Forsyth, *Old Enemy*.

15. Daise, *Biblical Creation Motifs*, 300.

16. Translated from Kramer Maier in Leick, *Sex and Eroticism*, 31. In Enki and Ninhursaga, creation begins with the sexual union between heaven and earth since Enki's promise to provide the origins of the city of Dilmun with "sweet fresh ponds" include his "phallus fill[ing] the ditches with semen." Leick also notes that "the double meaning of the Sumerian sign 'a' [can denote] 'sperm' as well as 'water'" (39). There could also be a fourth type of Sumerian/Mesopotamian creation motif—that of creation from the elements of earth (clay, etc.) through the craftmanship of the deity—who may also use the blood of slain "evil" and/or chaos-like deities—for instance, in the Enuma Elish, Marduk creates the universe from the corpse of Tiamat and the blood of Quingu. See Dalley, *Myths from Mesopotamia*, 4.

17. Leick, *Sex and Eroticism*, 55. In the myth of Enki and Ninhursaga, Ninhursaga impregnates herself with Enki's semen. Enki deceives Ninhursaga and has sex with

5

sheer act of reproduction results in the concomitant creation of "time," since there must necessarily be temporal space for the introduction of offspring into the world of the creator gods.[18]

There is an elemental relationship in the mythological texts of Sumer between the sexual reproductive aspects and behavior of the gods and the transmission of the ability for humans to mimic godlike sexuality. In the beginning, humans presumably have sex for procreative and pleasurable purposes since the gods who created them do.[19] In the same way, when humans are first created (the exact reason is not altogether clear in most Sumerian cosmogonies),[20] they are immortal. The immortality of humans is threatened when, due to human overpopulation—the din of humans reaches heaven and disturbs the sleep of the deities. The gods are then forced to create demons (sickness and disease) to truncate the length of human life.[21] The immortal life of humans first given by the gods is now curtailed. So, too, the sexual life of humans first given by the gods is then presumably circumscribed into categories that include productive sex (within the construct of marriage) and nonproductive sex (within the construct of prostitution). The question remains: why do the deities create death to solve the problem of human overpopulation instead of modifying the reproductive outcome of human sexuality? The Sumerian ethos of human sexuality is apparently modeled on that of the gods, but the myths describe evidence to suggest a connection between human sexuality and human mortality.

---

his first daughter, his offspring, and this sequence continues.

18. The creation of time gives way to the chaos of birth, which is not painful for Sumerian female deities (Dickson, "Enki and Ninhursag," 12). Whether we can make a distinction between the painful birth of humans in the Genesis story and the easy birth of the Sumerian female deities will be discussed later.

19. As Leick notes, "Mesopotamian systems have a strong anthropomorphic component and with this conceptual framework the most persistent pattern is that of sexual reproduction" (*Sex and Eroticism*, 12).

20. See Bottéro, *Religion in Ancient Mesopotamia*, 98, who remarks that in the Mesopotamian legends "the eternal question, 'why do human beings exist?' appears in few mythological writings" with the exception of the Atrahasis myth.

21. In the Gilgamesh epic, however, the tavern keeper Shiduri tells Gilgamesh, "You will not find the eternal life you seek. / When the gods created mankind / They appointed death for mankind, / Kept eternal life in their own hands" (Dalley, *Myths from Mesopotamia*, 150).

Chapter One

CROSSING THE BOUNDARY BETWEEN HEAVEN AND EARTH IN SUMERIAN MYTHOLOGY

The ancient Mesopotamian worldview maintained a distinct boundary between heaven and earth, as well as a definite boundary between divine and human. The creation myths of Sumer and later Mesopotamia are populated with deities, but these ancient mythologies give only a very minor role to humans. With the exception of the Atrahasis epic (the Sumerian flood story) and the Inanna-Sukaletuda myth, "mortals play little role in the Sumerian myths."[22] The Epic of Gilgamesh also seems to be a mythic exception. The Sumerian stories posit an etiology of human origins and life in the role of the beginning of things within the world containing both deity and few mortals. Yet this world, as well as the interaction between them, is carefully gendered.

The Inanna-Sukaletuda myth offers descriptive insight into the gendered blurring of the sacred boundaries of divine and human. The myth recounts the travels of the goddess Inanna through land of Sumer. She falls asleep in the garden of the boy Sukaletuda who takes sexual advantage of the goddess as she sleeps. Upon awakening, Inanna vows to determine who violated her and sends plagues upon the land. Her first, and most symbolic plague, is to turn all water from springs and wells into blood. She, in turn, sends a flood, a sandstorm, and finally blocks all trade roads. Throughout the devastation, Sukaletuda remains undiscovered. Inanna turns to the sun god Shamash for recourse and decides instead to ask recompense from her father, the god Enki. Enki manages to dispel all the plagues visited upon the humans so that only Sukaletuda is affected. Inanna at last decides his fate by changing him into a frog.[23]

A closer analysis of the myth reveals details concerning the complex interplay between deity and mortal. As the "queen of all of the important ME (spiritual powers)"[24] wanders over the earth recognizing "falsehoods

---

22. Kramer, *Sumerians*, 163.

23. The story is also recounted in the Epic of Gilgamesh.

24. The Sumerian MEs are an intrinsic part of the Sumerian understanding in maintaining an orderly civilization connected to the divine. Some were actual physical objects, such as musical instruments, and some were concepts, such as "truth" or technologies like "basket weaving." Not all MEs were positive—some MEs included concepts such as "falsehood" and "destruction of cities." See Kramer, "Blood Plague Motif." Leick describes ME as "divine perogatives" (*Sex and Eroticism*, 26). The poem "Enki and the World Order" describes how Inanna took the MEs from Enki and brought them triumphantly into the city of Uruk (the city later ruled over by Gilgamesh).

and injustice," weary Inanna takes her repose in the garden of Sukaletuda.[25] Before she sleeps, she covers her vulva with the ribbon of the seven ME. Sukaletuda sees the goddess, removes the ribbon of the seven ME, and proceeds to "sleep with" and "kiss" Inanna as she sleeps. When Inanna wakes, Sukaletuda has fled and the goddess notices immediately that something is profoundly amiss:

> The woman looked at herself.
> The silvery Inanna looked at herself,
> Oh, the ruin this woman caused, because of the shame she felt now.[26]

The poem is clear on three points: Inanna's initial response upon awaking is to take notice of her body, to "look at herself," and to "feel shame." All her resulting plagues are sent forth as a direct and swift response to her "shame," but it is not clear how the ribbons of the seven ME are connected with Inanna's understanding of this "shame." Inanna's response seems initially to suggest that she believes she has been sexually violated without her consent or knowledge. Perhaps it is not only sexual violation that enrages Inanna, but also possibly Sukaletuda's failure (or inability) to return the ribbon of the seven ME to its original and proper placement on the body of the goddess, for in "looking at herself," in noticing her body, Inanna can "see" that the seven ME are not in their original place. What is certain is that "shame" is connected in some way with Inanna's destructive rage:

> What has the silvery Inanna done because of the shame she felt now.
> She fills the wells of the land (Sumer) with blood.
> She fills the wells of the land (Sumer) with blood;
> You let a servant leave to fetch firewood: he drinks blood.
> You let a servant leave to get water: she ladles blood.
> It is blood that the blackhaired people drink.[27]

Kramer sees Inanna's "blood plagues" as the metaphorical blood of the goddess' defloration which she sends as consequence of the "mortal sin" of the gardener Sukaletuda in order that she might "ferret out at all

---

25. As Inanna wanders her land "recognizing falsehood and injustice," she shows a similarity to the Egyptian goddess of truth, Maat. I am using Volk, *Inanna und Sukaletuda*, 125.

26. Volk, *Inanna und Sukaletuda*, 128.

27. Ibid.

costs the mortal who has so shamefully abused her."[28] Kramer also suggests that there may be a connection between this story with its "blood plague motif" and earlier mythic material possibly available to the writers of the book of Exodus.[29] I agree that Kramer is correct in his assessment that Inanna's changing water into blood is a fitting, if excessive, punishment sent to the mortal who caused her "shame." Why does the goddess of war not send among her plagues earthquake, fire, or famine?

It is also possible that the blood Inanna sends is somehow connected with "the defloration of the goddess . . . and that the rivers being filled with blood . . . represent . . . [the goddess'] blood."[30] I would similarly argue that the blood of Inanna is not the blood of defloration. In myths such as *Enki and Ninhursaga* and *Enlil and Ninlil*, the point is "precisely not to dwell on erotic preliminaries and the enjoyment of the female partner, but to focus on the result, the impregnation."[31] While there are poems that center upon the pleasure of the female during sex, the prevailing motif is one that assigns "the phallus . . . to reproductive sexuality and, by extension, to water-based fertility."[32] This motif is also present in the Epic of Gilgamesh, which "portrays sex and love as types of human knowledge . . . once this knowledge is attained, continued non-productive sex is no longer acquisition of knowledge . . . but characteristic of the street, or, at worst, reversion to the animal state."[33]

If it is the case that the Sumerian myths divide sexual encounters between "productive" and "nonproductive," then the reason for the goddess' plague of menstrual blood becomes clear.[34] In *Inanna and Sukaletuda*, sex that would result in reproduction would be viewed as morally and spiritually superior to sex that is merely for pleasure—especially pleasure denied to a sleeping goddess. Punishment using menstrual blood is Inanna's unmistakable sign, especially to Sukaletuda, that his virility is highly suspect. Her menstrual flow is proof that he is not able provide the goddess with offspring. Moreover, the goddess seems resolute in her attempt to punish Sukaletuda not only for his sexual violation of her, but for the

---

28. Kramer, *Sumerians*, 400–2).
29. Ibid., 405.
30. Leick, *Sex and Eroticism*, 53.
31. Ibid., 50.
32. Ibid., 54.
33. Foster, "Gilgamesh: Sex, Love," 22.
34. So Foster argues, but Leick does not agree entirely.

merest hint of touching or handling the MEs with the possible intent to steal them. Having the ability to place his hands on the MEs of the goddess suggests to Inanna how fragile her hard won confiscation of the MEs originally belonging to her father Enki truly is.[35] Even though Sukaletuda is able to violate the body of the goddess for his own sexual pleasure, he cannot impregnate her. This does not necessarily mean that perforating the boundary between mortal and goddess in *Inanna and Sukaletuda* is perceived as immoral by the poet (and one would presume also by the Sumerian reader). Perhaps the poet wishes to convey as morally suspect the sexual violation of male against female. The poem is interwoven with complicated mores attached to both the divine and human spheres: Inanna is preoccupied with her status as goddess and clearly enjoys her role as a female—especially as a goddess of war. Her shame and resulting anger seem to be a direct result of the seven ribbons of the ME and their (dis)placement on her vulva. Sukaletuda is preoccupied not only with his sexual arousal for the female goddess as a male, but also by his garden's scarcity and lack of fecundity, which as a human he hopes the divine goddess can alleviate. Ultimately, the poem raises important questions for Sumerians in their cosmogonies and mythologies concerning concepts surrounding possible divine origins for the human struggle between the genders as well as sanctioning (or at least permitting) sexual relationships between divine entities and mortal humans.

THE DIVINE-MORTAL CONTINUUM

In the ancient Sumerian example *Inanna and Sulkaletuda*, a female goddess engages in sexual activity with a human male. There is no direct literary evidence uncovered thus far for such a sexual transaction between a male god and a mortal woman. Even the ritualized sexual contact known as the "sacred marriage" occurs between the (male) ruler a (female and human) representation of the goddess Inanna/Ishtar.

Many scholars have questioned the existence of an actual ritualized cult known as "sacred marriage." Three hymns composed during the Ur III dynasty are "commonly supposed to provide evidence that the relationship of the king and the goddess as husband and wife was represented in a visible ritual, with the role of Inanna enacted by a mortal woman."[36]

35. The story of how Inanna steals the ME's is found in *Enki and the World Order*.
36. Sweet, "New Look," 95.

But the hymns in question are not a genre used to establish and sustain heavenly cosmogonies in the same way as myths of origin or mythic poems. Even if these hymns demonstrate a mythological equivalent to "as in heaven, so on earth," the coupling of a mortal woman (representing the goddess Inanna) with the human king does not mitigate the absence of literary instances where a god crosses the diving-human boundary to engage in sexual activity with a mortal women, no matter what her hierarchical status—royal queen or sacred tavern keeper. It is certainly the case that "some rulers claimed to have personal relations with the gods."[37] But while "fatherhood of [Sumerian Kings by the] gods is also well-documented," all are physical inscriptions on victory stele proclaiming the legitimacy of a king as the "human offspring" of a god who is his "metaphorical parent," and are not classified as literary myths.[38]

The period referred to as the dynasty of Ur III saw a revitalization in the office of EN (a priestly office) by the king to the goddess Inanna. Originally the Sumerian pantheon was "dominated by female deities," but the domain of governance was exercised through male kingship and thus the role of male EN became solely the prerogative of the king.[39] The EN was "traditionally always occupied by a person whose gender was complementary to that of the deity served," with Inanna having a male EN and the mood-god Nanna a female EN.[40] And it is possible that the relationship between the EN and the deity was an erotic one. However, there were no ruling queens in Sumer or later Akkad, and there is no extant literary myth extolling the moon-god Nanna's relationship to his mortal EN. The most famous female EN, the poet Enheduanna, was EN to the goddess Inanna, but was stripped of her office after her father the king's death.[41]

There are also geographical differences in the kind of patronage extended from gods within the boundaries of their various city-states. At Elba (in the north), there is a preponderance of "female consorts [associated with] male deities, in the form of DAM.DINGIR priestesses."[42] This phenomenon actually predates the priestess/poet/princess Enhueduana,

37. Leick, *Sex and Eroticism*, 102.
38. Ibid.
39. Steinkeller, "On Rulers, Priests, and Sacred Marriage," 113.
40. Leick, *Sex and Eroticism*, 108.
41. Scholars debate whether Pu-Abi, whose tomb from the first dynasty of Ur was discovered by Sir Leonard Wolley in 1922, was that of a queen or priestess.
42. Steinkeller, "On Rulers, Priests, and Sacred Marriage," 123.

"the first recorded consort of [the moon god] Nanna" and it may be the case that "the custom of providing male deities with human female consorts, who most commonly were royal princesses, represented a genuine Semitic tradition."[43]

As the Sumerian pantheon grew more masculinized, and the religious centers dominated by goddesses became ruling centers dominated by kings, the role and function of the EN shifted so that only one particular gender was able to function in the role of EN. This change of gender is not retroactively attached to previous myths of origin nor does the Sumerian literature seem to overtly rewrite its cosmogonies, but by the time of Herodotus, we have his description of a ritual of sacred marriage where there is some evidence (even if not literary) that a male god crosses the boundary between heaven and earth and has sex with a human woman. At a later period, Herodotus relates the presence of a human female in the ceremony as "one Assyrian woman, all alone, whoever it may be that the [Assyrian] god [Bel/Marduk] has chosen."[44] The gendered exchange between human king and human woman as representing the female goddess seems to be the norm for Sumer but there is no mythological evidence for a sexual relationship between a male god and a female human.[45]

This sacred marriage rite (as it as portrayed in Sumer between king and goddess) may not have been enacted for the production of an heir but was instead intended "to foster a reciprocal relationship between men and gods" since the "concerns" of the patronage, governance, and fertility of the gods is the reason "gods were created by men in the first place."[46] But attention to the significance for the particular gendering of the arrangement between deity and human is obscured by this sort of sociological explanation. It may provide some rationale for the sexual relationships between deities but does not provide a locus for tracing the development of the phenomena that will be our ultimate concern: an ancient mythological foundation for the occurrence of male gods/deities departing the divine world they inhabit in order to engage in sexual relationships with human mortal women.

The entire concept of "sacred marriage" has even been called into question by some scholars who suggest that "the sacred marriage ritual

43. Ibid.
44. Quoted in Ibid., 134.
45. Sweet, "New Look,"102).
46. Steinkeller, "On Rulers, Priests, and Sacred Marriage," 136).

itself should be considered . . . one way of objectifying the divine-human sexual metaphor."[47] Beate Pongratz-Leisten has suggested classifying "sacred marriage" into several forms: "cosmogamy: the union between the cosmic elements of Heaven and Earth; hierogamy: the union between a goddess and a king; [and] theogamy: the union between a god and a goddess."[48] I would suggest that the classification labeled "hierogamy" should be analyzed in further detail to include another (but parallel) aspect of the divine-human metaphor as it pertains to Sumerian mythology: the union between a goddess and a male mortal who is not royal, or who is not (yet) a king. This particular element of the divine-human sexual interaction will be examined more fully in the pages that follow.

THE PRECURSOR TO GILGAMESH

One other significant example in Sumerian myth describes more fully another possible aspect of Pongratz-Liesten's "hierogamy." The story of the hero Gilgamesh is well known, but the legacy of his father Lugalbanda has received far less attention, despite the similarities of his mythology to his more famous son. According to Alster, the plot of the Lugalbanda epics is concerned with the succession of kings in early Sumerian history.[49] Lugalbanda will eventually become the divinized king of Uruk, the city that will later be ruled by Gilgamesh. He is the subject of two early epics: *Lugalbanda in Hurrumkura* and *Lugalbanda and Enmerkar*.[50]

Lugalbanda is a cultural hero whose heroic journey marks early theological attempts by Sumerian poets to navigate the complex and intricate world of sexual relationships between deities and humans and the resulting the fate of their jointly produced offspring. Lugalbanda ("little lord") as he is described in *Lugalbanda and Enmerkar* is "eighth" in a line of sons descended from "the goddess Urash and a 'nobleman,'" sons who become leaders in the army of Enmerkar—an historical king who is found on the Sumerian King List and credited with the building of

---

47. Nissinen and Uro, *Sacred Marriages*, 3.

48. See Pongratz-Leisten, "Sacred Marriage and the Transfer of Divine Knowledge" in Nissinen and Uro, *Sacred Marriages*, 44.

49. According to Alster, the Lugalbanda epics also suggest trajectories and parallels similar to the Old Testament and noncanonical literature. See Alster, "Lugalbanda," 60ff. See also, Shields, "To Seek but Not to Find."

50. So named by Alster ("Lugalbanda," 63).

the city of Uruk.[51] Lugalbanda proves himself a clever and noble leader. In one tradition, Lugalbanda becomes the protector of the city of Uruk his son allegedly builds.[52] In the later Epic of Gilgamesh, Lugalbanda becomes the father of Gilgamesh by marrying the goddess Ninsum.

In the person of Lugalbanda, we are presented with another example of a female goddess coupling with a male (mortal) "nobleman," but in contrast with the example in *Inanna and Sukaletuda*, the sexual interaction between goddess and human results in the production of a male offspring. The divinized status of Lugalbanda does not affect his mortality even though he is descended from the goddess Urash. Even in some versions where Lugalbanda is divinized by Gilgamesh, he does not become immortal. Gilgamesh is also not fated to be immortal despite being the offspring of a goddess and the partially divine hero/human Lugalbanda.[53]

Within the Sumerian mythological literature we may classify at least three types of divine/human sexual interactions:

Divine/Mortal interaction	Example in Sumerian Literature
goddess – male mortal | son/hero	Urash and male 'nobleman' Ninsun and Lugalbanda
goddess – male mortal | no offspring	Inanna and Sukadetuda Ishtar and gardener Inshullanu (told in the Gilgamesh Epic)
god – goddess | gods and goddesses	The Sumerian Pantheon
god – female mortal	No examples

51. Alster, "Lugalbanda," 65.

52. Mitchell, *Gilgamesh: A New English Version*, 288.

53. It may, however, give some insight into why in the epic Gilgamesh is said to be two-thirds divine. The mother of Gilgamesh, Ninsum (goddess Lady Wild Cow) is a full goddess and his father Lugalbanda is descended from a human father and the goddess Urash. See Dalley, *Myths from Mesopotamia*, 40. This particular percentage of Gilgamesh's divinity is intriguing and unlike the Greek system, which allows for offspring of male gods and female mortals. Mitchell suggests that Gilgamesh's divine/human ratio may be connected to the figure of Urshankabi—the boatman who sails across the waters of death. Urshankabi's name means "Servant of Two-Thirds," a reference to Ea, the god of water "whose symbolic numerical value was 40, two-thirds of Anu's 60" (Mitchell, *Gilgamesh: A New English Version*, 290). An/u was the first offspring of the first pair of primeval gods and father of all the pantheon.

In the Sumerian cosmogony, when divine beings interact sexually with humans, the divine beings are always female and the humans are always male. Even if, as in the case of the goddess Inanna, there is sexual interaction with a human male, the production of offspring is not guaranteed and may be hopeless from the start.[54] But for "lesser" goddesses (who are not immediate offspring of An/u and/or are more maternal) such as Urash (as in the case of Lugalbanda) and Nimsun (as in the case of Gilgamesh), when there is sexual interaction with a human male, offspring may be produced. Whenever offspring are born of a goddess, they are always male and they retain the status of mortal. As far as we can determine from the literary evidence, there are no examples of any male gods in the Sumerian and later Akkadian pantheon crossing the divine boundary to have sexual interactions with human women.[55]

THE MYTHS OF UGARIT

Since the discovery of the texts in Ras Shamra in 1928, the Ugaritic Pantheon and the stories of gods such as Baal and Anath/Astarte are now famous.[56] The mythologies of the ancient Canaanite city-state of Ugarit have greatly expanded our understanding of the myth and literature of early Israel and the Hebrew Scripture. These "ancient cosmogonies were interested in the emergence of society, organized with patron gods and worship systems, divinely appointed kings or leaders [and], kinship and marriage systems."[57] The cosmogonies of Ugarit reflect a similarly gendered "'world' of men and women" created to serve the gods. In Ugarit, as in Sumer, the world of humans mirrors the divine world.[58]

In Ugaritic mythology, divine and human worlds are gendered because "the ancients . . . wished to explain or legitimate elements of their

---

54. Possibly Inanna's warlike nature prevents her from any kind of maternal role.

55. While the god Enki in "Enki and Ninhursaga" is almost predatory in his sexual interactions, he does not cross the divine/mortal boundary. His sexual intercourse is only with goddesses. Two excellent analyses of this myth can be found in Dickson, "Enki and Ninhursag" and Leick, *Sex and Eroticism*.

56. The scholarship on how the texts of Ras Shamra have affected biblical studies is vast. For scholarship on Ugaritic myth and its influence on the early Israelites as it pertains particularly to the sexuality of the gods and fertility, see Worden, "Literary Influence of the Ugaritic" and Colless, "Ba'al's Relations."

57. Clifford, "Cosmogonies in the Ugaritic Texts," 187.

58. Ibid.

world."⁵⁹ With the exception of the *Aqhat* and *Kirta* epics (where Baal "provides children to human progenitors"), the gods of Ugarit do not interact with humans.⁶⁰ In the seasonal *Baal/Anat Cycle*, for example, humans do not even appear. When Baal, as a divine being, does interact with humans, it is for the sole purpose of granting to humans the gift of fertility—the god provides "acts of assistance to [infertile] humans."⁶¹ He does not interact sexually with those humans. No god of Ugarit ever sexually crosses the boundary separating immortal and mortal.

The gods of Ugarit "perform no unseemly sexual acts," presumably with one another, but certainly not with humans.⁶² The head of the Ugaritic pantheon, the father of the gods El, displays what some commentators describe as sexual prowess with two immortal "maidens" in the poem *The Birth of The Gracious Gods*—additional evidence for gendered sexual interaction between the gods and goddesses of Ugarit, but not between gods and humans.⁶³

Also missing from the epics of Ugarit are associations made by the Sumerians and later inhabitants of Mesopotamia between human sexuality and human mortality. As we have seen previously in the Sumerian literature, the gods alone are immortal and humans (although in some versions once created with immortality) are fated to die—stories such as the Epic of Gilgamesh afford us a glimpse into the Sumerian vexation with human death, as we shall explore in further detail. Conversely in Ugarit, there is only a vague cosmogony of human mortality and much more extensive preoccupation with the mortality of the god Baal. Baal alone among the gods, associated with life and fertility and presumed to be as immortal as the rest of the Ugaritic pantheon, struggles at the hands the god associated with death and infertility (Mot/death) and ultimately loses the fight. While Mot/death "admits frankly . . . that he is an enemy of the human race" with an insatiable appetite for human mortals, the

---

59. Ibid.

60. Greenstein, "God of Israel and the Gods of Canaan," 50.

61. Ibid., 53.

62. Ibid. On the possbility that Anat sexually propositions the human Aqhat, see Ackerman, *When Heroes Love*, 61 n. 35. For a dissenting view, see Day, "Anat," 183.

63. For an excellent state of the argument for El's sexual prowess, or if the episode in the poem with the two maidens may be termed a "sacred marriage," see "Sacred Marriage in the Ugaritic Texts? The Case of KTU/CAT 1.23 (Rituals and the Myths of the Goodly Gods)" in Nissinen and Uro, *Sacred Marriages*, 93–113. See also Smith and Parker, *Ugaritic Narrative Poetry*, 205ff.

focus in Ugarit is not on the origin(s) of human death, but on the death of the god Baal—the self-proclaimed protector of mortals.[64]

It may be possible that the Ugaritic focus on death through the actions of a god created as immortal reflects an all-too-human understanding of the inevitability of the human condition since "the fertility that makes human life possible is precarious; death dealing infertility is always on the horizon."[65] Equating death for mortals to infertility is parallel to the mythological themes of Sumer. Death is the created state for humans in the myths of Ugarit whereas death in Mesopotamian myth is imposed on humans by the gods. Ugaritic myth does not concern itself with any other aspect of human sexual life, other than equating infertility with death. Death in Ugarit connects the failure to reproduce with the end of life. In this way, human sexuality and human mortality are tangentially related, but not with the complexity found in Sumerian mythology.

Both texts of Sumer and of Ugarit value the fertility of humans in the production of offspring to better serve the gods. Both texts have gendered divinity. Mythological texts from Ugarit seem to value human sexuality resulting in offspring and say nothing of human sexuality devoted to pleasure alone.[66] The epics of Ugarit do not make any distinction between "productive" and "nonproductive" sex commonly found in the Sumerian literature. There is no mention of gods or goddesses of Ugarit blurring the boundary between divine and human to form a sexual relationship. The gods of Ugarit are concerned only with the fertility of humans who are created to serve them—they have no interest in any other form of human sexual activity. Connections between sex, death, and knowledge (found in the Sumerian literature and discussed more fully below) are absent from the texts of Ugarit.

THE MYTHS OF EGYPT

The various cosmogonies of the ancient Egyptians are filled with gender ambiguity. In the Heliopolian myth cycle, while it is the male creator Atum who brings the world into being through the act of masturbation, "the very nature of the universe exists as a gendered metaphor, and the

---

64. Clifford, "Cosmogonies in the Ugaritic Texts," 195.

65. Ibid.

66. Sumerian mythology is much more nuanced on both the pleasurable aspects of the sexualites of both gods and humans. See Leick, *Sex and Eroticism*.

creator god [has] within him both the male and female potential."⁶⁷ The Egyptians, as all the ancient myths discussed thus far, understood the divine beings as having "specific gender traits . . . sometimes those gender traits could be ambiguous . . . including the physical appearance of both male and female genitalia."⁶⁸ The ancient goddess Neith, for example, "is sometimes described as 'the man who acts as a woman and a woman who acts as a man.'"⁶⁹

Like the earlier Sumerian and Mesopotamian creation stories, "the creation of humanity does not have a central position in Egyptian myth. Some creation accounts omit humans altogether."⁷⁰ The pantheon of Egyptian gods and goddesses does not sexually transgress the boundary between divine and human. Divine "gender ambiguity" does however pervade the very nature and work of the gods, not only in acts of creation, but most especially in the significant role the deities play in the formation of the afterlife for humans within the complex theological process known as rebirth.⁷¹

The method and objective of rebirth required all Egyptian rulers upon their death to become divine by being incorporated into the deity Osiris. Because "rebirth required both male and female [deities], androgyny was essential where creation was attributable to only one entity, such as a primeval god without a partner, or a king wishing to identify with a primeval god. It was also necessary for female rebirth where the woman needed to become the male god, Osiris" in attaining the afterlife.⁷² For mortals, access to the afterlife, while certainly constrained by status (such as profession or condition of royalty), was not hindered by gender.⁷³

---

67. Onstine, "Gender and the Religion of Ancient Egypt," 2.

68. Ibid.

69. Ibid. Interestingly, the goddess Neith is also described as "2/3 masculine and 1/3 feminine"—the same ratio given to the hero Gilgamesh in his status as two-thirds human and one-third divine.

70. Pinch, *Egyptian Mythology*, 66.

71. Graves-Brown, *Dancing for Hathor*, 104.

72. Even in the ruler's titulary, or list of divine epithets, royal titles conflate the king with gods and goddesses and, in the rare case where there is a royal title of queen, with the gods and goddesses as well (Graves-Brown, *Dancing for Hathor*, 104). Graves-Brown notes that the first woman Queen of Egypt, Queen Sobekneferu "carried the full king's titulary" and "was only one of two female kings to use the epithet *nb irt-ht* ('Lord of doing things'), the other being Hapshetsut" (*Dancing for Hathor*, 145).

73. The attainment of the afterlife was obviously available primarily to royalty and those connected with royalty by virtue of their profession or access to royalty—or at

Chapter One

The mythic literature of ancient Egypt primarily concerns itself with the nature and workings of the gods and with the process by which royal humans are divinized through the path of rebirth. There is virtually no sexual intercourse between the gods and their created humans apart from very specific exceptions that occur for the purposes of maintaining dynastic stability or for the legitimization of a particular ruler's sovereignty.

During the Twelfth Dynasty (Second Intermediate Period) there is preserved on the Papyrus Westcar (Papyrus Berlin 3033) a Divine Birth Cycle composed in order to sanction the transition of political power that took place between Fourth and Fifth dynasties (2686–2181 BCE).[74] The story of the divine birth of the rulers Userkaf, Sahure, and Neferirkare is a foundational political mythos—"an archetype . . . created during the Fifth Dynasty as a type of theological motivation intended for the seizing of power by people from outside the royal family."[75] In the narrative, the succeeding rulers of the Fifth Dynasty are not merely the children "of the pharaoh and his wife, but rather represented the fruit of the union of the pharaoh's first wife with a god."[76]

More famous is iconic legitimization of Queen Hatshepsut's "kingship" created a thousand years after the Papyrus Berlin and inscribed as a set of pictorial reliefs on the walls of her temple in Deir el-Bahari. Because Hatshepsut was required to make such an extraordinary claim for legitimacy (John van Seters remarks that "no other reign is so filled with propaganda") she refashioned the earlier fifth dynastic supernatural birth narrative and crafted it to further her own political purposes.[77] The fifteen stone carvings are sequential scenes narrated as a kind of "play" and describe "in an unusually suggestive manner . . . the conception and birth of the pharaoh [Hatshepsut]" whose father was none other than the supreme head of the Theban pantheon—Amum-Re.[78] In the earlier Fifth

least available to those who could afford the costly methods of embalming in addition to constructing and maintaining a suitable tomb. See Dunand, *Gods and Men in Egypt*, 174ff for a discussion on socio-economic reality concerning the theological aspect of the Egyptian understanding of the "false equality of death."

74. The term "New Kingdom Divine Birth Cycle" is described by Mia Rikala as "a set of temple inscriptions and reliefs that describe and illustrate the divine origin of the Egyptian ruler as the son of the supreme deity, Amun-Re, and the human queen" (Nissinen and Uro, *Sacred Marriages*, 117).

75. Mysliwiec, *Eros on the Nile*, 81.

76. Ibid.

77. Van Seters, *In Search of History*, 174.

78. Mysliwiec, *Eros on the Nile*, 84. Rikala notes the similarities between

Dynasty structure of the Divine Birth Cycle, it is only after the birth of the three sons that the god Amum-Re acknowledges the sons as his own. But in Hatshepsut's version, the sexual coupling of her mother queen Ahmose and the god Amum-Ra graphically places him at the actual conception of Hatshepsut:

> [Amun-Re] has made his appearance like the majesty of his husband [the current Pharaoh] . . . He went to [Queen Ahmose] immediately and wanted her. He let her see him in the appearance of his divine image after he had come to her and she rejoiced upon seeing his beauty. The love of him coursed through her body . . .[79]

Both cases of Egyptian royal propaganda myths also share connections to the myths of Sumer through their similar sanctioning of a human ruler's power through either adoption by a god, a ruler's "birth" from a divine parent, or espousal to a goddess. However, in the myths of Sumer, the legitimization of power always connects a goddess with a male mortal (the king). In Egypt, the process of legitimating kingly power evolved over time but continued to be connected with human rulers (usually male) who held the title of divinity (i.e., Pharaoh as *Son of the Sun*) as it was incorporated into the formation of a theological concept which justified the ruler's divinity—more akin to later concepts of the "divine right of kings." In Egypt, there is no previous cosmological mythology that allows for the sexual interaction between deities and humans as in the Sumerian mythology contained in *Lugalbanda and Enmenkar* and *Inanna and Sukaletuda*.[80]

Like its Sumerian counterpart for male rulers, the female ritual position "God's Wife of Amun" was common in the Late Period and

---

Hatshepsut's Divine Birth Cycle and the biblical birth announcement in the gospel of Luke: "The god Thoth, the divine herald, informs the queen of the pregancy and the impending birth of the heir to the throne, parallel to the angel's announcement to the Virgin Mary in much later Christian tradition (scene VII). The pregnancy, birth of the baby, and his/her recognition by his divine father follow; the father appoints the child as his successor on earth . . ." (Nissinen and Uro, *Sacred Marriages*, 118).

79. Rikala notes "it is possible that the word 'beauty' here refers to the erect phallus of Amun-Re" (Nissinen and Uro, *Sacred Marriages*, 117 n. 8. See also Mysliwiec, *Eros on the Nile*, 90.

80. The other three instances of the use of the Divine Birth Cycle occur later in the New Kingdom: in Luxor for Amenhotep III (father of Akenaten); in Medinet Habu for Ramesses II; and in Karnak at the temple of Mut for an unknown ruler. See Mysliwiec, *Eros on the Nile*, 88.

originally held "by royal women of the New Kingdom; famous queens like Hatshepsut, Ahmose Nefertari, and several royal princesses."[81] The title did not "refer to belief in an actual union between a human woman and god, but [was] instead a ritual role played by the female holder of the title."[82]

In addition to her "birth cycle" royal propaganda myth, Hatshepsut also manipulated the complex Egyptian ideology of the soul through her references to her *ka*, or soul double. In the earlier stages of Egyptian mythology, the *ka* was associated only with the king. "The king's *ka* is born with him, or rather it is created when he is conceived, perfect from the very beginning, flesh of god, and fully divine."[83] Hatshepsut was "the only New Kingdom ruler to include a direct reference to the *ka* in the part of her royal titulary designated as Her Horus name: Powerful of Kas."[84]

The Pharaoh's *ka* did not absent him (or her) from mortality, even as it imbued the monarch with divinity: "his human form is overtaken by this immortal element, which flows through his whole being and dwells in it . . . [and] he assumes his rightful place on the 'Horus throne of the living.'"[85] Despite the presence of the *ka* the king (or female ruler) would necessarily still die a human physical death and thus begin the process toward being transformed into Osiris.

There are some interesting tradents, however, in the roles, activities, and the iconographic depictions of the goddesses of Egypt that have parallels in Sumerian myths and in the later myths of Israel. Like the similarities between goddesses and the gender roles of human women of Sumeria, Egyptian goddesses "are often shown in ways in which a female human would never be: goddesses are shown suckling, elite women are not; goddesses are shown holding knives, women are not."[86] Such iconic separation between human women and goddesses may not depict the actual status of women in ancient Egypt, but it would seem to indicate that the ancient Egyptians maintained very distinct boundaries between

---

81. Onstine, "Gender and the Religion of Ancient Egypt," 8.

82. Ibid.

83. Bell, "Luxor Temple and the Cult," 258.

84. Ibid., 290. Hatshepsut's sucessor, Thutmose III, "was the most vehement in smashing [Hatshepsut's] statues at her birth porticos [in her temple] at Dier el-Bahari . . . and could nullify the legitimacy of Hatshepsut by denying that the royal *ka* had, in fact, descended upon her" (257).

85. Ibid., 258.

86. Graves-Brown, *Dancing for Hathor*, 161.

Fallen Angels and Fallen Women

the divine and human worlds, which the Egyptian deities did not cross sexually, except by means human manipulation (in order to effect royal propaganda myths) for the purposes of establishing divine sanction which maintained power.[87]

A myth found on the shrines of Tutankhamun, *The Destruction of Humanity*, relates the story of the "eye of Ra"—depicted in Egyptian mythology as the daughter of the sun god Ra—deserves mention. While not directly related to any sexual relationship between gods and mortals, the story shares distinct parallels to the Sumerian *Inanna and Sukaletuda* in the similarities between two powerful female goddesses—one Sumerian and one Egyptian—focused on their use in avenging humanity through the agency of blood.

In the cosmogony of *The Destruction of Humanity*, a golden age existed for both humans and gods—with Ra as the primary god—where night and death did not exist.[88] Humans plot against Ra and in anger the god sends his daughter—his eye—in the form of Hathor to destroy all humans: "Hathor the eye of the Sun, [goes] into the desert transformed into the raging lioness Sekhmet, the powerful one" and begins to slaughter humans and wade in their blood.[89] As we have demonstrated in *Inanna and Sukaletuda*, blood also plays a pivotal role in the resulting wrath of Inanna in her quest to punish humanity. In the case of Hathor, the blood the goddess wades through is human blood and not her own. In *The Destruction of Humanity*, Ra eventually decides against the wholesale destruction of humanity, but no one is able to quell the raging goddess. A plan is devised to disguise beer with red ochre that Hathor—as the eye of Ra—believes is genuine blood. She consumes the "blood" and becomes once again the pacified and docile goddess.[90] Both the human and the beer "blood," however, in the Egyptian myth are the result of the actions of a more powerful male god who sends his daughter to do the work of

---

87. Even as erotic as Hatshepsut's Divine Birth Cycle narrative seems to be, the pictoral depiction of its sexual nature is, as Graves-Brown notes, "never explicit, as this would reduced the dignity of the queen and god"(*Dancing for Hathor*, 133).

88. A synopsis of the myth can be found in Pinch, *Egyptian Mythology*, 74–75.

89. Quoted in Graves-Brown, *Dancing for Hathor*, 169. See also Kramer, "Blood Plague Motif."

90. The destructive aspect of the usually nurturing Hathor as the "daughter of Ra" may have parallels with one particular component of ancient Canaanite and Israelite mythology concerning the significance of the role of "daughters" in general in addition to such theological concepts as the "daughter of the voice" (בת קול), and the epithet "daughter of man," which will concern us in later chapters.

destruction. In the Sumerian myth, Inanna wreaks havoc through her own volition.

We have discussed how the myths of Sumer and (more tangentially the myths of Ugarit) connect the themes of divine/human sexuality to the origins of human mortality. The myths of Egypt also make this same connection, but more indirectly. Although the Pharaoh encompassed the divinity (in the form of the sun god, Ra), both the Pharaoh and the spouse(s) of the Pharaoh were always perceived as mortal, even if it was assumed theologically that they would eventually become divine during the process of becoming Osiris during the afterlife.[91] Due to the structure of the complex and gender-ambiguous Egyptian divine pantheon and the dependence upon the transformation of the (gender neutral) mortal ruler to the status of divine immortal Osiris, death is not connected explicitly to human sexuality. The earliest cosmological myths of Egypt do not forge a direct connection between human sexuality, mortality, and knowledge or wisdom. This is not to say that Egyptian cosmogonic myth does not greatly interact with and influence the formation of later mythologies in later cultures and traditions, especially in ancient Israel. In order to trace most directly the themes that connect human sexuality, mortality, and wisdom, we turn again to the myths of Sumer and to the Epic of Gilgamesh.

RETURN TO SUMER AND THE EPIC OF GILGAMESH

The most famous epic of Sumer provides the seeds for mythologies that will continue for thousands of years and encompass a wide influential range in the angelic mythology of ancient Israel. The oldest story on record concerns itself with some of the oldest questions: Why do the gods live and mortals die? Is it possible for humans to attain immortality? What gives meaning to the mortal nature of life? The epic not only gives insight into the human quest and continued hope for eternal life but provides connections between wisdom (knowledge), human sexuality, and death. Most, if not all, future mythological literature of the Middle East use some component of the Epic of Gilgamesh as a foundation for its development.

---

91. For a more detailed overview of these concepts, see O. B. Berlev, "The Eleventh Dynasty in the Dynastic History of Egypt in Polotsky, *Studies Presented to Hans*, 361–77.

THE EPIC BEGINS

Multi-layered, full of nuance and complexity, the Epic of Gilgamesh introduces us to Gilgamesh, hero and king of the city of Uruk whose tyrannical behavior causes the inhabitants of the city to cry out to the gods for relief. The goddess Aruru, the creator of all humankind, responds by creating a twin for the hero. Enkidu is made especially for Gilgamesh to be an equal warrior, friend, companion, and mirror. Enkidu is two-thirds animal to Gilgamesh's two-thirds divine:

> ... [Aruru] created inside herself
> the word (?) of Anu
> Aruru washed her hands, pinched off a piece of clay,
> Cast it out into open country.[92]

But Enkidu is savage and wild, he lives on the steppes and hunts animals, scatters game and compels the neighboring hunter to complain to his father who suggests he seek recourse from the king. Upon hearing the complaint, Gilgamesh commissions Shamhat, cultic prostitute, to return with the hunter and civilize the wild man and initiate him into the ways of domesticated human life.

Shamhat follows the hunter to the steppes and waits for Enkidu to appear. She engages in sexual intercourse with Enkidu for "six days and seven nights" and continues the process of humanizing Enkidu by teaching him language, clothing him with a garment, and introducing him to human food. Finally, Shamhat brings Enkidu into the city of Uruk where he finally meets Gilgamesh.

Mehmet-Ali Ataç compares the relationship between Gilgamesh and Enkidu to that of Horus and Seth in *The Contendings of Horus and Seth* from Egyptian mythology.[93] The Sumerian heroes are two "opposites in equilibrium," not unlike their Egyptian counterparts.[94] And whereas Seth and Horus actually engage in homosexual behavior, the Epic of Gilgamesh only briefly touches on the homoerotic encounters between

---

92. Dalley, *Myths from Mesopotamia*, 52.

93. Ataç, "Angelology,'" 6). For a discussion on the etymology of the name "Enkidu," see Wasserman, Nathan, Offspring of Silence, Spawn of a Fish, Son of a Gazelle ...: Enkidu's Different Origins in the Epic of Gilgamesh in Klein, *An Experienced Scribe*, 593–9. See also George, *Epic of Gilgamesh*, 138–44.

94. Ataç, "'Angelology,'" 10. Foster also agrees that Gilgamesh and Enkidu are paired opposites. See Foster, "Gilgamesh: Sex, Love," 25.

Enkidu and Gilgamesh.[95] Ataç also understands the significance of the Epic's themes of wisdom, human sexuality and death, but fails to underscore the significance of Shamhat and her important agency within the epic.[96] While it is true that Gilgamesh is initially responsible for procuring Shamhat for the purposes of civilizing Enkidu, I will demonstrate that Shamhat and also later in the text the tavern keeper Shiduri are the primary characters who connect themes of wisdom, sexuality, and death to the epic. Their roles and their interactions with the two main characters—Enkidu and Gilgamesh, respectively—are pivotal in understanding later mythological developments to the Son of Man.

SHAMHAT

Common meanings of Shamhat's name (voluptuous woman) associate her with Sumerian terms that connote engaging in sex for payment: *harimtu* and *samhatu*. Shamhat's name is "the typical professional name" for a prostitute but could also be a technical term for a woman associated with the goddess Ishtar. The name Shamhat is also synonymous with her role as *harimtu*, a technical term like *samhatu* whose function and role are currently believed by scholars to be that of prostitute but may also be assumed to be that of a devotee with some kind of status associated with Ishtar.[97]

---

95. Mitchell, *Gilgamesh: A New English Version*, 23, and in his notes section traces the development of tablet XII where the homosexual language appended to the poem is "sexually explicit." Ackerman also makes a case for a homoerotic connection between Gilgamesh and Enkidu. See Ackerman, *When Heroes Love*.

96. Mitchell calls Shamhat "one of the most fascinating characters in *Gilgamesh*" (*Gilgamesh: A New English Version*, 13).

97. Leick notices that "There is is no general agreement among Assyriologists as to what extent the titles [for 'prostitute'] implied professional sexual activity" (*Sex and Eroticism*, 162). The non-Assyriologist is more apt to do away with question altogether, or to anachonize. Witness the comment made by Stephen Moore in his analysis of Shamhat's profession in his book on the history of the novel: "[Shamhat has] a respected position that doesn't carry any of the modern, pejorative implications of 'prostitute.' Think of her as a sexual nun" (*Novel*, 54n30). Mitchell (following Bottero) gives Shamhat's name the meaning 'the joyous one' leaving aside any associations with sexual activity (*Gilgamesh: A New English Version*, 289). According to George, "the etymology of the word suggests that *samhatu* carries overtones of vivacity and voluptuousness," which he suggests (predicably) would enhance her profession (*Babylonian Gilgamesh Epic*, 148). According to Dalley, the name Shamhat "is used as a personal name . . . [meaning] 'volumptuous woman, prostitute,' in particular as a type of cultic

Fallen Angels and Fallen Women

It may be the case that because Shamhat's name is also her occupation or title "she is not fully a person; her function as a means, a tool, is thereby emphasized."[98] But because we have no other Sumerian/Akkadian examples of mythological characters having names that also describe their function, we cannot assume Shamhat's name exempts her from having a distinctive persona, or that her name in the epic is not as important as the name Gilgamesh or Enkidu.

Both Abusch and Foster have admirably charted the literary development of the Epic of Gilgamesh from its (not well preserved) Old Babylonian (OB) and later more complex Akkadian Standard Version (SV) which Foster refers to as the Nineveh Version (NV) in their analysis of the poem.[99] Foster contends that "the Nineveh poet portrays sex and love as types of human knowledge" of which unproductive (sexual intercourse that does not result in the production of offspring) or "baseless" sex is "reversion to the animal state."[100] Foster sees the purpose of the Epic of Gilgamesh with its "emphasis on love and sex as intermediary stages to perfect knowledge" as the work of the Nineveh poet.[101] Like Ataç, Foster does not believe that Shamhat is the purveyor of knowledge herself, preferring to note that, in the Nineveh recension, "the poet . . . tells the story of Enkidu's entrapment by the hunter and harlot with relish, passing lightly over the important point that it is Gilgamesh who provides the harlot."[102]

Foster also fails to notice that in the Nineveh recension, it is the hunter's father who provides the original idea for having Enkidu "tamed" by a woman in order to prevent the wild Enkidu from scattering his son's game.[103] Further, "there is never any mention that the huntsman might send the subdued Enkidu back to Uruk for Gilgamesh to encounter. This

devotee of Ishtar in Uruk" (*Myths from Mesopotamia*, 126). Leick notes that Shamhat's name is derived from the verb "to flourish" (*Sex and Eroticism*, 166).

98. Bailey, "Primal Woman in Gilgamesh," 141.

99. Foster, "Gilgamesh: Sex, Love." See also Abusch, "Development and Meaning of the Epic of Gilgamesh." Abusch charts three major divisions in the development of the epic: The Old Babylonian version contains the oral stories of Gilgamesh that took shape 1700 BCE; the Akkadian Standard Version in eleven tablets and the Akkadian Standard version with twelve tablets (614).

100. Foster, "Gilgamesh: Sex, Love," 22. See also Leick, *Sex and Eroticism*.

101. Foster, "Gilgamesh: Sex, Love," 22.

102. Ibid., 24. In the Old Babylonian version, the episode with the hunter is not extant.

103. Dalley, *Myths from Mesopotamia*, 53.

idea instead is unique to Shamhat."[104] It is precisely through the agency of Shamhat that Enkidu enters "the first stage of knowledge, sexual awareness."[105] As she sees Enkidu approaching:

> Shamhat unloosed her attire, opened her vulva, and he took her charms.
> She was not bashful, she took to herself his vitality.
> She stripped off her clothes and he lay upon her,
> She indeed treated him, man, to woman's work.
> His passionate feelings caressed her.
> Six days and seven nights was Enkidu aroused and made love to Shamhat.[106]

Abusch divides the sexual encounter between Shamhat and Enkidu into two parts. In the first encounter, Shamhat satisfies the purely "animal" nature of Enkidu. Shamhat subsequently initiates the second encounter by spreading out her garment in order to "humanize" the sexual act, thus making "intercourse . . . a human and not an animal act."[107] Shamhat then invites Enkidu to enter "to the second [stage of knowledge] represented by the ability to hear and understand language."[108]

Shamhat initiates the next sequence of events which propel Enkidu through further stages of awareness that began with his awareness of human sexuality. As Enkidu enters the second stage of awareness, that of knowledge/wisdom of the civilized human world, he sits at the feet of Shamhat:

> He turned back and sat himself down at the harlot's feet.
> The harlot looked into his face
> And to [the words (?)] that she was speaking did
> His ears give hearing.[109]

Shamhat's verbal instructions and her transmission of the knowledge of human affairs to Enkidu are concomitant with her sexual

---

104. Ackerman, *When Heroes Love*, 142ff, contra Foster. Abusch postulates that, in an earlier form of the epic, "originally the main character in the episode was the courtesan and that she seduced Enkidu without any involvement on the part of the hunter" (Abusch, "Courtesan," 425ff.).

105. Foster, "Gilgamesh: Sex, Love," 25.

106. Ibid., 24.

107. Abusch, "Courtesan," 421.

108. Foster, "Gilgamesh: Sex, Love," 25.

109. Ibid.

initiation. Shamhat continues to be an important character in the epic. If the character of Shamhat were a plot device, merely an instrument of the powerful king Gilgamesh, she would not appear again, which she does so dramatically in the epic. As we will see, Enkidu's future curse of Shamhat is proof of her enduring agency in the poem.

We should not interpret Enkidu's "sitting at the feet" of Shamhat as the Sumerian precursor to later Middle Eastern practices of discipleship, but it does seem that the relationship of Enkidu to Shamhat is profoundly disciple-like. Foster points to this in his analysis, since later in the poem, "Enkidu is apparently adopted as a *sirqu*, or devotee of Gilgamesh, and thus joins the ranks of prostitutes and temple women" of which Shamhat is already a member.[110]

In the earlier OB, Shamhat acts with even more agency as the spiritual channel between the two men. At the same time Gilgamesh is relating the dream of Enkidu's arrival to his mother, Shamhat is dispensing (sexual) wisdom to Enkidu:

> While Gilgamesh was relating the dream,
> Enki[du was seat]ed before the harlot
> The pair made love [together].[111]

In this way, when Shamhat narrates the dream of Gilgamesh's introduction to Enkidu, she also "becomes a seer."[112] While Shamhat and Enkidu are still on the steppes, before returning to the city of Uruk, Shamhat clothes Enkidu in the same garment she spread before him during his sexual initiation so that the garment that provided the humanizing aspect of his sexual nature now becomes the garment she shares with him as a means to introduce "him into human society and culture:"[113]

> She took off her garments,
> Clothed him in one,
> Dressed herself
> In a second garment...[114]

Both the act of Shamhat's dressing Enkidu and Enkidu's wearing of attire represents the former wild man's inclusion into human society.

---

110. Ibid., 27.
111. Ibid.
112. Bailey, "Primal Woman in Gilgamesh," 140.
113. Abusch, "Courtesan," 421.
114. Dalley, *Myths from Mesopotamia*, 138.

Chapter One

"It is this process of clothing along with his sexual encounter with the harlot Shamhat, that transforms him into a civilized being . . . a civilized (mortal) man is generally represented as a dressed man."[115] Now that Enkidu is clothed, Shamhat continues the process of enlightenment by bringing him to a shepherd's table and introducing him to the products of human civilization and achievement over the wild—prepared food and fermented beer—"as a god [leads a suppliant]" in language that sounds remarkably similar to later Christian eucharistic language:[116]

> The harlot made her voice heard
> And spoke to Enkidu,
> "Eat the food, Enkidu,
> The symbol of life.
> Drink the beer destiny of the land."[117]

Shamhat's role in Enkidu's enlightenment process is identical to later examples of personified Wisdom (Sophia) who is also a provider of food in the canonical Scriptures (Proverbs 9:2). Ataç mistakenly connects Gilgamesh to this role, arguing that that "in [the character of] Gilgamesh . . . we have . . . a bit of a Sophia."[118] He even makes the observation that "In Gnosticism, Sophia claims to be whore and holy at the same time," which is a role that Shamhat fulfills far more than Gilgamesh.[119]

Enkidu is partially divine, yet his full incarnation into humanity and subsequent paring with Gilgamesh is artfully guided and accomplished by Shamhat.[120] In her initiation of Enkidu, Shamhat has not only made

---

115. Bahrani, *Women of Babylon*, 59. Bahrani also notices the connection between the "ME's"—which she calls "arts" of the goddess Inanna to include "the adornment of the body" which further connects Shamhat with her role as the emissary of the goddess Inanna/Ishtar (*Women of Babylon*, 59). According to George, Shamhat is probably associated with the "temple of Anu and Ishtar" (*Babylonian Gilgamesh Epic*, 148).

116. Mitchell, *Gilgamesh: A New English Version*, 138. See also Dalley's translation in both the Nineveh Version and the Old Babylonian Version (*Myths from Mesopotamia*, 59 [Tablet 2 ii], and page 138 [OBV Tablet II ii]).

117. This is not extant in the Nineveh version, but in the Old Babyonian Version (OBV). See Dalley, *Myths from Mesopotamia*, 138 (Tablet II iii).

118. Ataç, "Angelology," 14.

119. Ibid., 14.

120. Mitchell comments that "Enkidu is ideed Gilgamesh's double . . . [B]ut he is also Gilgamesh's opposite and mirror image: two-thirds animal to Gilgamesh's two-thirds divine" (*Gilgamesh: A New English Version*, 11). In view of Enkidu's (at least, partial) divinity, this initiation by Shamhat is reminiscent of the encounter between Salome and Jesus in the *Gospel of Thomas*, logion 61. See Jarrell, "Gospel of Thomas 61

the "wild man of the steppe" into a human being, she has "divinized" his animal nature and brought him closer to divinity itself.[121] Shamhat leads Enkidu further into the process of becoming a civilized human being as someone who is partially divine herself or, at the very least, as someone who acts with the authority of a divine mandate given to her by virtue of her status as *samhatu/harimtu* of the goddess Inanna-Ishtar. Shamhat is the wisdom figure who transforms Enkidu to a godlike hero:

> "As I look at you, Enkidu, you are become like God.
> . . .
> Come on, let me lead you . . ."
> . . .
> He [Enkidu] heard her words, her speech he accepted,
> The woman's advice fell upon his heart.[122]

In the later recension of the poem, Shamhat informs Enkidu that Gilgamesh has already been prepared for the arrival of his soon-to-be companion in a dream, and literally leads Enkidu—as a god leads a suppliant—to the city of Uruk.

According to Foster, in the NV, Enkidu's relationship to Shamhat serves as plot device for the poem to "develop a polarity of Enkidu's harlot-like relationship to Gilgamesh."[123] For Foster, however, Enkidu's "harlot-like" relationship with Gilgamesh is transcendent to the original relationship of Enkidu to Shamhat, which even Foster admits serves as the template for the later bond forged between Enkidu and Gilgamesh. Shamhat is the cruces through which Enkidu must pass on his path from animal to human as he becomes "civilized."

ENKIDU'S CURSE OF SHAMHAT

The friendship between Enkidu and Gilgamesh is deep and instantaneous. Together the pair kill the monster Humbaba and then proceed to

---

and 62." A further similarity between Jesus and Gilgamesh/Enkidu will be discussed in a later chapter.

121. According to Bailey, Shamhat brings Enkidu "wisdom and a quality of divinity through sexual experience" ("Primal Woman in Gilgamesh," 139).

122. Foster, "Gilgamesh: Sex, Love," 28.

123. Ibid. See also Dalley's notes on the description of Enkidu as "metaphorical words . . . [which] may be puns of terms for cult personnel of uncertain sexual affinities who were found particularly in Uruk, associated with Ishtar's cult" (*Myths from Mesopotamia*, 126n10).

destroy the sacred Bull of Heaven, angering the goddess Inanna/Ishtar. Later, Gilgamesh understands in a dream that because he and Enkidu have angered the gods by these heroic deeds, one of them must die. The god Enlil wishes to spare Gilgamesh; therefore, it is Enkidu who is sentenced.

Enkidu experiences his own death dream and awakens to his mortality, once invisible to him in his original animal state in the wilds of the steppes but now painfully evident and even more immediately immanent. He curses the hunter who first discovers him and rails against the god Shamash who now fails to protect him from death. Finally, he pronounces a very specific and detailed curse on Shamhat whom he blames for the "gift" of his human sexual awareness that he now understands is inexorably linked to the realization of his own transience:

> Because you defiled me when I was pure
> Because you seduced me in the open country when I was pure.[124]

The bulk of Enkidu's curses relegate Shamhat to the fate of a common prostitute who must contend with shameful working conditions and no place to live:

> May the [abode] of your delight be a doorway,
> The crossroad of the potters' quarter be your dwelling,
> May a vacant lot be your sleeping place,
> The shadow of a wall be your station . . .[125]

The "curses of Shamhat that Enkidu utters . . . are similar to the curses that the goddess Ereshigal, the queen of the netherworld, utters against an *assinnu* [a male who is part of the cultic order of the goddess Ishtar] who has been sent to petition her . . . Ereshkigal . . . begins her tirade against the *assinnu* by claiming she will curse him with a great curse, just as Enkidu opens his invective against Shamhat by saying, 'let me curse you with a great curse.'"[126]

Even the god Shamash comes to Shamhat's defense, calling her "my *harimtu*," adding to the list of gods that include Ishtar who bestow upon Shamhat their divine imprimatur. It is not clear from the text if it

---

124. Dalley's translation (*Myths from Mesopotamia*, 87). Foster's translation "Because you [killed me] after marrying [me]" is equally blaming ("Gilgamesh: Sex, Love," 38).

125. Foster, "Gilgamesh: Sex, Love," 38.

126. Ackerman, *When Heroes Love*, 142.

Fallen Angels and Fallen Women

is Shamash who demands that Enkidu reverse his curse (the lines are missing). When the text continues, Enkidu now grants Shamhat a list of blessings:

> Come Sham[hat]
> My mouth which cursed you, let it bless you again.
> May generals and dignitaries fall in love with you,
> May [one] a league away slap his thigh (in frustration),
> May one two leagues away (already) be letting down his hair,
> Nor let the underling hold back from you, let him open his drawers for you.
> May he give you obsidian, lapis, and gold . . .[127]

Enkidu's blessing proposes to enhance not only Shamhat's profession as *harimtu* priestess of Inanna/Ishtar, one that clearly requires attractiveness and sexual power, but also proposes to supply Shamhat with an abundance of material goods to ensure her status as a wealthy courtesan and a woman of means. Enkidu's blessing concludes with one final gift:

> The diviner shall lead you into the palace (?) of the gods.[128]

Foster's translation reads: "May exorcists . . . (into?) the holy (of the?) gods bring you in."[129] George's translation: "Ishtar, [the ablest] of gods, shall gain you entrance to the man whose home [is established] and wealth heaped high" is particularly problematic coming so soon from the mouth of Enkidu, who in the previous tablet (SB) has gravely insulted the goddess.[130] In that episode, Enkidu hurls the haunch of the Bull of Heaven recently ripped from the newly killed beast toward Inanna/Ishtar with the words, "Had I caught you too, I'd have treated you likewise, I'd have draped your arms in [the Bull of Heaven's] guts."[131]

Enkidu's underlying motivation for such a pronouncement to Shamhat may be an atonement for his offense against the goddess though the act of blessing her emissary. But both Foster and Dalley's translation

---

127. Foster's translation ("Gilgamesh: Sex, Love," 40).

128. Dalley's translation (*Myths from Mesopotamia*, 88).

129. Foster, "Gilgamesh: Sex, Love," 40.

130. George, *Epic of Gilgamesh*, 59. His translation is slightly different in *Babylonian Gilgamesh Epic*, 643 and reads, "To the man whose household [*is well off*], whose storage bins are heaped high, may Istar, [the most able] of the gods, send you in!" (Italics in original).

131. It is immediately after this episode that Enkidu dreams of his own demise (George, *Epic of Gilgamesh*, 52).

for Enkidu's final pronouncement offer another solution. In certain cases, Sumerian women were known to be high ranking in the temple/palace, as well as in charge of economic matters.[132] Enkidu at first grants Shamhat material wealth and the ability to continue to reap financial gains as a *harimtu*. This he follows by sanctioning Shamhat's progression to a far greater spiritual status as well. Recall that earlier in the epic, Shamhat "leads" Enkidu to his destiny with Gilgamesh as "a god leads a suppliant." We might also make the same comparison with Shamhat at this point in the text: it is possible that Enkidu bestows Shamhat with "a diviner" who "leads" her as a god into the divine palace/temple. In short, Enkidu offers Shamhat divine status. Sanctioning the highest spiritual status for Shamhat underscores the epic's portrayal of Shamhat as divine and a dispenser of (sexual) Wisdom. Now that Shamhat has attained divinity, the reader is prepared for the death of Enkidu and the subsequent enlightenment of his brother/friend Gilgamesh by the tavern keeper Shiduri.

ENKIDU'S DEATH AND GILGAMESH'S INITIATION

Abusch calls Enkidu's death the crux of the Epic. Enkidu's death is so pivotal, that "without Enkidu's death, there is no development" either in the remaining portion of the narrative, or in the character of Gilgamesh.[133] In his despair over the death of his beloved friend, Gilgamesh asks the questions:

> Shall I die, too? Am I not like Enkidu?
> Grief has entered my innermost being,

---

132. See Bahrani, *Women of Babylon*, 96ff. Bahrani cites the last independent Early Dynastic ruler of Lagash, Uru'inimgina, who "changed his title from 'governor' to 'king' and radically reformed several aspects of the government. It was only then that he renamed his wife's household as the temple of the goddess Bau" and put his wife Sasha in charge of administrating the household/temple (Bahrani, *Women of Babylon*, 107). Since Enkidu's blessing of Shamhat is not extant in the OB, and only occurs the SV, we cannot know if the blessing was part of the earlier form of the epic when the Sumerian Pantheon was primarily female. See Steinkeller, "On Rulers, Priests, and Sacred Marriage" for a detailed discussion of the idea of the rising importance of male deities ("though never superceding that of the goddesses") and its effect on the status of priests/esses and rulers (114). For a discussion of the "hotly debated topic" of types of cultic prostitutes, and their division into "temple" verses "commercial," see Walls, *Desire, Discord, and Death*, 83n24.

133. Abusch, "Development and Meaning of the Epic of Gilgamesh," 616.

I am afraid of Death, and so I roam open country.[134]

Abusch notes that "it is significant that just as a prostitute, a woman, humanized and acculturated Enkidu at the beginning [of the OB version], so a tavernkeeper, another woman, humanizes and acculturates Gilgamesh at the end."[135] I would contend, however, that Shiduri and Shamhat are mirror aspects of one other as well as aspects of the goddess Inanna/Ishtar, whom they represent.[136] Enkidu's blessing of Shamhat, in the precursor to his death, raises Shamhat to the status that Shiduri now inhabits, that of tavern keeper. Such taverns "as Shiduri is depicted as managing . . . were places where men went to meet prostitutes like Shamhat."[137] And since "Gilgamesh takes Shiduri to be a form of Ishtar" we may draw all three women/goddesses into one role.[138]

Just as Shamhat integrates Enkidu from the wild place of the steppes to the civilized world of Uruk and prepares him for his intimate relationship with Gilgamesh, so Shiduri, Shamhat's twin, reintegrates Gilgamesh from his wild place of grief into the next part of his life journey and ultimately allows the hero to return to his own intimate relationship with his city of Uruk.

After the death of his friend, Gilgamesh is bereft. In the OB version of the poem, Gilgamesh's wilderness journey leads him directly to the inn of the "alewife" who is not named.[139] In the SV, Gilgamesh sets

134. Dalley, *Myths from Mesopotamia*, 95.

135. Abusch, "Development and Meaning of the Epic of Gilgamesh," 616.

136. Walls agrees that the three women (Shamhat, Ishtar, and Shiduri) are connected, although his post-modern thesis denies Shamhat and Shiduri the roles I have suggested. See Walls, *Desire, Discord and Death*.

137. Ackerman, *When Heroes Love*, 143.

138. Abusch, "Gilgamesh's Request and Siduri's Denial, Part II," 7n18, citing Lambert, "The Hymn to the Queen of Nippur." But see also Dalley, *Myths from Mesopotamia*, 132n6: "And Akkadian list describes Siduri as 'Ishtar of wisdom.'" See also George, *Epic of Gilgamesh*, 148 and his discussion of the name.

139. Gilgamesh's wandering journey after the death of Enkidu and his subsequent meeting with the tavern keeper Shiduri could have been the original terminius for the OB (Abusch, "Development and Meaning of the Epic of Gilgamesh," 617). Abusch's maintains that while the meeting between Shiduri and Gilgamesh was the original end of the epic, the seeds for the search for immortality were in place with the wordplay in Shiduri's advice that hinges on the wordplay (in the OB) "between (ul) uta balatam [I do not find life] and Utana'ishtim/Utnapishtim [He has found life]. Uta-Napishtim is the name of the human survior of the Sumerian deluge made immortal by the gods ("Gilgamesh's Request and Siduri's Denial, Part II," 11), but see his note 48 for a detailed survey of the assyrological scholarship on this point.

out to find the only mortal, Utnapishtim, who is given immortality by the gods. Upon seeing the approach of the hero Gilgamesh, Shiduri flees to her rooftop. Gilgamesh threatens a forced entrance and the two converse about the death of Enkidu and Gilgamesh's ongoing quest to find immortality.

The parallels between the Enkidu's encounter with Shamhat and Gilgamesh's encounter with Shiduri are noteworthy and deserve analysis. (Enkidu's encounter with Shamhat occurs in Tablet I and Gilgamesh's with Shiduri in Tablet X).[140]

Shamhat	Shiduri
(Then) Shamhat <u>saw him</u>,	The ale-wife was <u>watching him</u> in the distance ...
the man-savage, a murderous	For sure this man is a slayer of wild bulls;
...	...
Shamhat let loose her skirts, She bared her sex and he took in Her charms.	The ale-wife saw him and barred her gate Barred her gate and went up on the roof.
She showed no fear, she took in his Scent: she spread her clothing And he lay upon her.	[Gilgamesh speaking] 'Ale Wife, why when you saw [me did you bar] your [gate?] You barred your gate [and went up on the] roof.
She treated the man to the work Of a woman.	I shall strike the door, I shall [break the bolt.]
His love caressed and embraced Her	[The ale-wife spoke to] him, [to] Gilgamesh: [...]...[...I barred] my gate, [...]...[...I went up on] the roof. [...]...[...] let me learn of [your ...]
...	...
He came back and sat down at The feet of the harlot, Watching the harlot, <u>(observing)</u> Her features.	(OB Version) I keep roaming like a hunter In open country. Now, alewife, now that I <u>Have seen your face</u>, the death that I Constantly fear may I not see.
[*har-rim-tum i-na-at-la pa-mi-sa*]	[*i-na-an-na sa-bi-tum a-ta-mar pa-ni-ka*]

Translation by Abusch, *Gilgamesh's Request and Siduri's Denial Part II*, also found in (George, *Babylonian Gilgamesh Epic*, 279).

Both scenes begin with Shamhat and Shiduri noticing, or "seeing" (*i-mur-su-[a]/at-ta-al-sum-ma*) Enkidu and Gilgamesh, respectively. Both men encounter their representation of the goddess Ishtar within the context of wilderness. Enkidu is the uncivilized animal-like human who originally inhabits the wilderness and is "civilized" by Shamhat. Gilgamesh wanders in desolation from civilized Uruk after the death of his friend into the wilderness of grief and must be reintroduced into "civilization" by Shiduri. Both men are first perceived by the agents of Ishtar as wild and part of the wilderness itself.

---

140. Translation by George in *Babylonian Gilgamesh Epic*.

Fallen Angels and Fallen Women

Now the two scenes play out differently: When Shamhat sees Enkidu, her reaction is the opposite of Shiduri's fearful reaction to Gilgamesh—Shamhat does not recoil against Enkidu's advances. On the contrary, her actions show extraordinary courage.[141] She takes on the role of the careful, cautious hunter taking in the scent of her prey, Enkidu. Conversely, after her initial perception of Gilgamesh coming toward her from the wilderness, Shiduri is convinced that he is a hunter, "a slayer of wild bulls" and she must flee to her rooftop for safety. At the beginning of the epic, in order to facilitate the initiation of Enkidu, Shamhat bares her sex; at the end of the epic, in order to facilitate the reintegration of Gilgamesh, Shiduri bars her gate.[142]

Both Enkidu and Gilgamesh strive to be admitted to the physical space inhabited by the representatives of Ishtar—Enkidu lays atop Shamhat's garment and Gilgamesh threatens to break down Shiduri's door and shatter the bolt. Gilgamesh's threat is "restored from the Nineveh manuscript of *Ishtar's Descent* [to the Underworld]."[143] Strange that Gilgamesh should use the very words spoken by the goddess Ishtar (whom he has rejected previously in the epic), but these words of Gilgamesh mirror the words spoken by Enkidu to curse Shamhat, which we have seen were taken almost verbatim from another scene in the *Ishtar's Descent to the Underworld*.[144]

While certainly not as explicit as the sexual encounter between Shamhat and Enkidu, there is some evidence from the OB Version that Shiduri does interact sexually with Gilgamesh. If we read Shamhat and Shiduri as a pair—twin representatives and priestesses of Ishtar, because Shamhat provides Enkidu with sexual wisdom in order to civilize him,

---

141. Thus Wall's observation that "Shamhat is instructed [by the hunter] to show no fear" in her encounter with Enkidu obscures Shamhat's actual reaction during the event. If the poem has gone through several redactions (as both Foster and George suggest) the words of the hunter could well be a poetic foreshadowing of Shamhat's bravery rather than proof that Shamhat is merely "a female body for hire who silently obeys her employer's directions" (Walls, *Desire, Discord, and Death*, 21).

142. As Dickson points out, in this scene, "Gilgamesh is now an intruder in a strange world, just as Enkidu once was: Both of them 'savage,' potentially violent, ignorant, and vulnerable" (Dickson, "Other and Gilgamesh," 177).

143. George, *Babylonian Gilgamesh Epic*, 2:869.

144. See also George, *Babylonian Gilgamesh Epic*, 1:497). Abusch, however, says that in the OB, "Gilgamesh takes Siduri to be a form of Ishtar" despite the later version "where Gilgamesh rejects Ishtar's proposal" ("Gilgamesh's Request and Siduri's Denial, Part II," 7).

then Shiduri's attempts to resuscitate Gilgamesh from the wilderness to civilized Uruk would include sexual interaction. Abusch points out that Shiduri's "attempt to reintroduce Gilgamesh to normal life after his wandering in the wild recalls the humanization of Enkidu . . . And just as the human prostitute attracts and introduces Enkidu to normal human life by means of sex, just so the divine alewife who may once have made love to the traveler now suggests that Gilgamesh make love with a woman and thereby return to a normal state."[145]

In his lament over the death of his friend, and his fear of his own impending death, Gilgamesh tells Shiduri:

> Since his [Enkidu's] death, I have not found life . . .
> (but) now, alewife, that I have seen your face,
> The death that I constantly fear may I not see.[146]

In his pronouncement that he has seen the face of Shiduri, "Gilgamesh articulates what might perhaps be a formula of marriage or relationship . . . to see [Shiduri's] face is to have attained a degree of intimacy with her."[147] This process of "gazing" would also mirror the beginning of the poem when, after the sexual advances of Shamhat, Enkidu gazes on the face of his enlightener, and so continues the process that will eventually lead him to Gilgamesh. So the scene between Shiduri and Gilgamesh may be evidence that Shiduri has provided Gilgamesh, not only with wisdom, but with sexual intimacy as well. Gilgamesh's actions parallel those of his now dead friend Enkidu as the Shamhat/Enkidu scene repeats itself and Gilgamesh gazes upon the face of Shiduri, his enlightener. Gilgamesh's proclamation: "Now that I have seen your face" is an affirmation that enables Gilgamesh to continue his own process of enlightenment and will eventually bring him out of his grief and return him to the city of Uruk.[148] Thus Gilgamesh has been prepared by Shiduri (Shamhat's twin and raised to divine status by Enkidu) for the next stage in his development—the acceptance of his grief of Enkidu, and ultimately the certainty of his own death.

---

145. Abusch, "Gilgamesh's Request and Siduri's Denial, Part II," 8.

146. Ibid., 5.

147. Ibid., 6. Abusch says further that "Originally, [Shiduri] was veiled, and it is surely no accident that in her first appearance in the Neo Assyrian version, Siduri is associated with veiling or covering (GE X I 4: kutummi kuttumatma . . .)."

148. I follow Abusch here in agreeing that Gilgamesh's search for immortality is a later development of the epic.

The epic rounds out the themes of women's role in the obtaining of wisdom, the hope for immortality and the certainty of death through the actions of Shamhat and Shiduri. In Gilgamesh's interaction with the tavern keeper, we have come to the end of the limits of the harlot's ability to awaken, for nothing can conquer human death. And Enkidu's lament will continue to echo though time mythologically: although women's sexuality brings wisdom, it also brings the awareness of mortality. So that, as Ataç convincingly argues, the only place left in the later recensions of the epic for Gilgamesh to experience wisdom is through his own death, in his "post-mortem . . . ascent" as the ruler/god of the underworld[149]

THE MYTHS OF GREECE

The most subtle and nuanced sexual interaction between immortal deities and mortal humans occurs in Greek mythology. The sheer multitude and varied interactions between Greek deities and mortals that occur in both poetry and myth make a complete summary and analysis impossible. It is important, however, to discuss some of the ways Greek myths and cosmogonies display similar parallels to myths and cosmogonies already outlined and analyzed above.

Many scholars have noted that "Greek religion is a bisexual polytheistic system, i.e.—there are female and male gods, all of whom are powerful in some way."[150] Both Greek gods and goddesses freely transgress the boundary dividing immortal and mortal—vis-à-vis both genders. Gods have sexual relationships with human women and goddesses have sexual relationships with human men—couplings that have powerful and often dire consequences for mortals. The sharp gender delineation in the Greek system "is an important element in Greek thinking about the gods, even though the difference between the sexes does not play the same role on Olympus as in the world of mortals."[151] It is far more important for the myths of Greece to preserve the "distance between gods and mortals" than it is to be concerned with "the sexual identities of the partners," whether the partners are either gods or mortals.[152] The fluidity pervasive

149. Ataç, "Angelology," 23.
150. Lucia Nixon, "The Cults of Demeter and Kore" in Hawley, *Women in Antiquity*, 75.
151. Nicole Loraux, "What Is A Goddess" in Pantel, *From Ancient Goddesses*, 15.
152. Ibid., 21.

in the commerce between divine and mortal is also especially noteworthy because it underscores the strange dichotomy that exists in how Greek myth constructs ways for humans to exhibit divinity (and in some cases immortality) but allows those same gender roles to remain profoundly fixed.[153]

The Greek mythological system contains the added complexity of describing the ontological status of the resulting offspring of immortal deities and mortal humans. Progeny created through such unions is always a demigod who is either hero or heroine. Usually "heroines and gods mostly come together for erotic or procreative purposes" and progeny created through such unions is always a demigod who is either hero or heroine. It is typically the case that "the child of the god is male."[154]

PANDORA

The myth of Pandora is Hesiod's account of the creation of the first woman and appears in his *Theogony*. A slightly more elaborate version is found in *Works and Days*. Many feminist scholars have noted that "it would be difficult to overstate the degree of negativity in the Greek version of woman's creation."[155] It is not difficult to argue that, like his character's fabled "box," Hesiod's misogyny has very few bounds.

One of the most interesting and by far overlooked characteristics of Pandora is, in fact, her relationship to her πιθός (usually translated "storage jar"). Originally mistranslated as *pyxis* (box), Pandora's πιθός is the source of the world's evils.[156] Several scholars have noted the connection between the similar shape between a πιθός and a woman's womb.[157] While

---

153. Deborah Lyons offers a revelatory view of this particular aspect of divine-human interaction in Greek mythology, especially as it pertains to the heroine. See *Gender and Immortality*.

154. Lyons, *Gender and Immortality*, 92–93.

155. Froma I. Zeitlin "Signfying Difference: The Myth of Pandora" in Hawley, *Women in Antiquity*, 59.

156. A possible textual corruption lead Erasmus of Rotterdam in the sixteenth century to render *pythos* (jar) as *pyxis* (box).

157. See Jenifer Neils "The Girl in the *Pithos*: Hesiod's *Elpis*" in Barringer, *Periklean Athens* for the most extensive treatment on the *pithos* in Greek art and myth; see also Froma I. Zeitlin "The Economics of Hesiod's Pandora" in Reeder, *Pandora: Women in Classical Greece* and Froma I. Zeitlin, "Signifying Difference: The Myth of Pandora in Hawley, *Women in Antiquity*. Almost all these scholars refer to Hoffmann, "Pandora, La Jarre et l'Espoir."

some commentators assign the ownership of the πιθός to either Zeus or Epimetheus (the unfortunate and intended recipient of the "beautiful evil" (καλὸν κακὸν)), there is no evidence in the text that the πιθός belongs to anyone other than Pandora.

The recounting of the events surrounding Pandora and her πιθός occurs only in *Works and Days*:

(90)Πρὶν μὲν γὰρ ζώεσκον ἐπὶ χθονὶ φῦλ' ἀνθρώπων
νόσφιν ἄτερ τε κακῶν καὶ ἄτερ χαλεποῖο πόνοιο
νούσων τ' ἀργαλέων αἵ τ' ἀνδράσι κῆρας ἔδωκαν·
αἶψα γὰρ ἐν κακότητι βροτοὶ καταγηράσκουσιν.
ἀλλά γυνὴ χείρεσσι πίθου μέγα πῶμ' ἀφελοῦσα
ἐσκέδασ'· ἀνθρώποισι δ' ἐμήσατο κήδεα λυγρά.
μούνη δ' αὐτόθι Ἐλπὶς ἐν ἀρρήκτοισι δόμοισιν
ἔνδον ἔμιμνε πίθου ὑπὸ χείλεσιν, οὐδὲ θύραζε
ἐξέπτη· πρόσθεν γὰρ ἐπέμβαλε πῶμα πίθοιο
αἰγιόχου βουλῇσι Διὸς νεφεληγερέταο.

> For previously the tribes of men used to live upon the earth entirely apart from evils, and without grievous toil and distressful diseases, which give death to men. [For in misery mortals grow old at once.] But the woman removed the great lid from the storage jar with her hands and scattered all its contents abroad—she wrought baneful evils for human beings. Only Anticipation remained there in its unbreakable home under the mouth (χείλεσιν) of the storage jar, by the plans of the aegis-holder, the cloud-gatherer, Zeus.[158]

In her discussion of the artistic representations of Pandora in Greek art, Jenifer Neils argues that "many scholars wish to see a close analogy between Pandora herself, made from clay, and the clay *pithos* that dispenses evils ... They ignore, however Hesiod's description of Pandora's *pithos* as *arrektoisi* or unbreakable."[159] Neil's conclusion, presumably because she is working with the artistic objects themselves, is to focus on the unbreakability of *pithoi* made from metal as opposed to clay. There is another category of unbreakability not considered by Neils: a woman's

---

158. Heisod, *Theogony*, 95. This translation, however obscures several references to a woman's body. A more literal translation might read: "but the woman removed the great lid with her hands from her womb and loosed all its contents ... only anticipation remained there in its unbreakable home underneath the lips of her womb."

159. Neils "The Girl in the *Pithos*: Hesiod's *Elpis*" in Barringer, *Periklean Athens*, 41.

womb is made of flesh is thus scarcely able to be broken—at least in a literal sense. Clearly Hesiod's poetic imagery of Pandora's body plays with both metaphors. Pandora is constructed by the order of Zeus and fashioned from clay through the artisanship of Hephastos. This clay yields a womb of flesh that is unbreakable. Pandora's womb of clay (her *pithos*) will later be described as having χείλεσιν (lips). This unbreakable womb is responsible for ending the harmonic relationship between men and gods and for scattering all the evils into the world ("grievous toil and distressful diseases") which also bring death.[160]

Hesiod assumes the reader will make the strong connection between *pithos* and womb. His artistic use of *pithos* is also a symbolic metaphor not only for the reproductive capabilities of this new "race" of women, but for women's perceived insatiable sexual appetites. Through his poetic rendering of the actions of Pandora who "removed the great lid of the *pithos*" in *Works and Days*, Hesiod connects his salacious characterization of Pandora to the progenitor of that cursed race of women who is "a great woe for mortals dwelling with men" in *Theogony*.

> Works and Days (94) πίθου μέγα πῶμ' . . .
> Theogony (592) πῆμα μέγα θνητοῖσθμ μετ' ἀνδράσι ναιετάοθσαι . . .
> Lid of the great Pithos . . .
> Great woe to mortals living with men . . .

Thus Hesiod's comparison between "the lid of the great *pithos*" (μέγα πῶμ') found in *Works and Days* is rendered through word play to match the polemic "great woe," (πῆμα μέγα, i.e., "women") inflicted on mortals found in *Theogony*.

Hesiod also seems to connect the womb imagery in *Works and Days* with the introduction of death/mortality in *Theogony*. In *Theogony* he makes the distinction between the *alloi theoi* (the deathless immortal ones who are stuck with wonder at the sight of Pandora) and *anthropos* (who are mortal):

> (585) αὐτὰρ ἐπεὶ δὴ τεῦξε καλὸν κακὸν ἀντ' ἀγαθοῖο,
> ἐξάγαγ' ἔνθά περ ἄλλοι ἔσαν θεοὶ ἠδ' ἄνθρωποι,
> κόσμῳ ἀγαλλομένην γλαυκώπιδος Ὀβριμοπάτρης·
> θαῦμα δ' ἔχ' ἀθανάτους τε θεοὺς θνητούς τ' ἀνθρώπους,
> ὡς εἶδον δόλον αἰπύν, ἀμήχανον ἀνθρώποισιν.
> ἐκ τῆς γὰρ γένος ἐστὶ γυναικῶν θηλυτεράων,

---

160. Heisod, *Theogony*, 95.

τῆς γὰρ ὀλοιόν ἐστι γένος καὶ φῦλα γυναικῶν,
πῆμα μέγα θνητοῖσι, μετ' ἀνδράσι ναιετάοθσαι,

> Then when he (Zeus) had contrived this beautiful evil thing (Pandora) in exchange for that good one (Prometheus' gift of fire stolen from Zeus), he led her out to where the other gods and human beings were, while she exulted in the adornment of (Athena); and wonder gripped the immortal gods and the mortal human beings when they saw the steep deception, intractable for human beings. For from her comes the race of female women; for of her is the deadly race and tribe of women, a great woe for mortals, dwelling with men . . .[161]

The creation of Pandora is a stratagem devised by Zeus to separate gods and men; Pandora is not the mother of *anthropoi* (all human beings) or even of humanity, but is the mother only of that specific *genos gynaikon* (the particular "race" of women).[162] Pandora is made as "an artificial creation in the form of a *parthenos* . . . a mixed creature composed of god, man, and beast."[163] The question remains whether Pandora is "an evil for just those *anthropoi* who, in happy fellowship with the gods, still did not know they were just the *andres*, a mere half of humankind? Or [is Pandora] an evil for humanity as a whole—men *and* women."[164]

For his part, Hesiod gives few clues concerning the status of human mortality during this mythic time of "gods and men," saying in *Works and Days* (line 42) that the "gods guard the means of life from *anthropous* (human beings)." The reader might also assume that Pandora's creation marks the origin of the differentiation between the half of humanity found in those who are described as *anthropoi* (human beings) categorized further into some other type of male and thus separated into the class of *andres*. Hesiod mentions both categories (*anthropoi* and *andres*) before, during, and after the creation of Pandora without clarifying the status of mortality within the two groups.

It is true that in the *Theogony*, "the first woman is not called Pandora but remains anonymous. Furthermore, she has no jar. She creates

---

161. Ibid., 51.

162. Loraux, *Children of Athena*, 74.

163. Ibid., 76. See lines 60–67 in *Works and Days*. This is similar to the formation of Enkidu who is part divine, part human and part animal.

164. Loraux, *Children of Athena*, 76, her emphasis.

the world's evils all by herself."[165] Scholars agree that the two versions of the creation of Pandora in the *Theogony* and in *Works and Days* are two versions of the same story, but few explicitly connect the sexuality of women with the origin of mortality. Few connect Pandora's sexuality to her introduction of the evils that will include the actual causes of mortality. Hesiod seems to suggest in *Theogony* that death for mortals existed prior to the creation of the "race" of women. Here, the unnamed "woman" is Zeus' retribution; "an evil for mortal men" but not the bringer of mortality itself. While the poet treats death and evil as separate categories in both poems, in *Works and Days*, Hesiod provides a more sophisticated rendering—weaving together the two concepts adroitly by means of Pandora's πιθός.[166]

What remains clinging to the inside Pandora's πιθός once all the evils have been dispersed is *elpis*. Translated by many as "hope," *elpis* can more accurately be interpreted "anticipation of bad as well as good things," and thus, *anticipation* is a much more cogent rendering.[167] Neils translates *elpis* specifically as the *false hope* that is prevented from escaping into the world by the plans of Zeus. "Since the other evils have escaped to do damage among mankind, false hope must have been retained" because "in this new, harsher world order in which man must labor for his living . . . false hope would be a formula for extinction . . . hence, to preserve man, Zeus . . . imprisons Elpis."[168] It is also instructive to examine Hesiod's word choice for the "home" of *elpis*, which is described as ἐν ἀρρήκτοισι δόμοισιν . . . πίθου ὑπὸ χείλεσιν "in its unbreakable home . . . under the lips of the *pithos*."[169] Hesiod's equation here between Pandora's *pithos* and her sexual nature is unmistakable. And given his strident misogyny, if the *pithos* is the womb/vagina of Pandora (complete with χείλεσιν "lips" that also attest to proof of her rampant sexual nature), then what remains not given to the world of men must be the sheer anticipation of women's sexuality. This anticipation, this *elpis*, is both good and evil—good in the

---

165. Sissa, *Greek Virginity*, 155.

166. Clay even realizes that "the jar itself is a doublet of Pandora, attractive on the outside, but a bane within" but does not make the connection between Pandora's bane and Pandora's sexual body. For Clay, Pandora's *pithos* is merely storage jar. See *Hesiod's Cosmos*, 103, 122ff.

167. Hesiod, *Theogony*, 95, see note 7.

168. Neils, "The Girl in the *Pithos*: Hesiod's *Elpis*" in Barringer, *Periklean Athens*, 40.

169. My translation.

sense that the poet understands too well that most men will always find sexual pleasure with women. The evil exists because, while the progeny that come from the womb are essential, women's sexual voracity, according to Hesiod's philosophy, will ultimately disappoint.

PANDORA AND THE SUMERIAN MYTHS

Charles Penglase draws many similarities between the Sumerian myths of Enki and the creation of Pandora. He connects Pandora's chthonic entrance into the world (fashioned from the earth by Hephaestos and pictured rising from the earth in artistic representations) with the "emerging head of mankind in Enlil's myth of the creation of mankind, 'Enlil and the Pickaxe.'"[170] He also connects the creation of Pandora to the Sumerian myth *Inanna's Descent to the Netherworld* and notes that Pandora's "*pithos* seems to be symbolizing, on a mythological plane, the netherworld."[171] He associates Inanna's return to earth and her subsequent "releasing the hostile evils from the netherworld on to mankind" with Pandora's scattering the world's evil by opening her πιθός.[172] But as we have seen, in *Works and Days* Pandora's πιθός is also associated with her genitals and, by extension, her sexual attributes—an association absent in *Inanna's Descent to the Netherworld*.

There are also similarities between Ishtar's adornment scene following her return to the upper world to Pandora's adornment by Athena in *Theogony*. It may help to clarify matters if we look more closely at the characters in the myths who are performing the actions of adorning. In *Ishtar's Descent to the Netherworld*, it is the gatekeeper who removes Ishtar's clothing at the command of the underworld goddess Ereshkigal, and it is not clear from the text whether it is Namtar (a lesser god and vizier of Ereshkigal) or the gatekeeper who re-dresses Ishtar upon her return to earth.[173] Neither Namtar or the gatekeeper are themselves gods.

I argue that a closer parallel to Pandora's adornment scene is found within the Epic of Gilgamesh in Shamhat's clothing of Enkidu (see above) because it is Shamhat who represents the goddess Inanna/Ishtar (and is later treated by the text as an actual deified goddess). Shamhat's

---

170. Penglase, *Greek Myths and Mesopotamia*, 205.
171. Ibid., 210.
172. Ibid., 211.
173. Dalley, *Myths from Mesopotamia*, 161n19.

counterpart is the goddess Athena who performs "all the dressing and adorning" for Pandora.¹⁷⁴

Penglase's point, however, that "the diseases and evils which come out of the jar [of Pandora] seem to be netherworld effusions, and this can be understood especially clearly in view of the Mesopotamian concept of the netherworld as the place from which demons and diseases emanate" is appropriate with some modifications.¹⁷⁵

Jane Harrison notes that Pandora's πιθός must be accounted "a very large jar, that either stands on or is partly buried in the earth" which she connects to the Greek practice of using large pithoi to bury the dead.¹⁷⁶ The practice of the *Anthesteria* or the release of spirits of the dead may be connected to more ancient versions of the Pandora myth. While Harrison is reticent to argue that Hesiod connects Pandora's πιθός to the practice of releasing "maleficent ghosts from the grave," I argue that he does indeed wish to make that association. In fact, Hesiod is making the claim that the genitals of his progenitor of the female race are the locus of evil. One of Pandora's ancient functions (one who releases evil) pairs her with Hermes Psychopompos whose purpose is to "let loose the κῆρες [ghosts, demons, spirits of the dead] from the grave-pithos."¹⁷⁷ In his story of the creation of the first woman, Hesiod reshapes the older tradition of Ge (mother earth).¹⁷⁸ In his poems, Hesiod conflates earlier chthonic associations of Pandora not just with an earth/birth-giving goddess, but now includes the more malicious aspects of her nature by combining her sexual "womb" with death and the origin of evil. Thus, the polemical phrase μέγα πῶμ' ("the mouth of women's womb") is semantically paired with πῆμα μέγα ("woman as a great woe") and has some similarities with the later Platonic saying *soma sema* ("the body is a tomb").

One aspect of the story of Pandora that remains to be compared with Sumerian myth in addition to her connection to sex and death (as we have seen), is her connection to wisdom and knowledge. In *Theogony*,

---

174. Penglase, *Greek Myths and Mesopotamia*, 221.

175. Ibid., 210.

176. Harrison, "Pandora's Box," 100, 112.

177. Ibid., 105.

178. Joan O'Brien also points out that "by Hesiod's time, Zeus had replaced the [earth goddess] as the dominant deity; and Pandora, now separated from her, would become the *pema*, scourge . . ." ("Nammu, Mami, Eve and Pandora," 35). She also suggests that the name of Pandora, "Hesiod's 'giver of all gifts' must have been attached to Ge, Demeter, or another earth goddess in the pre-Hesiodic Aegean" (40).

Hesiod does not name Pandora, nor does he mention any particular description of her mind, suggesting only that "a cherished wife is well-fitted in her thoughts."[179] It is only in *Works and Days* that Hesiod has Hermes place into Pandora the mind of a dog and a thieving disposition. He repeats the exact phrase ἐπίκλοπτον ἦθος ("thievish character") a few lines later and adds "lies and guileful words" to her final list of character traits.[180]

Some have argued that for the poets Hesiod and Homer, Pandora and Helen (of Troy) are "construct(s) specifically designed to bring misery to mortals" and that Helen, in the *Illiad*, like Pandora in *Theogony*, is described as πῆμα.[181] Helen's connection to Pandora deepens when we notice that "Helen does what no other Homeric character does: she insults herself" by using the terms that includes referring to herself as a dog (κυνὸς).[182] Many scholars argue that "the semantics of κύων / κυν in metaphor have not been well understood in general."[183] And I am not entirely convinced that there is no implication of sexual immorality when these terms are specifically used of women and/or goddesses (bitches, dogs, doglike, dogfaced, etc.) However, only Pandora has the term κύνεόν (doglike) applied specifically to her νόον (mind).[184]

The description of Pandora's mind as "doglike" may be Hesiod's attempt to disabuse the reader of any notion that Pandora could in any way be connected with wisdom or knowledge, unlike her Sumerian counterparts. Conversely, it may be the poet's attempt to see women's minds (and especially the mind of their progenitor) as partially wise to some extent, but focused on satisfying bodily desires by means of stealth and cunning. In the poems of Hesiod, Pandora's sexual nature and her intellect are common, bestial, and operate through guile and deception.

PANDORA AND ERICHTHONIUS

The two versions of the creation of Pandora describe "On the one side [*Theogony*], the presentation of an artificial creation in the form of a *parthenos*, and on the other [*Works and Days*], the emergence of a mixed

---

179. Hesiod, *Theogony*, 53.
180. Ibid.
181. Mayer, "Helen and the ΔΙΟΣΒΟΥΛΗ," 9, 10.
182. Graver, "Dog-Helen and Homeric Insult," 41.
183. Ibid., 42.
184. Ibid., 51.

creature composed of god, man and beast.[185] But the creation of Pandora also has several mythological threads that connect her to Erichthonius—the offspring of Haephaestus and (by proxy) Athena.

The story of Erichthonius is recounted in several poems and in prose. According to Apollodorus, Hephaestus pursued Athena but was unsuccessful in his sexual advance toward her—his semen spilled onto the Ge (Earth) and Erichthonius was born from the soil. Wishing to make the child immortal, Athena raised him without the knowledge of the other gods by hiding him in a chest and forbidding his caretakers, the sisters of Pandrosus, to open it. Their curiosity aroused, the sisters opened the chest, beheld the child—part human, part serpent—and were driven mad.[186]

Clearly, Greek tradition links Pandora with Erichthonius. First, they share the same "parents"—Pandora is created by Hephaestus on command of Zeus to be a *parthenos*. Pandora is adorned by Athena with a diadem fashioned by Hephaestus and decorated by wild animals; Erichthonius, part serpent, is created by Hephaestus (via Ge/earth), nurtured and protected by Athena who is the *Parthenos*, par excellence. Athena strives to make Erichthonius immortal; Zeus strives to unleash additional evils that bring mortality to humans through Pandora.

Both Pandora and Erichthonius occupied a place on the acropolis in Athens. Pausanias, in "describing the chryselephantine statue of Athena Parthenos, observes after just a single glance that there is a snake at her feet, who 'would be Erichthonios,' and that 'sculpted on the base of the statue is the birth of Pandora.'"[187] Pandora's associations with Erichthonius may also be connected to the older worship of the goddess Ge, which is the "ancient haunt of the snake-hero Cecrops" who in some mythic versions is the father of Erichthonius.[188] The association between Pandora and Erichthonius has been virtually ignored by most biblical scholars but will provide insight into the relationship between women's sexuality, death, and wisdom found in the second chapter of Genesis.

---

185. Loraux, *Children of Athena*, 76.

186. Apollodorus. See www.theoi.com/Text/Apollodorus3.html. In some versions of the myth, the snake-hero Cecrops is the father of Erichthonius and his caretakers are Cecrop's three daughters.

187. Loraux, *Children of Athena*, 114.

188. Harrison, "Pandora's Box," 114.

Fallen Angels and Fallen Women

Chapter Two

In order to understand how ancient mythologies were incorporated into later literary conceptions concerning Daughter of Man/Son of Man, we must read the character of Eve both within and against the other myths discussed thus far. We will compare the story of the "garden of Eden" found in Genesis 2 and 3 with a particular focus on how the role of Eve intersects with the role of the women previously surveyed in other ancient cosmogonies (Shamhat/Shiduri in the Epic of Gilgamesh and Pandora in Hesiod's *Theogony* and *Works and Days*). This chapter will illustrate how Eve is both similar to Shamhat/Shiduri and Pandora, but also how the text of Genesis 3 provides its own theological hermeneutic in its portrayal of the "mother of all living." As Shamhat/Shiduri and Pandora have been the focus for connecting themes of sexual knowledge, wisdom, loss of immortality and death—so Eve invites us to examine more closely those ideas whose trajectory continues throughout the Hebrew scriptures and into other myths of women and fallen angels.

The text of Genesis 2 and 3 may appear to be simple, but it is astonishingly complex.[1] Mesopotamian and Greek mythologies have been used widely for decades to provide evidence of earlier literary material underlying the story of the garden of Eden. I argue that Genesis 2 and 3 has not been examined with sufficient detail in order to discern many unmistakable thematic and linguistic parallels with the Epic of Gilgamesh and Hesiod's myth of Pandora. James Charlesworth has listed some fifty-seven "questions, even absurdities" generated by modern scholars connected to the famous story, which he believes is authored by J or the Yahwist writer and is "indebted to Akkadian, Canaanite, Egyptian,

---

1. I agree with Phyllis Trible's assessment that "if the story is simple, it is not, at the same time, neat and tidy. Abrupt, terse, elliptic, tentative . . . riddled with ambiguity . . ." quoted in Veenker, "Forbidden Fruit," 69.

Hittite, North Arabian, and Ugaritic" sources.[2] Charlesworth's attention is focused mainly on the symbolism and function of the *nahash*, or serpent, in the story, but his excellent exegesis and cross-disciplinary approach and methodology provides illumination upon several points of contact in Genesis with the themes described above.

GENESIS 2 AND 3

The first chapter of Genesis contains the shorter and later version of the creation myth usually ascribed to the Priestly writer and is dated to 500–400 BCE. The earlier and longer myth that concerns this chapter begins in Genesis 2:9, includes God's creation of Adam, and concludes with the expulsion of Adam and Eve from the garden (Gen 3:24). A brief summary of the myth is essential for our analysis because the story of "Adam and Eve" has been used (typically for biased agendas) to construct and uphold monolithic theological opinions concerning the role of women and men to the divine, their gendered relationship to each other, to the created order, and to sexual awareness, wisdom, and death.

After God creates heaven and earth, God creates a garden in Eden and fills it with trees. We are told in the narrative that the Tree of Life is located in the middle or center of the garden and the Tree of the Knowledge of Good and Evil is somewhere nearby. God creates Adam (man) from the dust/ground/earth in order that he may cultivate the garden. God places Adam inside the garden and charges him with an injunction: He may eat the fruit from any tree in the same garden with the exception of the fruit from the Tree of the Knowledge of Good and Evil. Eating from his tree will cause death. God creates from the earth wild beasts of the field, birds, and cattle which Adam duly names, but does not find among them a suitable partner. God creates woman from Adam's rib or side.[3] The recently created Serpent (נהש), described as the wisest of all the beasts of the field, engages the woman in conversation concerning the injunction given to Adam and by extension, to her as well. She repeats the injunction to the serpent who assures the woman that if she does eat from

---

2. Charlesworth, *Good and Evil Serpent*, 282–5. Most scholars accept the "Documentary Hypothesis" for dating the various authorial layers that comprise the Hebrew bible. For an alternative approach, see Cassuto, *Documentary Hypothesis* and Kitchen, *Reliability of the Old Testament*.

3. For a thorough account of the specialized linguistic relationship in Hebrew between "man" and "woman" אִשָּׁה כִּי מֵאִישׁ, see Meier, "Linguistic Clues."

the exempted tree, not only will she not die, but she and her partner will be like God—knowing good and evil. The woman consumes the fruit and gives the fruit to Adam which he also consumes. The woman and Adam perceive that they are naked and fashion leaves to cover themselves. The pair hear God walking in the garden and attempt to remain hidden. God calls Adam who responds and explains that the pair are hiding because they are naked. God inquires how the pair know this. Adam explains the consummation of the fruit and God pronounces a series of curses against the serpent, the woman and Adam. Adam names the woman Eve (Mother of All Living) and God clothes Adam and Eve in garments of skin. God announces that Adam has become perilously close to being like God—knowing good and evil—and in order to prevent Adam and Eve from eating again from the Tree of Life and becoming immortal, God banishes the pair from the garden by stationing two guarding cherubim and a revolving sword at the entrance to bar their return.

Many scholars warn readers against the idea that "a story such as Gen. 3 has only one meaning."[4] Indeed, as I intend to argue, "the writer [of Genesis 3] could have deliberately transformed a story that was initially more similar in outlook to that of Enkidu or Pandora, in order to highlight the distinctive *theological* understanding of life entailed by Hebrew faith in Yahweh."[5] I contend that a comparative reading of Genesis 2 and 3 with the mythologies of the Epic of Gilgamesh and Hesiod's two versions of Pandora yields insight into many aspects of the text. Such a comparative reading provides evidence that "the story of Eden" is the creation of an ancient Israelite mythos that is both dependent upon content originally found within the cultures of ancient Mesopotamia and Greece combined with content crafted from its own culture and creative theological discourse.

THE TREE OF THE KNOWLEDGE OF GOOD AND EVIL

According to Genesis *Rabbah*, Adam is warned against eating the fruit of the Tree of the Knowledge of Good and Evil because God wants to convey that sex is "more than carnal relations . . . [it is] an outward manifestation of the creative impulse. Thus, the meaning of the biblical idiom 'knowledge of good and evil'" suggests that "the creative impulse as manifested

---

4. Moberly, "Did the Serpent Get it Right?," 3.
5. Ibid., 23n64, italics original.

in sex (knowledge) can either build a world (good) or destroy it (evil)."[6] The enigmatic phrase "knowledge of good and evil," used four times in Genesis, is explicit "Biblical code phrase for sexual experience."[7] But the phrase also occurs in 2 Samuel 19:36 where King David's quartermaster general Barzillai, nearing the end of his life, laments "I am now eighty years old. Can I distinguish between good and evil? Can your servant taste what he eats and drinks? Can I still listen to the singing of men and women?"[8] Barzillai's meaning is implicit. He means to say that he can indeed "distinguish between good and evil" in making moral determinations but due to his old age, he cannot taste food or enjoy music. As Milgrom puts it, "one need not know Omar Khayyam to realize the third element [in Barzillai's lamentation] after wine and song is—women."[9] Therefore, when Barzillai asks "Can I distinguish between good and evil?" he is essentially putting forward the euphemism that means he can no longer enjoy sexual encounters. In his second example that argues for "knowing good and evil" as sexual euphemism, Milgrom notes that (after the Exodus when the Israelites are in the wilderness) "Moses reminds his people that they will not enter the [promised] land, [but that their] 'children who do not yet know good from evil, they shall enter it.'"[10] Milgrom contends that "since these 'children' are under the age of twenty (see Num 14:29–31), and many of them know the difference between good and evil, Moses probably means *unmarried* children, that is, those who have had no sexual experience."[11]

Themes connecting wisdom, sexuality, and death are also found in various Mesopotamian cultures by employing terms such as "fruit" and "eating" as explicitly sexual metaphors.[12] As we have seen, in the Epic of

6. Milgrom, *Sex and Wisdom*, 52.
7. Genesis 2:9, 17, 3:5, 22. See Milgrom, *Sex and Wisdom*, 21.
8. Milgrom, "Sex and Wisdom," 21.
9. Ibid.
10. Ibid.
11. Ibid.
12. Veenker, "Forbidden Fruit." For the opinion that "knowledge of good and evil" is moral only, see Eiselen, "Tree of the Knowledge." But compare Narrowe whose thesis is that the fruit of the Tree of the Knowledge of Good and Evil "did not reveal the nature of good and evil to Adam and Eve," it merely reveals that "the insight acquired [by the actions of eating from the tree] was limited to a recognition that it was improper for a man and a woman to be naked in each other's presence, a behavioral pattern that just about every Middle Eastern culture and civilization has retained to this day" (Narrowe, "Another Look," 187).

Gilgamesh "carnal knowledge is the first rung of the ladder of human knowing."[13] There are also many examples in the Hebrew Scriptures (for example Song of Songs 3) that combine "fruit" and "gardens" as sexual metaphor:

> Like the apple in the wildwood,
> So is my love among boys.
> In his shade I become sexually aroused; I crouch down
> And his fruit is sweet to my taste.[14]

Proverbs 30:18–19, 20 provides further evidence for such "overt eroticism."[15] There are additionally "several metaphors drawn from orchards, gardens . . . as well as the image of sexual eating" especially in the parallel poetic stichs in Song of Songs 4:16b:[16]

> Let my love enter his garden
> Let him eat its delectable fruits.

With these lines, the "female here invites her lover to 'enter his garden'; since garden is well established as 'vulva' and the verb 'to enter' has a straightforward sexual connotation . . . [meaning] 'to initiate coitus with her' . . . [and] since 'eating' is now established as sexual intercourse and 'fruit can serve as the metaphor for the sexual organ, [the male lover] has been invited to 'enjoy making love to her.'"[17] While such erotic language in Genesis 3 is more "covert," the phrase "eating from the fruit of the tree in the midst of the garden" is "laden with erotic connotations" and there can be no doubt that the term implies "sexual congress between Adam and Eve."[18] Not only does the metaphor and morphological elements of the myth point to its overall sexual connotation, but the structure of the narrative itself suggests that eating fruit is equated with engaging in sex. Genesis 2:25 (the transition from the second to the third chapter) and 3:7 taken together "form an inclusio marking a separate unit:"

> And the man and his wife were both naked,
> And they were not ashamed.

---

13. Veenker, "Forbidden Fruit," 57.

14. This he compares with Ishtar's invitation to Gilgamesh: "Come on Gilgamesh, be my lover and grant me your fruit" (Veenker, "Forbidden Fruit," 63).

15. Veenker, "Forbidden Fruit," 66.

16. Ibid.

17. Ibid.

18. Ibid.

> Then the eyes of both were opened,
> And they knew they were naked ...[19]

In 2:25 Adam and the woman have "no awareness of sexuality" but later in the narrative (3:7), Adam and the woman "are cognizant of their sexual nature."[20] Since the "solitary act in the interim is the 'eating of fruit,'" the only interpretation possible is that "'the transgression,' or the 'eating of the fruit,' is the sex act and nothing less" and that the "very structure of the narrative" attests to this fact.[21]

It is possible that the meaning of the "knowledge of good and evil" may be focused primarily on wisdom rather than sexual awakening, since "within the context of Mesopotamian fertility religion it is understandable that sexual experience would be considered the means of initiation into civilization. But in the context of the religion of Israel, which does not see fertility as the ground of all being human and divine, there is no such place for an initiation."[22] Yet as we have found in the Epic of Gilgamesh and the in mythology of Pandora, the portrayal of sexual awareness and human initiation into sexuality is a multivalent and complicated process, especially as it concerns the relationship between various creator deities of Mesopotamia, Greece, and Egypt. I would argue that Genesis is no less complicated and no less adept at conveying these same themes.

The sexual motif found within the woman and Adam's gaining of wisdom or "knowing good from evil" is encapsulated within a wider rhetoric of the Yahwist writer whose own theological contribution to the text reshapes or reframes the "animonies between Yahwism and the Canaanite fertility cult."[23] While general commonalities between the Yahwist writer and Canaanite myths certainly exist, I will argue that there are far more actual thematic as well as semantic correlations between Genesis 2 and 3 and the Epic of Gilgamesh in addition to correlations connected with Hesiod's myth of Pandora.

---

19. Ibid., 66.
20. Ibid.
21. Ibid., 67.
22. Bailey, "Primal Woman in Gilgamesh," 147. See especially 145ff.
23. Boomershine, "Narrative Rhetoric in Genesis," 127ff.

Chapter Two

THE EPIC OF GILGAMESH AND GENESIS 2–3

While there is plethora of work by scholars comparing Mesopotamian creation myths and especially the Epic of Gilgamesh to Genesis 2–3,[24] very few discuss in detail the similarities between the woman/Eve and Shamhat/Shiduri. But when the two texts are read in tandem, we find not only very close congruencies between the woman/Eve and Shamhat/Shiduri, but also between the other characters mentioned in both stories. When we transcribe both texts side by side, these similarities become apparent.

Earlier, we noted that Shamhat's *nomen* was in fact her title as well as her role as *harmintu*, which certainly included her significant status as a representative of the goddess Ishtar. In the same way, the name "Woman" given to the female human in Genesis serves to define her role and provide her with a title.[25] Below are sections from the second chapter of Genesis paired with corresponding sections of the Epic of Gilgamesh:

Genesis (trans. from Rashi commentary)	Gilgamesh (trans. Andrew George)
	1.95 [(Aruru) it was created them,] mankind so numerous:
2:7 Yhwh Elohim <u>formed the man of soil from the earth</u> . . . (*Adam* from *Adamah*)	1.101 The goddess Aruru, she washed her hands, <u>took a pinch of clay</u>, threw it into the wild.
2:8 <u>Yhwh Elohim planted a garden</u> in Eden to the east, <u>and placed there the man whom He had formed.</u>	<u>In the wild she created Enkidu</u>, the hero . . .

---

24. For example: Stordalen, *Echoes of Eden*, 243ff; Moberley, "Did the Serpent get it Right?"; Bailey, "Initiation and the Primal Woman"; Watson, "Tree of Life"; Walsh, "Genesis 2:4b—3:24"; Westermann, *Genesis 1–11*; etc.

25. Meier notes that "it is only in Israel that one can intimately connect specific features of woman's creation from man with the respective names applied to man and woman" through the linguistic use of the 'locative' or 'directional' *he* (the *he* locale) which describes and connects the creation of *adam* (man) from *adamah* (earth) and *isha* (woman) from man *ish* ("Linguistic Clues," 19).

Fallen Angels and Fallen Women

2:22 Yhwh Elohim built the side he had taken from the man into the woman	
	1.187 [Shamhat] spread her clothing and [Enkidu] lay upon her.
	1.202 [Now Enkidu] had reason, and wide understanding.
[The woman 'sits at the feet' of the Serpent, i.e. and "listens intently" to its words.]	1.204 [Enkidu] came back and sat at the feet of [Shamhat]...then to [Shamhat's] words he listened intently.
[The Serpent] said to the woman...	1.206–207 [...Shamhat] talked to him, to Enkidu:
2:4 for Yhwh Elohim knows that on the day you eat of [the Tree of the Knowledge of Good and Evil] your eyes will be opened <u>and you will be like Yhwh Elohim</u>.	You are handsome, Enkidu, <u>you are just like a god!</u>
2:6 And the woman saw that the tree was good for eating and... that it was desirable for comprehension...	P.66 [Shamhat's] words [Enkidu] heard, her speech found favor: the counsel of the woman struck home in his heart.
	P.70 [Shamhat] stripped and clothed Enkidu in part of her garment, the other part she put on herself.
and she took of its fruit and ate; and she gave also to her husband with her	2.36 By the hand [Shamhat] took [Enkidu], like a god [she led him].
	P.96 [Shamhat] opened her mouth, saying to Enkidu:
and he <u>ate</u>.	'<u>Eat</u> the bread, Enkidu, essential to life...'
2:7 And the eyes of both were opened and they realized that they were naked; and they sewed together a fig leaf and made themselves aprons.	

It may be impossible to argue that the writers and compilers of the second creation story in Genesis had textual or oral access to the Epic of Gilgamesh. Nevertheless, as Charlesworth explains in his work on the role of the serpent found in the myth, the authors of Genesis were immersed in the symbolic world of their age and used various themes and tropes important to the culture.[26] It is also not possible to determine that the authors and compilers of Genesis shaped their version of the creation of humankind as a polemic to be read counter to the concepts contained within Epic of Gilgamesh or other similar myths. But it is instructive to investigate both the comparative and divergent aspects between both stories for the purposes of tracing the mythological antecedents that will ultimately contribute to a more complete understanding of the concept "son of man."

In the Epic of Gilgamesh, we are not told what material the goddess Aruru employs to create all humankind, only that she fashions the hero Enkidu from a pinch of clay. In like fashion, Yhwh creates Adam from *adamah* (earth/soil). Aruru places Enkidu "in the wild"; Yhwh places Adam in a garden (Eden).

The creation of Woman in Genesis parallels the action of Shamhat in her instruction/civilizing/enlightenment of Enkidu. The sexual engagement between Shamhat and Enkidu forms a shared structure comparable to the sexual engagement of Adam and the woman (see chart). Both stories have as their focus the topic of sexual enlightenment. Enkidu, recently made a virtual disciple of Shamhat (in her role as the representative of the goddess Inanna/Ishtar) "sits at the feet of Shamhat." While the compilers of the Genesis story do not explicitly use language for discipleship in their portrayal of the relationship between the woman and the serpent, the implicit meaning is clear: the woman gives ear to what the serpent is saying—she listens and heeds the words of the serpent. Shamhat and the serpent speak to their respective "disciples" and both the woman and Enkidu receive their counsel. The woman "sees" that the fruit is desirable and able to make one wise, and Shamhat's words "strike home" in Enkidu's heart. In both cases, the woman and Enkidu follow their respective sage's advice. Finally, both the woman and Shamhat share a form of comparison with divinity. Shamhat declares that through his sexual engagement with her, Enkidu is now "like a god" while the woman—once she has eaten from the fruit of the tree of the Knowledge

---

26. Charlesworth, *Good and Evil Serpent*, 315ff.

of Good and Evil, i.e. (participated in sexual engagement with Adam), "will be like Yhwh." Both "godlike" states are related to sexual congress.

Obviously, both stories view the intimate sexual connection between Shamhat and Enkidu, and the woman and Adam in vastly different ways. Shamhat, under the agency of Inanna/Ishtar, brings enlightenment through sexual contact with Enkidu. His enlightenment is positive: he dissociates himself from the wilderness and his animal nature and becomes a civilized human and eventual hero. Enkidu's act of "eating" proves his status as civilized human and is confirmation of his partial divinity. The woman and Adam's act of "eating" is a loss of status with the divine. Like Shamhat in the Epic of Gilgamesh, the woman in Genesis acts through the agency of the serpent, and brings sexual enlightenment to Adam, but her action is seen as pejorative. Her consumption of the fruit gives her sexual enlightenment that she literally "gives" to Adam. But such "knowing" of sexuality brings shame and guilt to both the woman and Adam and ultimately disbars the couple from the garden and immortality.

Within the larger section mentioned above there is a smaller thematic unit. In the Epic, Shamhat's creation of Enkidu's garment from her own clothing may be compared to the first couple's manufacture of garments in Genesis. Enkidu's garment, however, symbolically depicts his protection by the goddess Inanna/Ishtar and is a celebration of his entry into the civilized world. In contrast, the fashioning of garments by the woman and Adam are a direct result of their guilt and shame brought about by their sexual awareness couched euphemistically as "eating" the fruit of the Tree of the Knowledge of Good and Evil.

THE TRIPLE CURSE

Although the woman has been the instigator in facilitating the pejorative if enlightening sexual knowledge to Adam, when the couple hear the voice of Yhwh and retreat among the trees in the garden, it is Adam alone who is addressed by Yhwh. When Adam explains to his maker the reason for his concealment (that he is naked, i.e., he and the woman "know good and evil,") Yhwh first queries Adam how it is that he understands his own nakedness, ("who told you that you were naked?") but does not wait for a response before issuing a second question: Have you eaten from the tree which I commanded you not to eat?[27] Adam implicates the woman for his

27. Rashi, *Rashi 'al ha-Torah*.

(and their) culpability in disobeying the injunction: "The woman whom you gave to be with me—she gave me of the tree, and I ate."[28]

To Yhwh's query "what is this you (feminine singular) have done" the woman answers that the serpent is the cause of her (their) culpability in disobeying the injunction: "The serpent deceived me, and I ate."[29] In his quest for answers, Yhwh does not even attempt to question the serpent. Instead, Yhwh's set of queries to Adam and the woman conclude with the serpent and become the focus of a tripartite "curse."[30]

Yhwh ⟶	Adam ↓
Yhwh ⟶	The Woman ↓
Yhwh (tripartite curse) ⟶	The Serpent

Now the order is reversed. Beginning with the serpent, Yhwh then curses the woman and finally Adam:

Yhwh			
	adamah ≠ Adam	≠ The Woman	≠ The Serpent
	▶ 3	▶ 2	▶ 1

Yhwh's first curse is directed to the serpent. Its goal is to disrupt the relationship established between the serpent and the woman forever: "I will put enmity between you and the woman, and between your offspring and her offspring."[31] The next curse is directed to the woman and effectively disturbs the relationship between the woman and Adam: "I will greatly increase your suffering . . . and your craving will be for your

---

28. Ibid. The Hebrew נתן (gave) is used by both times by Adam and seems to suggest another attempt by Adam to deflect culpability: because the woman was a gift from You, I assumed that anything she gave me would be an extension of Your original gift.

29. Ibid. It is also interesting to notice the wordplay here: in the beginning of Genesis 3, the serpent is described as ערום (wisest) a word that plays upon the later ערים (naked). Both words are visually similar to ארור (cursed).

30. The order of Yhwh's curses is slightly out of sequence from which the created beings are made: Adam, serpent, beasts of the field, and the woman. Savran connects the cursing in Genesis 3 with the story of Balaam. See Savran, "Beastly Speech," 41 ff.

31. Rashi, *Rashi ʿal ha-Torah*.

Fallen Angels and Fallen Women

husband and he will rule over you."[32] Finally, Yhwh addresses Adam and terminates the once harmonious relationship between the earth/soil (*adamah*) from which he was formed and Adam himself: "Because you have listened to the voice of the Woman ... accursed is the ground because of you ... by the sweat of your brow you shall eat bread until you return to the ground from which you were taken"[33] In each curse, the woman figures prominently: beginning with Yhwh's "מַה־זֹּאת עָשִׂית" (what is this you have done?) all of the deity's curses, even when they are directed at the other characters, mention the woman. The serpent and the woman will be enemies, as will their offspring; the woman will endure pain in childbearing and be ruled by Adam; and because Adam "listened to the voice" of the woman, even the very ground is cursed.

THE CURSES OF ENKIDU AND YHWH

There are both thematic and linguistic similarities between Tablet VII in the Epic of Gilgamesh and Genesis 3:13–21. In the Epic, Enkidu, faced with his own morality, seeks retribution by cursing Shamhat, whom he holds accountable for his predicament. In Genesis, Yhwh, upon discovering that the first couple has disobeyed his only injunction, seeks both retribution and banishment.

Epic of Gilgamesh (George Translation)	Genesis 3[A]
VII Line 100 [After][Enkidu] had cursed the hunter to his heart's content, he decided [also] to curse Shamhat [the harlot:]	
104 [I will] curse you with a mighty curse my curse shall afflict you now and	:13 ...more cursed are you than all the animals and all the beasts of the field ...

---

32. Ibid.

33. Ibid. It is interesting to note that in eating from the fruit of the forbidden tree, we are not told explicitly (in the text) whether the woman communicates directly to Adam. The only instance Adam in the text has "listened to" the woman's voice is when she speaks to the serpent (by way of explaining the original injunction which neither she nor the serpent have directly heard because they were not yet created) and again when the woman (in the presence of Adam) speaks to Yhwh.

forthwith! A household to delight in [you shall not] acquire, [never to] Reside *in the* [*midst*]of a family!	:16 I will greatly increase your suffering and your pregnancy; in pain shall you bear children.
	:17 Accursed is the ground because of you
119 [Thorn and]briar shall skin your feet!	:18 Thorns and thistles shall it sprout for you
130 Because [you made] me[weak who was undefiled!] Yes, in the wild [you weakened] me, who was undefiled!	:20 The Man called his wife's name Eve, because she had become the mother of all the living.
134 (Shamash the sun god speaks to Enkidu) O Enkidu, why curse Shamhat (my) harlot, who fed you bread that was fit for a king, who clothed you in a splendid garment . . .	:21 And Yhwh made for Adam and his wife garments of skin, and He clothed them.
152 (After Enkidu reverses Shamhat's curses) May you be led into the [palace] of the gods (George): Ishtar, [the ablest] of gods, shall grant you entrance . . . ᴮ	
A. Rashi, *Rashi ʿal ha-Torah*. B. See chapter 1 for commentary on Enkidu's reversal of Shamhat's curse and his possible divinization of her.	

The characters of Yhwh and Enkidu are functioning from opposite degrees of mortality. Enkidu, despite his hero status, cannot escape his mortality and his cursing Shamhat will have no effect on prolonging his life. Yhwh is immortal and his curses will impose future conditions on the quality of the (now certain) mortal life of his creatures. Yhwh and Enkidu's initial motive for retribution, however, is driven by the sexual action of a woman. Yhwh's preoccupation with connecting the woman to each portion of his tripartite curse is similar to Enkidu's twenty-four lines of vitriol specifically aimed at Shamhat and her vocation.[34]

It is possible to compare Adam's impugning the woman solely for the shared crime of eating from the Tree of the Knowledge of Good and Evil to Enkidu's deathbed cursing of Shamhat. Such dissembling by

---

34. George, *Epic of Gilgamesh*, page 58ff.

Adam serves to underscore "the importance of [the Woman's status and] position."³⁵ The same may be said of Enkidu's obsession with Shamhat. Enkidu seems, however, to share the motif of cursing more with Yhwh than with Adam. A close reading of the text provides evidence that Enkidu's articulation concerning the magnitude of his curse toward Shamhat contains parallels with Yhwh's declaration leveled against the serpent that he become "more cursed" of all the creatures. Enkidu would rob Shamhat of children altogether; Yhwh only dooms the woman to suffer painful childbirth.³⁶ Both Enkidu and Yhwh (in his invective toward Adam) refer to the harshness of the ground. In the Epic, the god Shamash connects Shamhat's garments to her almost sacred treatment of Enkidu. In contrast, Yhwh's creation of "garments of skin" serve as a visible reminder to first couple of their disobedience to Yhwh and their enduring shame.

Enkidu's final lament—"naming" his motive for cursing Shamhat—may be paradoxically parallel to Adam's "naming" the woman.³⁷ Adam's first "naming" of the woman is reported in Genesis 2:23, and contains a semantic play on the Hebrew similarities between "man" and "woman."³⁸ Now that the woman has become sexually aware, she will be known as Eve "the mother of all living." Just as Enkidu traces his impending death and mortality to his sexual awakening by Shamhat, Adam must trace his mortality to the sexual awakening of the woman. The end result for both women is diametrically opposed: Shamhat becomes divinized and may even have escaped mortality, but Eve will be driven from paradise and kept from the tree that might have given her eternal life.

Thus we see that the wider view of the relationship between created humans and civilization found in Genesis is at odds with the view found within the mythology of Mesopotamia. "In Mesopotamian myths, civilization arises via the intervention of gods or other divine beings . . . in Genesis 1–11, on the other hand, there are no divine mediators . . . rather, civilization is the product of human endeavor."³⁹ What we see by comparing the texts of Gilgamesh and Genesis is that "particularly through the Eden narrative's portrayal of civilizing knowledge as illicitly acquired

---

35. Bailey, "Primal Woman in Gilgamesh," 149.

36. Some scholars note the parallels in the ability of Sumerian goddesses to give birth "without pain or travail" but mortal women are known as "the screaming one" (Jongsma-Tieleman, "Creation of Eve," 180n18).

37. It may also be parallel, contra Bailey see above to Adam's "blaming" the woman.

38. See Meier, "Linguistic Clues."

39. Melvin, "Divine Mediation and the Rise of Civilization," 2.

divine knowledge" the two texts are radically at odds with humanity's participation in the sexual life of divine beings.⁴⁰

THE TREE OF LIFE AND GILGAMESH

It is not clear that either Adam or Eve are created to be immortal.⁴¹ And, in fact, it is nowhere supported by the text.⁴² Yhwh's prohibition to Adam against eating the fruit from the Tree of the Knowledge of Good and Evil (that he "shall die") does not necessarily indicate Adam's created condition includes his immortality; Yhwh is warning Adam that death will be the consequence of eating its fruit. If it is the case that both Adam and the woman are created to be immortal, why does Yhwh later lament his fear that (Adam, at least) will eat from the Tree of Life and live forever?⁴³

In describing to the serpent the prohibition given by Yhwh against eating from the Tree of the Knowledge of Good and Evil, the woman (not yet named) refers to the Tree of Life, which she says is in "the middle" of the garden. Twice when the Tree of Life (ועץ החיים) is referred to in the text, it is modified by "in the midst of" or "in the center of" (בתקך) as its designation and location (Genesis 2:9 and 3:3). The Tree of the Knowledge of Good and Evil has no such linguistic marker.⁴⁴

---

40. Ibid.

41. Milgrom cites the problem with eventually overpopulating the garden as the logic behind his pronouncement that "After all, Adam and Eve are immortal" Milgrom, "Sex and Wisdom," 21. Cf., however, Narrowe, "Another Look"; Watson, "Tree of Life." An excellent analysis on the mortality of Adam is given by Stordalen, *Echoes of Eden*, 229ff.

42. Moberly, "Did the Serpent Get it Right?," 14ff.

43. Charlesworth notes that the Yahwist "does not suggest that Adam was created with immortality" but must be allowed to eat at least periodically from the Tree of Life in order to gain immortality—something not possible after the exile from Eden (*Good and Evil Serpent*, 315). But Moberly observes that such a view, while possible, creates new problems ("Did the Serpent Get it Right?," 15n39). In addition, Moberly notices that the mention of the Tree of Life found in the introduction and conclusion to the story, but which is absent through much of the text, "gives the impression of being an interpretation of what is entailed by human obedience and disobedience to God that has been joined to the tradition, yet not fully integrated into it" ("Did the Serpent Get it Right?," 2). And see Westermann, *Genesis 1–11*.

44. Rashi, *Rashi 'al ha-Torah*, 25n2: *Targum Onkelos*. "If הגן בתוך meant 'within the garden,' and tells us only that the tree of life grew within the area of the garden, it would have appeared at the end of the verse, after ועץ הדעת טוב ורע, for the Tree of the Knowledge of Good and Bad also grew within the area of the garden. The positioning

Fallen Angels and Fallen Women

It appears that the woman desires wisdom even at the expense of her possible immortality. One question arises: previously in her conversation with the serpent the woman has given the location of the forbidden tree (the Tree of the Knowledge of Good and Evil), which she believes she must not even touch, "in the center of the garden." But the only tree with that linguistic marker ("in the center") is the Tree of Life. The fruit of the tree the serpent is suggesting the woman eat is not in the center because the Tree of the Knowledge of Good and Evil does not have that location (see above).

A synchronic approach to the text of Genesis 2:4b—3:24 reveals "a highly structured unit [whose] principal pattern is a concentric arrangement of seven scenes, each of which is tightly organized"[45] that may be further divided into "narrative" and "dialogue."[46] I argue, in addition, that the text of Genesis 2 and 3 also exhibits nesting sets of highly complex linguistic structures whose interrelated form and function have not been adequately examined. While such an undertaking is beyond the scope of this chapter, it may be instructive to compare and contrast sections of direct discourse in Genesis 2 and 3 in a manner similar to a synchronic analysis. By focusing solely upon the linguistic component of three specific sets of conversational exchanges between Yhwh and Adam and between the serpent and the woman, we may understand more fully the significance of the relationship between the woman and the two trees in the garden.

In the whole of Genesis (apart from naming the animals, naming the woman, and finally calling her "Eve") Adam has direct discourse with Yhwh twice, both in answer to Yhwh's queries. The woman (apart from naming "Cain" and Seth" later in Genesis) has direct discourse with the serpent and Yhwh, both in answer to queries. In the text, Adam and Eve never converse with one another.[47] We begin by comparing the injunction of Yhwh to Adam with the recollection of that injunction by the woman:[48]

---

of הגן בתקך after החיים ועץ and before הדעת ועץ וטוב ורע indicated that it describes a quality particular to the tree of life; thus, it is understood as 'in the center of the garden' (*Levush HaOrah*)."

45. Walsh, "Genesis: 2:4b—3:24," 177, 161.

46. Ibid., 161. For a similar analysis using direct and third person discourse, see White, "Direct and Third Person Discourse."

47. It is interesting to notice that Yhwh's first words to Adam is a command, while Yhwh's first words to the woman is an accusation: מַה־זֹּאת עָשִׂית "What is this you have done?" See Moberly, "Did the Serpent Get it Right?," 4.

48. Rashi, *Rashi ʿal Ha-Torah*.

Woman (to Serpent)	Yhwh (to Adam)	Serpent (to Woman)
Of the fruit of any tree in the garden we may eat. Of the fruit of the tree which is in the middle of the garden God has said: 'You shall not touch it, lest you die.'	Of every tree of the garden you may eat; but of the Tree of the Knowledge of Good and Evil, you must not eat thereof; for on the day you eat of it you shall surely die.	Did perhaps God say 'you shall not eat of any tree of the garden?'
		You will not surely die; for God knows that on the day you eat of it your eyes will be opened and you will be like God knowing and evil.

Taking the woman's recounting of Yhwh's injunction as our standard, if we align the thematic elements in all three discourses, we find that certain word-for-word correspondences exist:

Woman	Yhwh	Serpent
of the fruit of any tree of the garden we may eat	of every tree of the garden you may freely eat	did perhaps God say you shall not eat of any tree of the garden
from the fruit of the tree	but of the tree of the Knowledge of Good and Evil	knowing good and evil
which is in the center of the garden		
God said		And you will be like God
you shall not eat of it	and you must not eat of it	
and you shall not touch it		
lest you die	you shall surely die	you will not surely die

In the Masoretic text and in the LXX by following the order of the woman's discourse, the similarities become more apparent:.

Woman	Yhwh	Serpent
מִפְּרִי עֵץ־הַגָּן נֹאכֵל	מִכֹּל עֵץ־הַגָּן אָכֹל תֹּאכֵל	הַגָּן לֹא תֹאכְלוּ מִכֹּל עֵץ
וּמִפְּרִי הָעֵץ	וּמֵעֵץ	
	טוֹב וָרָע הַדַּעַת	יֹדְעֵי טוֹב וָרָע

Fallen Angels and Fallen Women

אֲשֶׁר בְּתוֹךְ־הַגָּן		
אָמַר אֱלֹהִים		וִהְיִיתֶם כֵּאלֹהִים
לֹא תֹאכְלוּ מִמֶּנּוּ	לֹא תֹאכַל מִמֶּנּוּ	כִּי בְּיוֹם אֲכָלְכֶם מִמֶּנּוּ
וְלֹא תִגְּעוּ בּוֹ		וְנִפְקְחוּ עֵינֵיכֶם
פֶּן־תְּמֻתוּן	מוֹת תָּמוּת	לֹא־מוֹת תְּמֻתוּן

In the MT text, a preponderance of exact word matches are found within the discourse between Yhwh and the serpent, followed by a lesser number of exact word matches in the discourse between the woman and Yhwh, and two exact matches in the discourse between the woman and the Serpent. The only exact word match between the serpent and the woman occurs with the serpent's phrase that the pair "will surely not die," reproducing the verb form used by the woman, possibly to shade his words using her voice.[49]

In answering the serpent's query, the woman is obliged to "cite the prohibition [of Yhwh], and consequently make both God and his words into objects of reference of a third person statement."[50] The compiler would have had no other alternative for the woman's answer since she does not have direct experience of Yhwh's prohibition concerning the Tree of the Knowledge of Good and Evil at the time it was delivered to Adam. The woman was created after the prohibition was given. Since Adam is noted in the text (after the direct discourse between the serpent and the woman) as being physically present (with her) (עִמָּהּ),[51] it is difficult to imagine that the woman would have received direct discourse from Yhwh, both because Yhwh would not have repeated the prohibition to the pair after it was given to Adam, and Yhwh is not present to give

---

49. Thematically, however, allowing for changes in verb form due to origin of speaker and resulting reportage, all three discourses are in complete congruence concerning "from all the trees" the pair may eat and that the result of violating the injunction is death.

50. White, "Direct and Third Person Discourse," 98.

51. According to Phipps, "In the Vulgate, Jerome omitted translating from either the Hebrew Bible or the Greek Septuagint the prepositional phrase which establishes Adam's presence" ("Eve and Pandora Contrasted," 35). Jean Higgins points out that Adam's being (with her) (the woman) was noticed by early feminist theologians such as Elizabeth Cady Stanton and Katherine Sakenfeld, who contributed to *The Woman's Bible*. In her article, Higgins lists five possibilities for suggesting "Adam was present at the serpent-Eve dialogue," but makes her strongest case by citing the presence of the Hebrew word "*immah*" "with her" ("Myth of Eve," 645n47; see also 646ff.).

Chapter Two

such a repetition.[52] It seems the case that the woman has received knowledge of the prohibition from Adam.

The failure of the woman to adequately report Yhwh's injunction to the serpent against eating from the Tree of the Knowledge of Good and Evil has been construed as "an indicator of Eve's stupidity, immorality, or lack of confidence in God's words."[53] But when the direct discourse between all the characters in the text is viewed schematically, it is difficult to conclude that the woman is any of these. We must set aside the bizarre fact that during the woman's conversation with the serpent Adam does not attempt to correct the woman's factual errors. Even if the woman has heard the prohibition from Adam and skewed the details, the fact that Adam does not correct the woman implies that Adam recalls the prohibition exactly as the woman recounts it to the serpent. But this suggestion creates entirely new problems, so we must assume that, because the reader of the text is "present" when Yhwh gives the prohibition to Adam, that Adam does indeed know the details of the injunction. Why then the woman's confusion? We are left with few alternatives. Either the woman does, in fact, get Yhwh's injunction wrong, or she is under the impression that it is the Tree of Life (the only tree in the center of the garden), as opposed to the Tree of the Knowledge of Good and Evil, she must avoid.[54]

We return again to the curious fact concerning the preponderance of exact word and phrase matches between Yhwh and the serpent. Some commentators have suggested that the serpent's clever wordplay is an ingenious method of persuasion. In order to encourage the woman to eat from the Tree of the Knowledge of Good and Evil, the serpent assumes Yhwh's authority by employing the very words spoken by Yhwh. However, Yhwh did not create the serpent until after he has given the prohibition to Adam. How is it possible for the serpent to use Yhwh's

---

52. It is possible that between the time of her creation and the time of the serpent's query, the woman had her own private discourse with Yhwh, but this cannot be supported in the text for the reasons given above.

53. Kvam, *Eve and Adam*, 33. According to Bal, however, the woman's rehearsal of Yhwh's command to the serpent show where the woman's priorities lie, quoted in Kvam, *Eve and Adam*, 33. According to Rashi, the woman's adding to Yhwh's commandment was a violation of the commandment itself. See Rashi, *Rashi 'al ha-Torah*, 31n3.

54. White's statement that the woman "uses what appears to be a circumlocution for 'tree of knowledge of good and evil'" does not take into account the specificity of the carefully chosen language. See White, "Direct and Third Person Discourse," 98. See also Moberly, "Did the Serpent Get it Right?," 6n13. A fuller discussion follows.

exact words if he has not heard them and presumably does not know they exist? If the serpent is merely questioning the woman concerning the details of Yhwh's injunction (the question arises as to why he would know about the injunction at all), why does he not use words that are not spoken by Yhwh?[55] We cannot avoid the conclusion that the serpent is not merely asking a simple question.

Both the Masoretic text and the text of the LXX display the same exact word and phrase matches with one interesting difference. In the Masoretic text, the serpent combines both Yhwh's initial *qal* infinitive absolute construct with the masculine plural form of the verb used by the woman which he negates (לֹא־מוֹת תְּמֻתוּן) "You [both] shall surely not die." In the text of the LXX, however, both Yhwh and the serpent use the same grammatical construction (a dative noun masculine singular common, paired with the indicative future second middle person plural):[56]

Woman[c]	Yhwh	Serpent
ἀπὸ καρποῦ <u>ξύλου τοῦ παραδείσου</u> φαγόμεθα	ἀπὸ παντὸς <u>ξύλου τοῦ</u> ἐν τῷ παραδείσῳ βρώσει φάγῃ	οὐ μὴ φάγητε ἀπὸ παντὸς <u>ξύλου τοῦ</u> ἐν τῷ παραδείσῳ
<u>ἀπὸ δὲ καρποῦ τοῦ ξύλου</u>	<u>ἀπὸ δὲ τοῦ ξύλου</u> τοῦ	
	γινώσκειν καλὸν καὶ πονηρόν	γινώσκοντες καλὸν καὶ πονηρόν
ὅ ἐστιν ἐν μέσῳ τοῦ παραδείσου		
εἶπεν ὁ θεός		καὶ ἔσεσθε ὡς θεοὶ
<u>οὐ φάγεσθε ἀπ' αὐτοῦ</u>	<u>οὐ φάγεσθε ἀπ' αὐτοῦ</u>	
	ᾗ δ' ἂν ἡμέρᾳ φάγητε ἀπ' αὐτοῦ	

55. Yhwh's command is given to Adam using all masculine singular verb forms, which the serpent changes to masculine plural (to include the woman) in asking the question 'did God, in fact say"; the woman uses both first common plural and masculine plural verb forms in her report to the serpent.

56. In Greek, there is no grammatical construction similar to the one used in Hebrew, so the compilers of the LXX translate the Hebrew literally: "Death, you will not die!" By aligning the grammatical constructs used by both Yhwh and the serpent, the text of the LXX seems to anticipate the creation of the woman by having Yhwh use the plural form of the verb when he is addressing only the masculine singular Adam.

οὐδὲ μὴ ἅψησθε αὐτοῦ		διανοιχθήσονται ὑμῶν οἱ ὀφθαλμοί
ἵνα μὴ ἀποθάνητε	θανάτῳ ἀποθανεῖσθε	οὐ θανάτῳ ἀποθανεῖσθε
c. Grammatical correspondences between the woman and Yhwh are underlined; between Yhwh and the serpent italicized; between the woman and the serpent bolded.		

EATING FROM THE TREE OF LIFE

The Tree of Life is mentioned in Genesis three times (2:9; 3:3; 3:22). At its creation, the tree's location is marked—it is found in the center (or midst/middle) of the garden (MT and LXX):

וְעֵץ הַחַיִּים בְּתוֹךְ הַגָּן וְעֵץ הַדַּעַת טוֹב וָרָע:

καὶ τὸ ξύλον τῆς ζωῆς ἐν μέσῳ τῷ παραδείσῳ καὶ τὸ ξύλον τοῦ εἰδέναι γνωστὸν καλοῦ καὶ πονηροῦ

When the woman is recounting Yhwh's injunction to the serpent, she identifies the forbidden tree as "in the center" but does not call it specifically "Tree of Life" (MT and LXX):

וּמִפְּרִי הָעֵץ אֲשֶׁר בְּתוֹךְ־הַגָּן אָמַר אֱלֹהִים לֹא תֹאכְלוּ מִמֶּנּוּ וְלֹא תִגְּעוּ בּוֹ פֶּן־תְּמֻתוּן

ἀπὸ δὲ καρποῦ τοῦ ξύλου ὅ ἐστιν ἐν μέσῳ τοῦ παραδείσου εἶπεν ὁ θεός οὐ φάγεσθε ἀπ' αὐτοῦ οὐδὲ μὴ ἅψησθε αὐτοῦ ἵνα μὴ ἀποθάνητε

Is it possible that the tree the woman believes she and Adam must avoid is not the Tree of the Knowledge of Good and Evil but the Tree of Life? While Yhwh does not specifically tell Adam that he could eat from the Tree of Life in particular, Yhwh does allow Adam to "freely eat" from any tree in the garden, with the exception of the Tree of the Knowledge of Good and Evil. In the verse before Yhwh's prohibition, we are told that the Tree of Life is at the center of the garden and that the only tree whose fruit may not be eaten is the Tree of the Knowledge of Good and Evil.

Although it is of significant theological concern to be able to ascertain whether Adam had been eating from the Tree of Life until he and the woman were exiled from the garden, it may not be possible to determine. It is difficult to imagine the compilers of the myth giving Adam such a duplicitous character that he would eat from the Tree of Life but allow the woman (once decried as "flesh of my flesh") to avoid the same tree (and possible eternal life) because she believes it to be forbidden. The other option is equally untenable—that Adam is unable to recall the exact tree named so recently in Yhwh's prohibition.

We will examine the serpent's role in the couple's acquisition of sexual awareness below, but now our purpose is to determine the relationship of the woman to the Tree of Life. It is also possible to argue, although nowhere seemingly documented in scholarship, that the woman is persuaded by the serpent to eat from the Tree of the Knowledge of Good and Evil because she does not classify it within the category of the tree from which it is forbidden to eat. It is possible that she understands she is not to eat from the tree "in the center" of the garden because the only tree given the term "center" as its location is the Tree of Life.

The woman knows only the prohibition (or a confused version of the prohibition). Some scholars have argued that the woman's phrase "neither shall you touch" the fruit of the Tree in question is "little more than a stylistic variation by the writer."[57] It may be that "some ancient versions tend to assimilate the woman's wording in 3:2 to the wording of Yhwh's command in 2:16 . . . which suggests that the translators were not aware of any particular significance [at this point in the narrative]."[58] What is certain is that the woman knows only what the punishment of the violation is, not what benefits the tree may ultimately provide. However, the woman is obviously convinced by the serpent's argument for "knowing good and evil" and is attracted to the fruit because she "sees" it will make her "wise," not that it will give her eternal life.[59] Even if the woman believes that it is the Tree of Life which will make her "wise," she is in some sense choosing wisdom before immortality.

In the much older Yahwist account of the creation of humankind, the sequence of events is thus: immediately after the injunction against eating from the fruit of the Tree of the Knowledge of Good and Evil, Yhwh announces that it is not appropriate for Adam to be alone and then creates "out of the earth all the beasts of the field and all the birds of the

---

57. Townsend, "Eve's Answer to the Serpent," 400. Townsend contends that the woman's phrase, far from being "presumptuously added to God's word," is, in fact, "that Eve's statements might be original to the story and indicative of the story's dependence on the cleanness code found in Leviticus 11" (405).

58. He cites the BHS: Moberly, "Did the Serpent Get it Right?," 6n13.

59. And it is also possible that both trees are in close proximity to one another and that both may be said to be in the "center." But see footnote 36 above.

sky" and brings them to Adam to name.⁶⁰ Adam gives names "to all cattle, and to the birds of the sky, and to every beast of the field, but for the man was not found a helper as his partner."⁶¹ Presumably, the serpent is created when Yhwh makes "out of the earth all the beasts of the field," for later in the myth, we read that the serpent is given the designation "beast of the field."⁶² Indeed, the serpent is given a superlative description: of all the beasts of the field, the נהש is the wisest.

Charlesworth has written convincingly regarding the characteristic of wisdom associated with the serpent. Some of his major points are recounted below. First, after tracing ophidian texts, realia, and iconography throughout many ancient cultures, Charlesworth points out that the authors of the Genesis myth had recourse to symbolic ideas about the *nahash* that were adapted and/or borrowed in the formation of the story.⁶³ He argues that the role of the serpent in ancient cultures was a complex and multivalent one, but one particular trait that marks its function is wisdom. The exact word ערום "wise" or "shrewd" used in Genesis to describe the *nahash* is also found in Proverbs to express someone who displays wisdom and prudence.⁶⁴

In addition to being wise, the serpent in the Genesis story also exhibits the power of speech—a characteristic that only the serpent shares with the created humans and not with the other beasts of the field.⁶⁵ Charlesworth notices that the commentators of the *Tosephta* surmised that the *nahash* was not originally a serpent, but was some form of angelic or divine being. The question remains: how is it that the serpent apparently knows what Yhwh knows? Despite not being created until after Yhwh's injunction to Adam, but before the creation of woman, the serpent understands that when the woman and Adam eat from the Tree

---

60. My translation.

61. My translation.

62. It is interesting to notice that the serpent is also in the category of not being a suitable partner for Adam.

63. Charlesworth, *Good and Evil Serpent*, 58–258. According to T. Stordalen, this creates in the serpent "jealousy towards the woman who took 'his' position and reduced him to a mere animal ruled by the humans" but the serpent exhibits qualities (speech, foreknowledge) that are if not comparable to, surpassing human abilities (*Echoes of Eden*, 239).

64. See Proverbs 12:16, 23; 13:16; 14:8; 22:3; and 27:12.

65. Charlesworth points out that the Serpent's power of speech is unlike Balaam's ass, whose mouth was "opened by God" (*Good and Evil Serpent*, 297).

of the Knowledge of Good and Evil, their "eyes will be opened" (i.e., they will gain sexual awareness) and they will be like Yhwh.[66]

How, then does the serpent attain such knowledge? According to Charlesworth, the serpent's privileged "supernatural knowledge . . . aligns it with the gods and reveals the world of mythology and lore . . . central to worship" in ancient Israel.[67] One possibility for the serpent's possession of such divine knowledge has been proposed by Veenker and Milgrom who both conclude that story is concerned with the intersection of wisdom and Yhwh's apprehension of sexual awareness between Adam and Eve. Hence the serpent, who has more experience as a created being, exhibits an awareness of sexuality that he advances to the woman.[68]

Scholars have debated the omission of the complete name of the deity found earlier in the narrative by the serpent during his discourse with the woman. The term יְהוָה is never used by the serpent when he speaks to the woman regarding Yhwh. The serpent uses only the name אֱלֹהִים and not יְהוָה אֱלֹהִים to refer to the deity and the woman does not correct him.[69] It is also clear that the serpent's revelatory comments to the woman ("God knows . . . you will be like God) puns on the Hebrew word for "God" (אֱלֹהִים) and that by referring to Yhwh as *elohim*, the serpent plays upon the plurality of the word אֱלֹהִים that can also sometimes refer to lesser divinities (such as angels, e.g., *bene elohim*), or to rival gods, especially in the Canaanite pantheon.[70] The omission of יְהוָה and the exclusive use of אֱלֹהִים for the divine name used by the serpent may be a possible description for the type of god the woman and Adam would be in their becoming "like" Yhwh but also binds the woman to the serpent linguistically. She follows his naming example and thus shares with him the same word for the deity.

---

66. Ibid., 293.

67. Ibid., 294.

68. See Milgrom, "Sex and Wisdom" and Veenker, *Forbidden Fruit*. The command "Be fruitful and multiply," used twice in the Priestly account, does not occur in the Yahwist version.

69. There is no account in Genesis of direct discourse whereby Adam has a need to "name" God. We have only the woman's third-person account of the specific name we assume Adam called Yhwh when he relayed to her the injunction. But see Walsh, "Genesis 2:4b—3:24," 165.

70. Such plurality is also found earlier in Genesis 1:26 with the "priestly" account of the creation of humankind: "Let us make Adam in Our image after Our likeness."

RETURN TO GILGAMESH

W. F. Albright, using one of the earlier translations of the Epic of Gilgamesh by P. Haupt, (*Das babylonische Nimrodepos*) argues that the character of Shiduri (the "alewife") is the goddess "Siduri Sabatu who is depicted in the earliest recensions of the myth inhabiting a garden surrounded by trees where "the vine is the centerpiece."[71] As Albright points out, "if Siduri was in one story the goal of the hero's quest for life, she must have been regarded as the goddess or nymph in whose hands lay its disposal."[72] We have already surmised earlier that Shiduri is the counterpart to Shamhat, but Albright further strengthens our claim that Shiduri is not merely associated with Ishtar/Inanna but is actually a goddess in her own right. In the incantatory series Surpu, II, 172, Shiduri is called "goddess of wisdom, genius of life."[73] Albright notes that the goddess Siduri is associated not only with vines and trees, but also with serpents:

> ". . . we can hardly avoid the conclusion that Siduri Sabatu was also a serpent-goddess in one or more of her forms. Her intimate association and virtual interchange with serpent deities, her character as goddess of life and wisdom as vine deity and as genius of life . . . all point in that direction."[74]

Albright thoroughly agrees with Charlesworth's assessment that serpents and snakes are ancient and universal and understands that such a connection exists between ophidian imagery associated with the goddess Shiduri and Genesis 3:1 since, "it is not easy to see how a genius of wisdom, like [Siduri] Sabatu can fail to appear in serpent form, as the snake is the wisest of animals (Gen. 3:1)."[75] On a linguistic note, Albright argues that "it is hard to overlook the paronomasia between Old Sumerian *mus*, 'serpent,' and *mus*, 'tree' (later *gis*), which may have aided the association between the tree of life (as the symbol of the goddess Shiduri Sabatu) and the serpent."[76]

Albright makes a convincing case that Shiduri the "alewife" in the Epic of Gilgamesh is the same goddess Shiduri Sabatu but most

---

71. Albright, "Goddess of Life," 259.
72. Ibid., 260.
73. Ibid.
74. Ibid., 274.
75. Ibid., 275.
76. Ibid., 279.

importantly, that she is associated with ophidian imagery to the extent that she often takes ophidian form. I argue that the woman in Genesis assumes the role once assigned in the Epic of Gilgamesh to the *harimtu* Shamhat and the goddess Shiduri Sabatu.[77] This is the primary reason for the woman's linguistic connection to the serpent in Genesis, not only through her dialogue with him and shared use of the "diminished" term for Yhwh, but also through her transferring the fruit of the forbidden tree to Adam. The woman in Genesis functions as a combination of Shamhat (sexual/spiritual initiator) and Shiduri (giver of life and wisdom) who is also often found in other mythologies in the form of a serpent.[78]

In the Epic of Gilgamesh, Shamhat/Shiduri both participate in sexual initiation that brings wisdom to her initiates. Both are identified with the tree of life that symbolizes the gift of earthly existence. The woman in Genesis is intimately related to the Tree of the Knowledge of Good and Evil which will bring sexual awareness to the couple. The woman is also significantly connected to the Tree of Life (both in Genesis and in the Epic of Gilgamesh) because her mythological antecedents are goddesses who are symbolically represented by life giving trees and the promise of immortality. The woman clings to the (once considered mistaken) belief that the tree she must not consume, or even touch, is the Tree of Life because in more ancient mythologies, she is profoundly associated with such a tree. Through his insight into the ramifications of eating from Tree of the Knowledge of Good and Evil (in making the couple "like God,") the serpent seemingly displays almost supernatural powers. But by the same logic, the serpent in Genesis is functioning as another form of the woman whose distant ancestor in the Epic of Gilgamesh is a goddess of sexual awakening, wisdom and life who also often appears in the form of a serpent.

If the woman and the serpent are twin vestiges of Shamhat/Shiduri, it becomes evident why the tripartite curse of Yhwh is thus thematically structured.[79] By creating two separate characters (the woman and the

77. For my argument on connecting Shamhat with Shiduri, see chapter 1.

78. Previously, I argue that Shiduri's sexual initiation of Gilgamesh brings about the hero's ability in the OB version to be reintegrated back into civilization and the city of Uruk.

79. According to Boomershine, "the basic opposition in the sexual code is related to the antithetical programs of Yahweh and the serpent. The antimony is between male/female as creations of God and as a competitive god/goddess" ("Narrative Rhetoric in Genesis," 127). It is tempting to draw analogies between the competitiveness of Ishtar/Inanna and Gilgamesh to the relationship between the serpent and Yhwh.

serpent), the compilers of Genesis manage to completely dissociate the woman in her guise as the goddess Shiduri from that of her divine serpent form. Through his invective, Yhwh removes from the serpent any remnant of previously held divinity ("more cursed than any beast of the field . . . dust shall you eat,") and creates as much "enmity" between the woman and the serpent as possible, not just in the present, but in the distant future. Such enmity even includes the descendants of the woman and the serpent.[80] While the serpent (as a beast of the field) cannot be expected to produce offspring painfully, Yhwh's curse totally eliminates the possibility that the hatred of the descendants of the serpent and the woman will ever heal. Further, in order to prevent the woman from (re)assuming any kind of goddess/divine status, Yhwh narrowly circumscribes the attributes of her birth experience: giving "life" is removed from the sacred realm of the goddess Shiduri and is replaced, "cursed," with travail and pain. As Adam will confirm (Gen 3:20), the woman must now be named "the mother of all the living" because she has initiated Adam into sexual awareness and will be able to bear children. But their initiation, while it has brought sexual awareness, has come at a great cost.

Eve's ancient and intrinsic relationship to the mythos and theology within other cultures associating her with sexual awareness, life, wisdom and death is never entirely excised from the text of Genesis and remains not only in the symbolism of the first temple, but appears in various parts of canonical and extracanonical Israelite mythology, often quite dramatically.[81]

HESIOD'S PANDORA AND EVE

In our attempt to explore the ancient ideas concerning the relationship between the sexual world inhabited by divinities and the human world of mortals, we have already reviewed the story of Pandora and its connection with Mesopotamian mythology. It cannot be possible, however, to determine a specific trajectory (if one can be proven to exist) between Hesiod's versions of Pandora found in *Theogony* and *Works and Days* and

---

80. No doubt playing upon the ancient Israelite importance on progeny which will feature so prominently especially in the remainder of Genesis and in the remainder of the Hebrew scriptures.

81. See, for example, Barker, "Life-Bearing Spring"; Brenner, "Tree of Life as a Female Symbol"; and Long, "Asherah, the Tree of Life and the Menorah" who see strong vestiges of goddess typology through the symbolism of the first temple of Solomon.

the text of Genesis 2 and 3. It is possible the Pandora myth provided no influence on Genesis at all. Later writers (Philo and the Greek *Life of Adam and Eve*, for example) as well as other patristic literature certainly incorporated Greek ideology concerning Pandora which they combined with the story of Eve, but even if there are parallels between Hesiod's Pandora and Mesopotamian mythology such as the Epic of Gilgamesh, it is not clear whether Pandora shares such distinct correspondences with Genesis 2 and 3.[82] In surveying the antecedents and tradents surrounding the role of women in ancient Israelite mythology and their (sexual) relationships to divine beings, it is worth pursuing some elements of the Pandora myth which have similarities to Genesis 2 and 3.

WISDOM

One scholar argues that Pandora is created to be the antithesis of wisdom in contrast to Athena:

> As the representative Woman, she is (potentially) promiscuous whereas Athena is virtually asexual. She causes helplessness whereas Athena is resourceful and invents for human beings technologies of all sorts. She is unknowing whereas Athena is wise. She is artifice whereas Athena is artificer. She is passive whereas Athena is active. Pandora is, in effect, the Anti-Athena.[83]

But this does not necessarily remove Pandora completely from any context of wisdom, at least on some symbolic level. The first woman Pandora is the creation of both Hephaistos and Athena; the serpent god Erichthonios and avatar of Athena is the creation of the same two parents. Accordingly, "Pandora is repeatedly described in Hesiod as παρθένος, like the goddess of the temple itself, and since she was formed of earth or clay she was, literally, autochthonous—another motherless creature, a child of the earth . . . in the sense that she was the creation of Hephaistos and Athena, Pandora would thus have been a counterpart to Erechtheus/Erichthonios . . ."[84] It might seem that Pandora's creation from clay would

---

82. Phipps surmises that "it might reasonably be inferred that Hesiod had made use of some variant of a narrative that was also utilized in the story of the Garden of Eden" ("Eve and Pandora Contrasted," 34).

83. Hurwit, "Beautiful Evil," 134.

84. Ibid., 183. We have already reviewed Pandora's artistic depiction as a *pithos* rising from the earth (see above).

place her in a thematic position similar to Adam, but she is created much later than "man," so such a comparison can hardly be apt.[85] Other scholars argue that "the first woman is the fruit of a cooperation between Athena and Hephaestus" and that Athena and Hephaestus were "associated in myth, which related the birth of Athena's autochthonous ancestor Erichthonios from the only partially consummated union of the two divinities."[86] Through her connection with the serpent-like Erichthonius, who was nurtured by Athena, Pandora does exhibit a particular symmetry with Eve, not only, as we have seen, through Eve's encounter with the serpent in Genesis 3, but also considering Eve's connection to the serpent-goddess Shiduri.[87] Several scholars have also demonstrated that Pandora's relationship to her *pithos* in addition to her chthonic nature reveal an earlier earth-goddess mythological substratum that Hesiod reshaped.[88] Thus, Pandora's fundamental goddess nature is also parallel to Eve's ancient association with the serpent-goddess Shiduri.

Pandora's identity as maiden is directly connected to her sexuality. "If Pandora is παρθένος, it is in the sense that she is a maiden ready for marriage—[a] 'sexually available,' one who has not *yet* lost her virginity..."[89] Both Pandora and Eve in their respective myths progress from *parthenos* into sexual awareness. One important divergence is that in Hesiod's myths, Pandora is created for the distinct purpose of becoming sexually aware, whereas in Genesis, Eve is not.[90] Pandora is created imbued with erotic attributes and intended by Zeus to be a creature who is both a deception and trap for men—"a beautiful evil"; Eve is created with none of Pandora's sophisticated erotic overtones but as an anthropo-

---

85. Another shared comparison between Eve and Pandora is that Pandora's voice contains "lies and guileful words" (Hesiod, *Theogany*, 93) and while Eve never speaks to Adam, paradoxically Yhwh curses Adam because he "listened to the voice" of Eve.

86. Bremmer, "Pandora," 23.

87. Erichthonius, according to various sources, is depicted with either a half or complete serpent form. Erichthonius as coiling serpent was portrayed on the interior of Athena's shield in the Parthenon.

88. Brown, "Aphrodite and the Pandora Complex," 27. See also Hurwit, "Beautiful Evil," 177.

89. Hurwit, "Beautiful Evil," 185, italics original.

90. Unlike Hesiod, the writers of Genesis do not provide the same sophisticated psychological motives for Eve as Hesiod assigns to Pandora. In Hesiod's view, "the threat posed by women, however, is psychological as well as economic, for Pandora's deceptive beauty inspires 'cruel longing'" (Marquardt, "Hesiod's Ambiguous View of Women," 289).

morphic twin of Adam. It could be argued that if Yhwh's initial plan was to provide eternal life to the pair through the fruit of the Tree of Life, it is possible that Eve was never expected to ever bear progeny. Both Hesiod and Genesis, however, focus almost exclusively on the sexual aspects of women than on their ability to bear children. In Genesis Yhwh curses the process of birth and in *Theogony* Hesiod contends that women are a distinct and separate race (γένος) without providing any information about the process of childbearing.

Some scholars insist "the myths [of Pandora and Eve are] two versions of the same primeval story of the first woman. Both show that woman is a divine 'afterthought' and is, in Hesiod's words, 'a curse and a bane.'"[91] Thus, "the creation of Pandora guaranteed man's never-ending struggle with the earth to obtain a meager living" and that Hesiod does "envision the agricultural pithos as the source of the evils which Pandora set upon men."[92] The same similarity exists in the Genesis myth through Eve's initial action. Adam and his descendants are consigned to wrestle a "meager living" from the soil, which Yhwh has also cursed. It is clear that "with the arrival of woman man is no longer alone, but at the same time he no longer can share the company of the gods."[93] Genesis makes clear that it is Eve's action which prompts expulsion from the garden and exile from the presence of Yhwh. Pandora's creation marks a fundamental shift in the relationship between human and divine. Thus both Eve and Pandora function in their respective myths as agents separating humans from gods. Such separation is not at all metaphorical, for in the case of Genesis the exile from the garden is due explicitly to Eve's initial sexual awakening: separation from the presence of the divine, woman's sexual awareness, and the resulting human mortality are all inextricably linked. Hesiod's Pandora traces the same thematic premise: she is created to terminate commerce between gods and men, and it is her sexual (mis) understanding that unleashes evil into the world and brings mortality to humans.

---

91. Phipps, "Eve and Pandora Contrasted," 34.
92. Marquardt, "Hesiod's Ambiguous View of Women," 288.
93. Bremmer, "Pandora," 24.

GARMENTS

In *Theogony*, it is Pallas Athena herself who adorns Pandora "with silvery clothing and with her hands . . . [hangs] . . . a highly wrought veil from her head," inviting comparison to the act of Shamhat dressing Enkidu in the Epic of Gilgamesh and to Adam and Eve fashioning garments for themselves.[94] It is also Athena who places on the head of Pandora a "golden headband" crafted by Haephaestus. Pandora's divinely crafted golden diadem is described as "immediately . . . attractive to the eye, but on closer inspection . . . deeply disturbing."[95] Like the Tree of the Knowledge of Good and Evil, whose fruit is described as "a delight to the eyes" but which contains something infinitely more dangerous, the intricate design on Pandora's diadem "becomes an encoding of Pandora herself . . . as on the diadem, so in the flesh, the divine power of art can make beauty out of what should seem terrifying."[96] In like fashion, the serpent's words to Eve take on a divine power by making the dangerous fruit appear attractive and proscribe the same type of negative encoding to Eve by the writers of Genesis.

The diadem's depiction of animals underscores Pandora's past association with the goddess of wild animals and is Hesiod's "acknowledgement of the fostering and destructive power of the old goddess of nature who lies behind the Olympian creation."[97] Pandora's diadem with its finely wrought depiction of wild animals (ζωοῖσιν) in *Theogony* suggests a connection to the name Adam finally bestows upon Eve in Genesis 3:20 found in the LXX: Ζωή (Life), a name that puns on Adam's previous declaration that Eve is "μήτηρ πάντων τῶν ζώντων (mother of all living)." Pandora's association with the beasts and wild animals is usually given to Aphrodite as πότνια θηρῶν (goddess of wild animals/nature), but "there is no evidence that Aphrodite regularly played the role" in Greece.[98] Hesiod's final crowning of Pandora with the diadem is further proof that "Pandora is being remodeled to accommodate her to the Olympian system."[99] Eve's title is also reminiscent of the wild beasts found on the diadem of Pandora and corresponds to both women as not only "first women" but

---

94. When the goddess Shiduri is first seen by Gilgamesh, she is also attired in a veil.
95. Brown, "Aphrodite and the Pandora Complex," 29.
96. Ibid.
97. Marquardt, "Hesiod's Ambiguous View of Woman," 287.
98. Ibid.
99. Ibid., 286.

also "Mother" of all that lives, including the wild animals. It also should be noted that neither Pandora's nor Eve's creation is predicated directly upon the existence of wild animals, i.e., Eve is created for Adam because, in fact, there were no "τὰ θηρία" (beasts) considered suitable partners for him, yet both women gain an association with beasts/wild animals/all that is living because of their mythological ancestry and connection to more ancient goddess figures.

Finally, Pandora's diadem is described in *Theogony* as having intricately carved "designs, highly wrought, a wonder to see, all the terrible monsters the land and the sea nourish . . . wondrous, similar to living animals endowed with speech."[100] Although the serpent in Genesis is the wisest of "πάντων τῶν θηρίων" (all the beasts of the field) he is also similar to the depictions on Pandora's diadem of "living animals endowed with speech."

In summarizing the similarities between Pandora and Eve, it becomes apparent that the writers of both myths manipulated ancient narratives for their particular purposes and that later writers such as Philo were easily able to draw numerous connections between them because the roots of these ancient stories were analogous.

GENESIS 6

> Now it came about, when men began to multiply on the face of the land, and daughters were born to them, that the sons of God saw that the daughters of men were beautiful; and they took wives for themselves, whomever they chose. Then the LORD said, "My Spirit shall not strive with man forever, because he also is flesh; nevertheless his days shall be one hundred and twenty years." The Nephilim were on the earth in those days, and also afterward, when the sons of God came in to the daughters of men, and they bore *children* to them. Those were the mighty men who *were* of old, men of renown (Gen 6:1–4, *NASB*).

Scholars have noted that this passage "has been a center of controversy for at least two millennia."[101] In wrestling with the Genesis 6:1–4, both ancient and modern exegetes are particularly divided in determining how the phrase "the sons of God" should be interpreted. For the

100. Hesiod, *Theogony*, 51.
101. Newman, "Ancient Exegesis of Genesis 6:2,4," 13.

most part, the precise meaning of בני האלהים is divided into several ideological categories occupying various positions along the divine/human continuum.

It is possible to assert that "among the extant materials interpreting Gen. 6:2, 4, the supernatural view" of the "sons of God" is the oldest. The LXX translates בני האלהים as οἱ υἱοὶ τοῦ θεοῦ.[102] Other interpretive sources outside the canonical text (among them *I Enoch, Jubilees* and the *Genesis Apocryphon*) assign the phrase "the sons of God" not only to the supernatural status of "angels" but to the category of "fallen," malevolent, or rebellious angels.[103]

The "nonsupernatural" interpretation of the phrase "the sons of God" begins in the first century CE, and includes works by Philo and Pseudo-Philo, the *Targumim*, and other Rabbinic literature.[104] All such sources understand the phrase בני האלהים in terms of human men, either as morally degenerate rulers ("the sons of the nobles"), tyrannical kings, or human judges.[105]

Modern exegetes are equally divided,[106] but in recent decades the debate has had difficulty in ignoring the evidence from the Qumran texts. Some scholarly opinion has conjectured that Genesis 6:1–8 is a mythological fragment awkwardly inserted as a precursor to the flood

---

102. The Alexandrine Codex translation is "ἄγγελλοι," although the majority reading supports "οἱ υἱοὶ τοῦ θεοῦ." See Newman, "Ancient Exegesis of Genesis 6:2,4," 15n5 who discusses the priority of "ἄγγελλοι" over "οἱ υἱοὶ τοῦ θεοῦ," whereas Coleman (who claims that the "sons of God" are human) argues for "a corrector . . . [who] changed the text to read *angels*" (Coleran, "Sons of God in Genesis 6:2," 488, italics original). See also Ruiten, "Interpretation of Genesis 6:1–12."

103. Newman, "Ancient Exegesis of Genesis 6:2,4," 14ff. We will discuss these extracanonical texts in greater detail in later chapters and the issue of "rebellious" angels.

104. Ibid., 23ff.

105. There is also the opinion which Newman claims began in the Christian era that the "sons of God" were descendents of Seth and the "daughters of men" were the descendents of Cain. See Newman, "Ancient Exegesis of Genesis 6:2,4," 27 ff.; Marrs, "Sons of God," 219; VanGemeren, "Sons of God in Genesis 6:1–4," 320. See also VanGemeren, "Sons of God in Genesis 6:1–4," 332–3, who argues against the "daughters of man" being assigned to either Sethite or Cainite lineage exclusively because "they belong to the category of human beings of the feminine gender."

106. Among those who support the "angelic" interpretation, see Kooij, "Peshitta Genesis 6"; Newman, "Ancient Exegesis of Genesis 6:2,4"; VanGemeren, "Sons of God in Genesis 6:1–4"; Marrs, "Sons of God"; Greig, "Genesis 6:1–4: The Female and the Fall." Those who support an "human" interpetation include Coleran, "Sons of God in Genesis 6:2"; Fockner, "Reopening the Discussion"; Kline, "Divine Kingship and Genesis 6:1–4"; Gilboa, "Who 'Fell Down' to our Earth?."

story.[107] Other scholars argue that "Gen. 6.1–8 is a carefully structured unified section which was consciously inserted to inform the reader about the developments that led to the flood."[108] Logically, however, the unity of Genesis 6:1–8 emphasizes strongly that "the sons of God can no longer be treated in isolation from the flood narrative—they are part of the introduction to the flood . . . [and] the reason for the flood." [109] This insight should not preclude the possible interpretation that the "sons of God" are supernatural or angelic beings. The conjecture that Genesis 6:1–8 is a disjointed remnant of mythology cannot be properly substantiated through evidence of direct appropriation in any case. While the story of the flood in Genesis has been shown to have been influenced by Mesopotamian mythology (the Atrahasis myth and the later editions of the Epic of Gilgamesh), the odd narrative concerning the "sons of God" and the "daughters of men" has no specific parallels in the surrounding culture(s). Certainly, "the *bn ilm* of the Ugaritic texts are almost indisputably the equivalent of 'the sons of god' in Gen. 6:1–4 [but] these beings are to be understood not as the offspring of the gods, but as lesser deities subordinate to the chief Canaanite god, El."[110] As we have noted earlier, there are no examples of sexual congress between the divine and human worlds in Ugaritic mythology.

The antecedents of the strange story in Genesis 6:1–8 (and especially 6:2) is found within the extracanonical literature of Qumran among religious and sectarian texts of the Dead Sea Scrolls (DSS), most notably in the story of *1 Enoch* and the myths of the Watchers. *1 Enoch*'s retelling of Genesis provides the reader an alternative perspective concerning the problem of evil as well as an aetiology on mortality. In place of a serpent whose advice to one woman results in the loss of immortality, *1 Enoch* attributes theodicy to the actions of a cadre of rebellious and "fallen"

---

107. See especially VanGemeren, "Sons of God in Genesis 6:1–4," 323 and Kline, "Divine Kingship," 187.

108. Fockner, "Reopening the Discussion," 435. I disagree with his view that of the "sons of God" should be interpreted as human.

109. Ibid., 448.

110. Greig, "Genesis 61–4," 490. Greig mistakenly suggests that El "impregnates two females who give birth to Dawn and Dusk," but as we have argued, (see above) those females are themselves divine beings and not mortal women. Van Gemeren's proposal that a Hittite myth "detailing the battles between the weather god and Illuyankas, the dragon" has some semblance with Genesis 6:1–4 is totally unconvincing. See "Sons of God in Genesis 6:1–4," 322.

angels who impregnate the "daughters of man."[111] We will explore the mythology found in *I Enoch* (and similar myths) more precisely the next chapter. Before examining those texts, however, it is essential to analyze the connections between Genesis 6:2 and the previously mentioned text of Genesis 3:6.

GENESIS 3:6 AND 6:2

When the woman saw that the tree was good for food, and that it was a delight to the eyes, and that the tree was desirable to make *one* wise, she took from its fruit and ate; and she gave also to her husband with her, and he ate. (Genesis 3:6)
... that the sons of God saw that the daughters of men were beautiful; and they took wives for themselves, whomever they chose. (Genesis 6:2)

The multivalent story of Genesis 6:1–8 is "among other things, *a comment on immortality* rather than *morality*."[112] Evidence for such a reading is found in verse 6:3: Then the LORD said, "My Spirit shall not strive with man forever, because he also is flesh; nevertheless his days shall be one hundred and twenty years. The statement "is the only one in which the persona God makes his remark and, thus, *mortality* is its theme."[113] Other scholars view the theme of mortality as the connection between 6:1–8 and Genesis 3:6ff since "'life-span' is the reason given for the expulsion of Adam and Eve from the Garden of Eden, where immortality ... was presented in the text as an essential factor distinguishing God from God-like humans who acquired a certain kind of godly knowledge."[114]

Indeed, the entire episode of Genesis 6:1–8 recapitulates in exacting detail the previous text of Genesis 3:6ff. The presence of the words ראה, טוב, לקח ("see," "good," "take") in both texts indicate "the similarity between Eve's sin and the action of the sons of God ... Both Eve and the sons of God see something, consider it good, and take it."[115]

In both the MT and the LXX, the correspondences are as follows:

---

111. Loader points out that in *1Q20* (*Genesis Apocryphon*), there is a possible reference to "that version of the myth found in *Jubilees* which understood the Watchers as having been sent to earth on a divine errand" which we will discuss in greater detail below ("Beginnings of Sexuality," 288).

112. Gilboa, "Who 'Fell Down'?," 66, italics original.

113. Ibid. 73.

114. Ibid.

115. Fockner, "Reopening the Discussion," 438–9.

(Genesis 3:6)

וַתֵּרֶא הָאִשָּׁה כִּי טוֹב הָעֵץ לְמַאֲכָל וְכִי תַאֲוָה־הוּא לָעֵינַיִם וְנֶחְמָד הָעֵץ לְהַשְׂכִּיל וַתִּקַּח מִפִּרְיוֹ וַתֹּאכַל וַתִּתֵּן

καὶ εἶδεν ἡ γυνὴ ὅτι καλὸν τὸ ξύλον εἰς βρῶσιν καὶ ὅτι ἀρεστὸν τοῖς ὀφθαλμοῖς ἰδεῖν καὶ ὡραῖόν ἐστιν τοῦ κατανοῆσαι καὶ <u>λαβοῦσα</u> τοῦ καρποῦ αὐτοῦ ἔφαγεν καὶ ἔδωκεν καὶ τῷ ἀνδρὶ αὐτῆς μετ' αὐτῆς καὶ ἔφαγον

(Genesis 6:2)

גַּם־לְאִישָׁהּ עִמָּהּ וַיֹּאכַל׃
וַיִּרְאוּ בְנֵי־הָאֱלֹהִים אֶת־בְּנוֹת הָאָדָם כִּי טֹבֹת הֵנָּה וַיִּקְחוּ לָהֶם נָשִׁים מִכֹּל אֲשֶׁר בָּחָרוּ׃

ἰδόντες δὲ οἱ υἱοὶ τοῦ θεοῦ τὰς θυγατέρας τῶν ἀνθρώπων ὅτι καλαί εἰσιν <u>ἔλαβον</u> ἑαυτοῖς γυναῖκας ἀπὸ πασῶν ὧν ἐξελέξαντο

What Eve and the sons of God "see" is unmistakably linked to the aspect of desire. Eve desires the fruit because she "sees" that, not only is it good, it will make her wise. The sons of God desire the daughters of men because they "see" that the women are good, just as Eve's fruit is good. The sons of God's discernment regarding the daughters of men is not only a lustful perception but also an insight into the "quality" of the women.[116] Eve "takes" the fruit and "eats" (becomes a sexual being), the sons of God "take" from among the daughters of men and impregnate them. In both instances each section of the text describes a moment of sexual awakening from vastly different perspectives. The violations by Eve and the sons of God are sexual violations and result in the diminishment of immortality (or some portion thereof) by Yhwh. In the first instance, Eve and Adam's sexual infraction produces the loss of eternal life. In the second instance, the effect from the sexual action of the sons of God reduces the lengthy span of human life to one hundred twenty years.

The sons of God share a similarity with the ancient role of the woman/Eve: both have divine mythological ancestry associated with wisdom that potentially threatens Yhwh.[117] Both their sexual actions result in the circumscription of immortality by varying degrees. But the daughters of men are also assigned to Eve's role. The compiler of Genesis 6:2 is definitive in connecting the "daughters of men" to Eve. The result of Eve's sexual awakening results in the original birth of the "daughters of men" who are sexually awakened by the "sons of God" producing "giant"

116. Gilboa, "Who 'Fell Down'?," 74.
117. In the Book of Enoch, the angels bring metallurgy and other arts to humans.

children whose violence will eventually lead to the demise of all living creatures.[118] In these passages, the Yahwist's narrative demotes again the once powerful first female by referring to the role of her daughters in the destruction of earth and pointing the reader to Eve's initial compliance to the serpent's instruction which has ultimately led to the reason for the flood.

---

118. One final correlation to the text of Genesis 6:2 may be ascribed to the Epic of Gilgamesh. Gilboa ingeniously sees a connection between Gilgamesh's "brutal attitude to women" and the sons of God who mate with human women. See Gilboa, "Who 'Fell Down'?," 74.

Chapter Three

THE WIFE OF LAMECH and mother of Noah appears as a named character in *The Book of Jubilees* (*Jubilees*) and the *Genesis Apocryphon* (*1Q20*) but is not named in *The Book of Enoch* (*1 Enoch*). Her name is the feminine Aramaic equivalent of אנשא (בר) "son of man" (or some variant: i.e., (א) נש (א) בר). The name *Bat Enosh* (בתאנוש), means literally "daughter of man," and can only be identified with the "daughters of men" found in Genesis 6:2. Scholarly consensus is that "Lamech's wife's name probably means 'daughter of man' and ... is a reflection of Gn 6:2, which otherwise underlies the account [in *1Q20*]."¹ Other scholars connect the episode between the sons of God and the daughters of men to the name *Bat Enosh* by observing that since "Noah and his line are the only survivors of the flood ... it hardly seems coincidental that the mother of Noah is *Betenosh*, from the Hebrew *bt'nws*, 'the daughter of man.'"²

BAT ENOSH AND THE GENESIS APOCRYPHON (1Q20)

Part of the DSS corpus known as *1Q20* found in cave 1 in Qumran retells much of Genesis 6–14 in addition to material found in sections of Enoch literature as well as the book of *Jubilees*. In analyzing the meaning of the name, it is misleading to emphasize, as Fitzmyer has done, the etymology of the particular vowels associated with the consonants in the name.³ Such a reconstruction merely obscures the most salient feature and profound feature of the character in question. Fitzmyer's linguistic analysis

---

1. Fitzmyer, *Genesis Apocryphon*, 127.
2. Rook, "Name of the Wives," 113.
3. Fitzmyer vocalizes the name as "bitenosh." See *Genesis Apocryphon*, 127.

may account for the correct pronunciation, but ultimately draws focus away from the unambiguous meaning of the name *Bat Enosh*. To focus solely on the phonetic details is to obfuscate the metaphorical significance of the name "Daughter of Man." It reduces her character to a mere foil for the patriarch Lamech and places her in the role of aberrant female rather than foundational archetype. Nor should the name *Bat Enosh* be given solely generic value. Unlike other Hebrew naming conventions for abstract feminine nouns (such as *bat* for "daughters,") *Bat Enosh* is both an historical personage as well as metaphorical archetype whose *nomen*, like Shamhat, Shiduri, and Eve, is carefully crafted to alert the reader to her mythological ancestry.[4]

In *1Q20*, an entire scene between Lamech and *Bat Enosh* develops after the birth of Noah in which Lamech seeks to determine the cause of his infant son's miraculous appearance and abilities. Lamech confronts *Bat Enosh* with the accusation that the birth of Noah has been accomplished through the agency of one of the Watchers, or perhaps one of the sons of the angels in heaven. *Bat Enosh* is emphatic in her denial that this is not the case, swearing an oath to Lamech that the child is indeed his. She then describes, in explicit sexual detail, Noah's conception. The especially graphic nature of *Bat Enosh's* speech has been puzzling to many scholars.[5] Some scholars emphasize that the nature of *Bat Enosh's* erotic speech indicates a high regard in *1Q20* for sexuality in general and for women specifically. As I will argue below, this cannot be the case.

Below is the section that includes her speech:[6]

8   [Then Bitenosh, my wife, spoke to me with great vehemence; she cr[ied]
9   and said, "O my brother and my lord, recall my pleasure. [ ]
10 [in the hea]t of the time, and my breath in the midst of its sheath. For [I shall tell you] everything truthfully [ ]."
11 [the b]irth." And then my mind was much changed within me. [ ]
12 When Bitenosh, my wife, noticed that my expression had changed [ ],

---

4. For the use in Biblical Hebrew of *bat* daughter followed by a geographical name or location, see Dobbs-Allsopp, "Syntagma of Bat."

5. See Fitzmyer, *Genesis Apocryphon*; Loader, "Beginnings of Sexuality"; Nickelsburg, *1 Enoch: A New Translation*.

6. Fitzmyer, *Genesis Apocryphon*, 69.

13 then she suppressed her emotion, speaking to me and saying to me, "O my lord and [my brother, recall]
14 my pleasure. I swear to you by the Great Holy One, by the King of H[eaven]
15 that this seed is from you; from you is this conception, and from you the planting of [this] fruit [ ],
16 and not from any stranger, or from any of the Watchers, or from any of the sons of hea[ven.[7] Why is the expression]
17 of your face so changed and deformed: (Why) is your spirit so depressed? [For I]
18 am speaking to you truthfully.

One scholar observes that "the stormy emotional scene between Lamech and his wife in *1QapGen* 2 (2) has no counterpart in *1 Enoch* 106–107."[8] Nor is there any mention of a scene of this type in *Jubilees*. While it is true that the words, emotion, and length associated with women specifically in these types of narratives are not generally reported with such elaborate detail, the purpose underlying *Bat Enosh's* conversation with Lamech fulfills two distinct purposes. First, *Bat Enosh* must contend with the issue of the miraculous child's paternity. She accomplishes this by her assurance to Lamech that despite his angelic appearance and demeanor, Noah is his child. Second, *Bat Enosh* negates any other possible candidates for Noah's paternity, including "strangers," "Watchers," and the "sons of God." That *Bat Enosh* orders the list of candidates is revealing. She begins by commenting that no other human male is the father of Noah and then moves to the angelic realm by her mention of the Watchers. Finally, she includes all types of heavenly beings in her use of the euphemistic phrase "sons of heaven" which is typically used as "a substitute for [the phrase]'sons of God' in Gen. 6:2,4 (בני אלוהים) . . . [since] the Hebrew equivalent of this phrase . . . designates angelic beings of some sort."[9]

---

7. Wise translates line 16 as "not by any stranger, neither by any of the Watchers, nor yet by any of the Sons of Heaven" no doubt seeing the triple use of ו as a linguisitic intensifier of לא. See part 3 "Parabiblical Texts" in Parry, *Dead Sea Scrolls Reader*, 5.

8. Nickelsburg, *1 Enoch: A New Translation*, 180.

9. Fitzmyer, *Genesis Apocryphon*, 128.

Bat Enosh is named "daughter of man" by the compilers of *1Q20* for the specific purpose of connecting her to that group of women (the daughters of men) who were among those taken as wives by the angelic beings in Genesis 6:5ff. As such a "daughter of man," *Bat Enosh* must deny any possible association with the women who consorted with the fallen angels by recalling her sexual "pleasure" to Lamech. She must convince him that the conception of Noah is through his "seed." What scholars have missed however, is the compiler's insistence that *Bat Enosh* swear an oath to answer Lamech's accusation, even though such an oath does nothing except intensify the reader's continued suspicion of *Bat Enosh's* veracity. Ancient readers were all too aware that for any woman, paternity is relatively easy to falsify. Only later in the narrative will the reader be assured, through Enoch's authoritative assessment, that despite all appearances to the contrary, Lamech is indeed the father of Noah.

The association of *Bat Enosh* to the "daughters of men" remains present throughout the narrative and will continue to cast a "fallen" angelic shadow upon Noah throughout the remainder of the story.[10] The argument can be made that the continued ambiguity surrounding Noah's mysterious birth and *Bat Enosh's* suspected veracity could indicate a lost tradition where Noah is fathered by some sort of angelic being who exhibits the positive characteristics of a "holy one" rather than the negative characteristics of a "fallen" angel. But the shadow of Noah's potential angelic heritage exists in other works. Even the compilers of *Jubilees* anticipate questions concerning Noah's paternal lineage by mentioning Lamech's paternity and reporting the birth of Lamech "with reference solely to the paternal line—'he (Methuselah) begat a son' (Lamech) (4:28)."[11] Scholars have noticed that "immediately preceding this birth, the author [of *Jubilees*] describes how Enoch bore witness against 'the Watchers, the ones who sinned with the daughters of men so that they might be polluted' (4:22)."[12] It seems clear that this "reference is sufficient to raise the question of its impact on the purity of the line coming to Noah. Hence, although the author presents a full identification of Methuselah's wife ('Edna, daughter of 'Azri'al, his father's brother' [4.27]), he

---

10. Scholars have suggested the section in *1Q20* following the scene with *Bat Enosh* and Lamech is connected to an earlier "Book of Noah." For a summary of the arguments for and against the existence of such a book, see Loader, *Enoch, Levi, and Jubilees on Sexuality*, 75n211.

11. Amaru, "First Woman," 618.

12. Ibid.

designs a paternal birth notice that explicitly indicates that Methuselah, that is, not a Watcher, is Lamech's father."[13] It may be the case that the author's intention is to infer that Lamech's mother interacted sexually with the Watchers, but it is more likely that the author of *Jubilees* wishes to disassociate Lamech's future son from any kind of angelic being since there is no indication that Lamech's birth is remarkable (unlike his son).

The tradition of the two "Lamechs" found in Genesis 4 also possibly attests to the existence of a polemical remnant now lost in which Lamech is connected to polygamy and murder. The first Lamech is mentioned in the generations of the "Cainite" line while the second Lamech is found within the generations of the "Sethite" line.[14] Some scholars observe that the doubling of Lamech is in some form dependent on "a single 'stock genealogy.'"[15] One possibility is that the doubling of the tradition indicates two separate antecedents that were only partially combined since "the individuals that are morphologically identical have ancient traditions concerning them that indicate they are not to be confused … [for example] the Enoch of chapter 4 built a city or at least had a city named after him, while his counterpart walked with God. Lamech, the descendent of Cain, was an infamous murderer, while Seth's descendent fathered the righteous flood hero."[16] In either case, the possibility of polemic cannot be dismissed.

In the "song of Lamech" found in 4:23, we read:

> And Lamech said to his wives
> 'Adah and Tzila, hearken to my voice,
> wives of Lamech, give ear to my saying:
> aye—a man I kill for wounding me,
> A lad for only bruising me![17]

13. Ibid.

14. According to Hess, Lamech serves as the transitional figure between the Cainite and Sethite lines. See Hess, "Lamech." Some scholars argue that Genesis 4 mirrors the Sumerian king lists. For example, see Bryan, "A Reevaluation of Gen 4" and Barton, "Sumerian Source of Genesis." For a summary of the differences between the chronological genealogies in the MT, LXX, and Samaritan Pentateuch, see Klein, "Archaic Chronologies."

15. Miller, "Descendents of Cain," 172.

16. Bryan, "A reevaluation of Gen 4," 187.

17. Stanley Gevirtz notes that the "song expresses Lamech's overweening pride [and] his refusal to suffer hurt," quoted in Miller, "Yeled in the Song of Lamech." Brigitte Kahl calls the poem, "the first military hymn in history, the birth of the great narrative of war" ("She Called His Name Seth," 20n5).

The translation demonstrates the reason the last two lines have garnered attention from scholars who notice the couplet's "outlandish parallelism" that joins "man" with "lad."[18] This particular couplet "is the only instance of this word pair in parallelism ('man' is usually paired with 'son of man')."[19] Scholars have also remarked that "it is odd that Lamech should boast of having slain a mere boy."[20] The possibility exists that in some other source the original might have contained the more usual wording: "a man I kill for wounding me, a *son of man* for only bruising me" alluding to the conflict that already exists in *1Q20* between Lamech and the angelic beings whose giant offspring are the ultimate cause of the flood.[21] Such conflict may underlie the diametrically opposed "twin" fathers of Noah. One version of Lamech in Genesis, associated with the fallen angels and gigantic offspring, composes a song of violence and brutality, while the other version of Lamech names his righteous son "Noah" in verse 29. It seems logical to find in Genesis the same tension found in other extracanonical texts which struggle with determining the identity of a "good" angel verses a "fallen" one. The theological question concerning sexual encounters between angels and human women continues to develop in extracanonical texts and will greatly influence the development of Christian mythology. This point will be explored more fully in the following chapters.

It should be obvious by now why the defense of *Bat Enosh* takes on its unusual and highly erotic tone. We have already pointed to the connection between the daughters of men in Genesis 6:2 and their associations with Eve through their sexual encounters. In *1Q20*, the author establishes a similar connection between *Bat Enosh* ("Daughter of Man") and her sexual "nature" in order to radically underscore her connection to Eve. Since it is the first woman who brings sexuality to humanity with dire consequences, so the character of "Daughter of Man" must secure her defense against improper behavior by providing evidence of her sexuality as the essential component of her *apologia*.

---

18. Miller, "Yeled in the Song of Lamech," 477.

19. Ibid.

20. Ibid. Miller also points out that the MT *yeled* could also be paired with the "Sumerian council of 'men' *gurus* who advised Gilgamesh, 'the young, arms-bearing males of the kingdom'" ("Yeled in the Song of Lamech," 477). The LXX has νεανίσκον Gen: 4:23, the only instance in the Hebrew Bible the MT translates *yeled*.

21. Ibid., 477.

That *Bat Enosh* denies Lamech's "allegation by reminding him of her sexual pleasure" is far from "obscure."[22] Her graphic sexual validation only proves to align her negatively with other "daughters of men" who engage in intimate encounters with angelic beings. In *1Q20* immediately after *Bat Enosh* refers to "lovemaking," she "employs a double oath to underscore a triple assertion that Lamech is the father and a triple denial that the child has not been conceived by an angel."[23] Such a reference to her sexual pleasure comes without a corresponding reminder to Lamech concerning his sexual pleasure during the conception of Noah and indicates a supreme irony in the text. Just as men who are comparable to the "good" angels do not experience sexual pleasure, women, who are comparable to the "fallen" angels, do. *Bat Enosh's* focus on her sexual pleasure does not demonstrate that *1Q20* views the sexuality of women in a positive light. On the contrary, by connecting the conception of Noah with the sexual pleasure of *Bat Enosh*, the author of *1Q20* has strengthened the initial paradigm found originally in Genesis 3 whereby feminine sexuality and awareness of that same sexuality is associated with the loss (or diminution) of immortality.

What is absent from *1Q20* is a concomitant acquisition of wisdom as the consequence of Eve's sexual "enlightenment" in Genesis 3. In Genesis 6, the sons of God and the daughters of men attain sexual wisdom granted to Eve in Genesis 3. However, in *1Q20*, *Bat Enosh's* acquisition of wisdom has been shifted to Lamech who instead is "enlightened" through Methuselah's visitation to the heavenly Enoch who assures Lamech that the child in question is actually his son.

---

22. Nickelsburg, "Patriarchs Who Worry," 183. And according to Dorothy Peters who cites Ida Frölich *Bat Enosh's* use of terms such as "recall my pleasure in the heat of the time" *1Q20*, line 10, see above, indicates that "the narrator [of 1Q20] was demonstrating knowledge of fourth century B.C.E. Greek medicine. In *On the Generating Seed and the Nature of the Child*, Hippocrates argues that female 'pleasure' and 'heat' during intercourse are offered as proofs of conception" (Peters, *Noah Traditions*, 117). But, as Peters also points out, even despite such information from *Bat Enosh*, Lamech still does not believe the child is his. What, also, are we to make of *Bat Enosh's* erotic phrase "and my breath in the midst of its sheath" if the only reason for mentioning "pleasure" and "heat" are pharmacological?

23. Nickelsburg, "Patriarchs Who Worry," 183.

Chapter Three

BAT ENOSH AND THE BOOK OF JUBILEES

Like 1Q20, *Jubilees* is also a retelling of much of Genesis and includes the creation stories, the creation of the first humans, and the story of the interaction between the "fallen" angels and human women. Originally composed in Hebrew in the first half of the second century B.C.E., *Jubilees* is preserved mostly in Ethiopic "which appears to have been a translation from a Greek version."[24] There are sections preserved in Latin (translated from the Greek) and Syriac. In the caves at Qumran, the DSS attests to fragments from at least fourteen different copies in Hebrew "earlier by far than the other witnesses and reflecting the original language."[25]

Jubilees 4.15 introduces the reader by way of a prologue to the descent of the Watchers coinciding with the birth of "Jared" (ירד "to go down" in Hebrew) and puns on his name: "for in his days the angels of the Lord descended on the earth, those who are named the Watchers that they should do judgment and uprightness on the earth."[26] Thus the original purpose of the descent of the "angels of the Lord" is described as positive. In *Jubilees*, the birth of Enoch inaugurates explicit interaction between divine beings and humans. Enoch is "the first among men that are born on earth who learnt writing and knowledge and wisdom"—not only is Enoch taught by the Watchers, but he also experiences mystical visions concerning "what was and what will be."[27] It is Enoch, moreover, who "testifies to the Watchers, who had sinned with the daughters of men; for these had begun to unite themselves, so as to be defiled, with the daughters of men, and Enoch testified against (them) all."[28] While the text of Genesis is obscure regarding the rationale for Enoch's disappearance from earth (for "God took him"), the text of *Jubilees* informs the reader that Enoch was "taken from amongst the children of men" and "conducted" into the Garden of Eden in preparation for his role in testifying against the Watchers. Enoch's entrance into the Garden of Eden occurs "in majesty and honor . . . [where] he writeth down the condem-

---

24. Loader, *Enoch, Levi, and Jubilees on Sexuality*, 113.

25. Ibid., 114. Loader notes that "in his extensive analysis [of the text] James C. Vanderkam concludes that the Ethiopic *Jubilees* 'is an extraordinarily precise reflection of the original Hebrew text'" (114).

26. The terms "Watchers" and "angels of the Lord" are used interchangably, at least in the Ethiopic text. See Charles, *Book of Jubilees*, 39.

27. Charles, *Book of Jubilees*, 39.

28. Ibid., 40.

nation and judgment of the world, and all the wickedness of the children of men," which is recounted before the birth of Lamech and Noah.[29]

Bat Enosh is mentioned in *Jubilees* only briefly. Noah is named after his birth by Lamech with a pronouncement that "this one will comfort me for my trouble and my work and for the ground which the Lord hath cursed" foreshadowing Noah's future salvific activities and connecting him to his ancestor Adam who is the reason for the curse on the earth's soil.[30] The subsequent section of *Jubilees* recounts the death of Adam (who was lacking "seventy years of one thousand years"), which connects Noah not only to the fact of Adam's mortality, but to the original cause of death, the sin of sexual awareness (eating from the "tree of knowledge").[31] This foreshadowing in the text alerts the reader that Noah will in some way attempt to mitigate the original first sin, even if he cannot erase it completely.

Some scholars have argued that "one of the more eye-catching aspects of *Jubilees* is the significance it assigns to women."[32] It is certainly the case that "the author of *Jubilees* demonstrates an interest in women which stands in sharp contrast to that shown by the Priestly biblical writer."[33] Women are seen as codes of morality rather than instigators of power. And it is "precisely" the (male) compiler of *Jubilees*' "regard for matters of purity and marriage that inspires the author's esteem for female characters."[34] While many points of blatant polemic against the earlier mythologies by the writers of Genesis are softened in *Jubilees*, the essential connection between women's sexual awareness and the origin of death remains. In the genealogies that occur before the flood, "wives and mothers are ignored, and the common pattern includes only the names of fathers."[35] By contrast, in *Jubilees*, the names of both parents are given, but it is the woman who gives birth to the male child and the father who names him. Even the purpose for the inclusion of the lineage for "Edna," wife of Methuselah (with the formulaic "daughter of his father's broth-

---

29. Ibid.

30. Ibid., 41.

31. Ibid. *Jubilees* explains the troubling fact of Adam's continued existance after eating from the Tree of the Knowledge of Good by interpreting "day" as one thousand years. See footnote 183.

32. VanderKam, *Book of Jubilees*, 420.

33. Amaru, "First Woman," 609.

34. Ibid.

35. Ibid., 615.

Chapter Three

er") is only to avoid tainting Enoch's lineage with any association to the "daughters of men."[36] Since it was Enoch who "bore witness against the Watchers, 'the ones who sinned with the daughters of men,'" the writer adds the lineage of Edna in order to confirm the fact that "Methuselah, that is, not a Watcher, is Lamech's father."[37]

In *Jubilees*, *Bat Enosh* is listed as "the daughter of *Baraki'il*, the daughter of her father's brother."[38] Later in the text we learn that "[*Bat Enosh's*] father is thus the same as one of the fallen watchers listed in *1 Enoch* 6–7."[39] Thus, the association between the *Bat Enosh* and the daughters of men is made explicit by the compilers: The name of the father of *Bat Enosh* (Daughter of Man) is identical to the Watcher "chief" *Baraki'il* who is reported to be slightly lower in the ranks from the head-leader of the fallen angels, *Semihazah*.[40]

In *Jubilees* 3.15, the holy angels who have been commissioned by God originally make their descent for the purpose of instructing humanity in all "uprightness on the earth" and spend seven years (a jubilee) teaching Adam and Eve to cultivate the garden of Eden. In Genesis, the rationale for the descent of the "sons of God" remains obscure. But in *Jubilees*, an addition to the story found in Genesis prepares the reader for the conduct of the angels who "descend [from heaven] originally on a positive mission" but whose righteous undertaking will "soon deteriorate rapidly."[41]

> 20. And the woman saw the tree [of the Knowledge of Good and Evil] that it was agreeable and pleasant to the eye, and that its fruit was good for food, and she took thereof and ate. 21. And when she had first covered her shame with fig leaves, she gave thereof to Adam and he ate, and his eyes were opened, and he was that he was naked.[42]

In *Jubilees* 3.21, the text makes clear that the sin of sexual awareness belongs, if not solely, then originally to the woman who takes the initiative to atone for "her" sin by covering "her shame with fig-leaves"

36. Charles, *Book of Jubilees*, 41.
37. Amaru, "First Woman," 618.
38. Huggins, "Noah and the Giants," 107.
39. Ibid.
40. Nickelsburg, *1 Enoch: A New Translation*, 24.
41. VanderKam, *Book of Jubilees*, 33.
42. Charles, *Book of Jubilees*, 35.

before she offers the fruit to Adam. While this act may appear to grant the woman the agency denied to Eve in the Genesis passage, it also intensifies her culpability, since her realization does not prevent her from giving the fruit to Adam. The process of her sexual awakening is thus stymied by the awareness of her "shame" even before she experiences her sexuality.

The sequence of blame in Genesis (i.e., from Adam to the woman, from the woman to the serpent) is excluded in *Jubilees*, but the same tripartite curse given by God remains. The turning sword barring the entrance to the garden is also omitted but the banishment from the tree of immortality remains. The subtle shift in *Jubilees* is directed from the emphasis in Genesis on the loss of immortality and is focused more on the author/compiler's preoccupation with "shame." These additions allow "the author of *Jubilees* to associate the Genesis story with Leviticus 12 which gives the different laws that apply to a woman depending on whether she gives birth" to a male or female child.[43] But this addition in *Jubilees* does not mitigate the associations made between the actions of the woman and the ultimate result of those actions. The woman's sexual awareness, i.e., her "shame" is only made more explicit.

Jubilees places the birth of Noah, his subsequent marriage, and the birth of his three children before the sexual encounters of the Watchers with the daughters of men. This chronology may be an attempt by the compilers to remove Noah and his mother *Bat Enosh* from any association with the marauding angels. But because the name *Bat Enosh* is listed in the genealogy of *Jubilees* in conjunction with the name of her father, *Baraki'il*, the reader is meant to associate *Bat Enosh* with the women in Genesis who mate with divine beings and give birth to "giants."

BAT ENOSH IN 1 ENOCH

In *1 Enoch*, the name Bat Enosh is not mentioned, nor is the mother of Noah featured in any specific passages. The text of *1 Enoch* 6.1–3, however, is subtly contrasted with the text of Genesis 6:1–4, which it recounts:

> When the sons of men had multiplied, in those days, beautiful
> and comely daughters were born to them. And the watchers, the

---

43. VanderKam, *Book of Jubilees*, 31. For a summary of scholarly works on the androcentricity of the Hebrew Scriptures, see Selvidge, "Mark 5:25–34." For a more detailed discussion of the role of sexuality as it relates to women in Leviticus and Deuteronomy, see Ellens, *Women in the Sex Texts*.

sons of heaven, saw them and desired them. And they said to one another, "Come let us choose for ourselves wives from the daughters of men, and let us beget children from them."[44]

In Genesis 6:2, the Hebrew words used to describe the daughters of men are כי טבת ("fair"). That same word is translated "good" earlier in the Genesis narrative (3:6) to describe the fruit of the forbidden tree. But the use of the word טבת in describing the daughters of men in 6:2 indicates that "the quality of moral goodness is not in view. The word 'good' is a shortened form of the idiom 'good in appearance'" that makes a strong linguistic connection between the daughters of men and the fruit on the Tree of the Knowledge of Good and Evil desired by the first Woman (כי טוב).[45] The linguistic pairing in both instances (כי followed by the masculine or feminine form of the word טוב) found in the narrative does not necessarily preclude any moral implications of the word used in these two specific cases. The moral "goodness" of the fruit taken from the Tree of the Knowledge of Good and Evil by the woman is an illusion, not immediately seen by the woman. For the sons of God, the moral "goodness" of the (now tainted) daughters of men is also illusion. For the writer of Genesis, what seems both morally and aesthetically "good," especially with regard to sexuality, will be proven false. In *1 Enoch*, the moral goodness of the daughters of men has been erased completely: the "good" found originally in Genesis has been eliminated in order to provide focus upon the women's sexuality—the daughters of men in *1 Enoch* are "beautiful and comely."

Unlike *Jubilees*, *1 Enoch* highlights the relationship between sexual awareness and knowledge found in Genesis by explicitly connecting the sexual behavior of the "sons of heaven" to the dissemination of knowledge: "and [the sons of heaven] began to go in to [their chosen wives], and to defile themselves through them, and to teach them sorcery and charms, and to reveal to them the cutting of roots and plants."[46] The leaders of the two hundred sons of heaven are listed in addition to the "secrets" they reveal to the daughters of men:

> Asael taught men to make swords of iron and weapons and shields and breastplates and every instrument of war. He showed them metals of the earth and how they should work

44. Nickelsburg, "Patriarchs Who Worry," 23.
45. VanGemeren, "Sons of God," 331.
46. Nickelsburg, *1 Enoch: A New Translation*, 24.

gold to fashion it suitably, and concerning silver, to fashion it for bracelets and ornaments for women. And he showed them concerning antimony and eye paint and all manner of precious stones and dyes.[47]

The connection between "weapons of war" and "bracelets and ornaments for women" can only be compared to the story of Pandora, where the finely wrought headband mentioned by Hesiod draws unsuspecting males not only toward seduction but to the eventual proliferation of evil and death after the manner of Pandora's opened *pithos*:

[And the sons of heaven] made [bracelets and ornaments] for themselves and for their daughters, and they transgressed and led the holy ones astray.[48]

According to scholars, these lines attest to the existence of "a form of the myth in which the angelic revelations are primary and lead to the seduction of the holy ones."[49] And in *1 Enoch* the "Asa'el tradition focused on the pre-diluvian dissemination of *reprehensible forms of knowledge* attributed to the 'fallen angels.'"[50] In *Jubilees*, the Watchers are sent to earth originally for the purposes of educating humanity but eventually consort sexually with human women. In *1 Enoch* the "fall" of the holy ones is result of the daughters of men who misuse divine knowledge given to them by the divine beings. *Jubilees* places the onus of the behavior of the sons of God squarely on the angels, but *1 Enoch* retains a mythological remnant which attached culpability solely to the daughters of men, a mythos more in keeping with Hesiod than Genesis.

1 ENOCH AND THE BIRTH OF NOAH

In *1 Enoch* 106:1ff, the actual birth of Noah is narrated with detail alluded to (or missing from) *1Q20* or *Jubilees*:

And when (Lamech) had come of age, he took for himself a wife, and she conceived from him and bore a child. 2/ And when the

---

47. 1 Enoch 8:1. The "chief" of the sons of heaven, Semihazah, is listed as teaching "spells and the cuttings of roots." On the possibility of the collation of two separate narratives concerning the leaders Semihazah and Asael, see Kvanig, *Primeval History*.

48. Nickelsburg, *Enoch: A New Translation*, 25.

49. Ibid., 25n. *i*.

50. Auffarth, *Fall of the Angels*, 99, italics original.

> child was born, his body was whiter than snow and redder than a rose, his hair was all white and like white wool and curly. Glorious <was his face>. When he opened his eyes, the house shone like the sun. 3/ And he stood up from the hands of the midwife, and he opened his mouth and praised the Lord <of eternity>. 4/ And Lamech was afraid of him, and he fled and came to Methuselah his father. 5/ And he said to him, "A strange child has been born to me. He is not like human beings, but (like) the sons of the angels of heaven. His form is strange, not like us. His eyes are like the rays of the sun, and glorious is his face. 6/ I think that he is not from me, but from the angels. And I fear him, lest something happen in his days on the earth. 7/ I beg you, father, and beseech you, go to Enoch our father and learn the truth from him, for his dwelling is with the angels."[51]

Lamech's fearful description of Noah's otherworldliness directs the reader to several important aspects of his birth. Only *1 Enoch* and *1Q20* mention Noah's strange appearance. Nothing is said in Genesis or in *Jubilees* which connect Noah explicitly to the (fallen) angels. In *1 Enoch*, Lamech draws the conclusion that Noah is (at least part) angel because he witnesses Noah stand "up from the hands of the midwife" and perform the angelic requirement of praising "the Lord <of eternity>." This detailed narrative reflects Lamech's same concern in *1Q20* where Noah's angelic appearance causes him to accuse *Bat Enosh* of infidelity.

Scholars have questioned the purpose underlying Lamech's doubting the paternity of his son and wonder if Lamech's "suspicion [is]based on the almost universal licentiousness that characterizes the final generations of the antediluvian era."[52] Yet it is strange that the supernatural signs of Noah's birth "are not immediately recognized as evident indications of God's favor" by Lamech and why the reader is "taken through the narrative detour that produces a refutation of the ascription of a 'Giant' status to Noah."[53]

One view is that since "the Jewish author(s) of the Book of Giants identified Utnapishtim, the Babylonian Noah, as one of the bastard Giants engendered by the fall," the Noah in Genesis should be classified as one of the "*gibborim*."[54] The *Book of Giants* "counters a view that appears to have

51. Nickelsburg, *1 Enoch: A New Translation*, 164.
52. Reeves, "Utnapishtim in the Book of Giants," 110. Reeves does not connect the name of "Batenosh" to the daughters of men.
53. Ibid., 112.
54. Ibid., 115.

given giants positive roles as beings who survived the flood, especially as mediators of information to Abraham."[55] It is very possible that "notions that perhaps Noah, himself, was a giant, may be in the background of *1 Enoch* 106–107, which is at pains to explain Noah's wondrous nature otherwise."[56] What is also remarkable about Noah's angelic appearance is that until Lamech receives confirmation from Enoch (who resides with the good angels and who is taught by them), Lamech cannot be certain whether Noah's angelic status is aligned with God or with the "fallen." The question Lamech must answer for his own reassurance and for the sake of the world according to *1 Enoch* ("lest something happen in his days on the earth") is whether Noah is good or evil. Lamech fears that if Noah is partially divine, his status could place him in the category of the הגברים (*ha-gibborim*) who are listed in Genesis 6:4 and who are a significant reason for the flood in the *Book of Watchers* and the *Book of Giants*.[57] The thesis that Noah is meant to be identified as a Giant cannot displace the evidence (as we will show in the chapters that follow), that there exists a real tension in Noah's status as a son who is "chosen by God" not only through his (extracanonical) supernatural appearance and behavior at birth but also by his (canonical) identity as the one who literally becomes a "savior" of the remnants of the inhabitants of the earth. The possibility that Noah is the offspring of an angelic being is intimately connected to the question of the moral identity of the particular type of angel from which he may be derived. And this underscores a more complicated issue for all the writers in describing the interaction between the divine and human worlds within the aforementioned mythologies. What are the moral/spiritual alliances of certain categories of angelic beings and how are they to be understood?

STRANGERS, WATCHERS, (NEPHILIM), AND SONS OF HEAVEN

In *1Q20*, when *Bat Enosh* lists the candidates for beings who are *not* the father of Noah, they include:

55. Loader, *Enoch, Levi, and Jubilees on Sexuality*, 82.
56. Ibid.
57. According to Stuckenbruck, "while the early Enochic traditions ... regarded the flood as but one component of God's judgement against the sons of God (watchers) and the giants. These biblical and apocalyptic traditions are fused by the authors of Jubliees..." (Auffarth, *Fall of the Angels*, 111).

Chapter Three

ולא מן כול זר ולא מן כול עירין ולא מן כול בני שמ[ין למא צכם

... and not from any strangers (foreigners), watchers nor sons of heaven.[58]

Stuckenbruck points out that "scholars have observed that in a number of early Jewish writings [fallen] angels were regarded as evil beings whose activities, whether past or even present, were inimical to God's purposes for creation."[59] But the delineation between good and evil angels is not precisely straightforward in Genesis. According to Stuckenbruck, despite "all the apparently one-sided emphasis of [early Jewish writings] with respect to their interpretation of 'the sons of god' and their progeny as evil, nothing in Genesis 6 itself unambiguously prepares us for such an understanding."[60] In contrast to Genesis which "distinguishes at least two, perhaps even three categories of beings: (1) 'the sons of God' . . . (2) 'the offspring of their union' . . . [and] (3) a somewhat indefinite mention of 'the Neph[i]lim,'" the *Book of Watchers* (within *1 Enoch*) "draws a clear line of demarcation between the rebellious angels who fathered the giants and introduced humans to rejected forms of knowledge, on the one hand, and those angels which instructed Enoch concerning the nature and structure of the universe, on the other."[61] Initially, *Jubilees* views all angelic beings as holy, until they become disobedient to God's mission, at which point, *Jubilees* "makes every effort to distinguish sharply" between what Stuckenbruck terms "reprehensible astrological knowledge" and "correct" astronomical knowledge which is "first taught to Enoch by the (good) angels . . . presumably transmitted through Noah . . . and [which] finally re-emerges as a component of the piety attributed to Abraham."[62]

In the sources mentioned thus far—Genesis, *1Q20*, *Jubilees*, and *1 Enoch*, and *Book of Giants*, classifying the moral identity of angelic beings is never completely straightforward. Any angelic being who violates the sexual boundary separating them from human women and who in addition imparts potentially dangerous knowledge reserved only for those in the heavenly realm to those women is considered "fallen." But

---

58. Fitzmyer, *Genesis Apocryphon*, 69. According to Fitzmyer "the watchers (עירין) are associated with the (קדישין), 'holy ones,' and the (נפילין), 'fallen ones.' In [*1Q20*] 2:16, they stand in parallelism to, 'sons of heaven'" (124).

59. Auffarth, *Fall of the Angels*, 87. See especially footnote 1.

60. Ibid., 88.

61. Ibid., 89 and 100.

62. Ibid., 114.

even if fallen angels engage in sexual activity with women, they are still perceived by the authors of these texts to be partially divine even though their actions are antithetical to the mandates of God.

NOAH

There is no need for an overview of the relationship between the flood story found in Genesis and the parallels to Mesopotamian and Babylonian mythology, or to review the parallels between Noah and Utnapishtim found in the Atrahasis myth or in the Epic of Gilgamesh.[63] In the mythological accounts of Noah's birth in *1 Enoch* and *1Q20* are more ancient narratives which suggest the flood hero "Noah was conceived through a romance between Lamech's wife and one of the watchers."[64] That Enoch must assure Lamech Noah has not been conceived from a union between *Bat Enosh* and a Watcher indicates that he must be "a figure of higher reputation than the flood hero" found in Mesopotamian mythology. It is also "not likely that the Enochic scribes here knew of Enoch's instruction by Uriel in the secrets of astronomy and cosmology in the Astronomical Book" of *1 Enoch* and clearly provide an early example for discourse between angels and humans.[65] These examples seem to prove that the traditions surrounding Noah's relationship to his angelic heritage are complex. Some scholars contend that "directions of influence" between Genesis and the Watcher account in *1 Enoch* intersect and "crisscross."[66] It is possible there were two simultaneous "growing text traditions"—one "story contains an echo of the priestly document in . . . Gen 6:1–4 [and one that] is dependent on the Semihazah narrative [found in *1 Enoch*]."[67] It also seems clear that *Jubilees* follows *1 Enoch* (and *1Q20*) and places Noah in the role of giant, but in Genesis the remnant of that tradition is very faint indeed.

While the mythology will continue to evolve, the criteria accorded to the figure who will be known as "son of man" originates with Noah. At

---

63. The scholarship on this issue is vast. But see especially Kvanvig, *Primeval History*; Forsyth, *Old Enemy*; Stanton, "Asking Questions"; Rendsburg, "Biblical Flood Story"; Frymer-Kensky, "Atrahasis"; Barton, "Sumerian Source of Genesis"; and Simoons-Vermeer, "Mesopotamia Floodstories."

64. Kvanvig, *Primeval History*, 499.

65. Ibid.

66. Ibid., 520.

67. Ibid.

its foundation is the emphasis placed upon the character and role of his female progenitor. As we have seen through the portrayal of *Bat Enosh*, especially in *1Q20*, the woman who gives birth to a son of man must be connected specifically to Eve; that is, she must be mythologically positioned according to her own concomitant sexual awareness, which is often directly related to the "Knowledge of Good and Evil" experienced by the first woman. Second, the female progenitor of a son of man is identified with those "daughters of men" (like *Bat Enosh*, "daughter of man") who gives birth to the *gibborim* and who gains not only sexual awareness but also knowledge (often secret or "reprehensible," to use Stuckenbruck's term), conveyed to them by their angelic "husbands."[68]

The "son of man" will also display vestiges of angelic paternity through an angelic and/or supernatural birth. A Son of Man is marked by imposing physical characteristics such as ones possessed by the *gibborim*, demonstrates signs of physical strength, prophetic witness, mystical ascents (Merkaba or Throne/Chariot visions) and miraculous and healing powers. Finally, a Son of Man demonstrates evidence of God's favor and engages in direct communication with God. And in only two canonical instances (Noah and Jesus), the title Son of Man is directly related to salvific attributes connected to themes of cosmic judgment.

NOAH AS (FIRST) SON OF MAN AND SAVIOR

Unlike the Mesopotamian Atrahasis myth, the flood story (in Genesis) is emphatically not about overpopulation and "seems to be an explicit rejection of the idea that the flood came as a result of attempts to decrease man's population."[69] The story of the flood in Genesis and its interpretation in the extracanonical versions discussed above is part of a mythology that locates the cause and focus of evil within Jewish apocalyptic tradition.[70] In Genesis, the flood narrative becomes intricately related to the problem of the origin of evil. The cause for the loss of immortality and exile from the presence of God rests entirely with Eve. In some sense, Genesis 6:1–4 seems to shift the onus for the origin of evil away from the

---

68. Eventually these concepts concerning the sexual availabilty of the female progenitors becomes both more nuanced and more polemically connected to ideas surrounding "honor" and "shame" as we shall see in later chapters.

69. Frymer-Kensky, *In the Wake of the Goddesses*, 150.

70. Auffarth, *Fall of the Angels*, 87ff.

first woman, but depicts her daughters as the culprits for the descent of the lustful fallen angels. The story of the rebellious watchers in *1 Enoch* does little to mitigate the narrative in Genesis 6:1–4. By locating "the inception of the watcher's disobedience on earth" in *Jubilees*, some scholars suggest that "the origin of evil is further removed from heaven where the God of Israel reigns."[71] However, the daughters of men are hardly exonerated. The connection between women's sexuality and lack of morality is made more prominent since "what the angels have done *inter alia* through both their sexual union with women and their teachings serves, by way of negative example, as a warning . . . thus the document [of *Jubilees*] has Noah exhort his children to 'preserve themselves from *fornication* and *pollution* and from all *injustice*.'"[72] Ironically, the salvific qualities of Noah as the first son of man are directly related to the consequences of the sexual actions and receipt of (forbidden) knowledge by the daughters of men who are also the daughters of Eve. Noah's angelic status enables him to provide a means for salvation, even if it is also the reason for the necessity for humanity's destruction in the first place.

Within the etiology of Noah's name in Genesis 5:29 "the figure of a savior appears . . . with a soteriological perspective . . ."[73] In verse 29 Lamech reports "this one will bring us ease (comfort/relief) from our work and from the toil of our hands, from the ground which Yhwh has cursed" and in the LXX, "the name is derived from the root נוח in the sense 'to rest, repose.'"[74] Another variant "derives the name Noah from another sense of the same root נוח, 'to remain, to be left,' an etymology that reflects Noah's career" as the "righteous remnant" and "prototype of the righteous at the End of Days" found in both *1 Enoch* and *Book of Jubilees*.[75] The concept of "righteous remnant" can also be found in *1Q20* where Noah explains:

מן עול ובבור הורתי יעית לקושט וכדי שפקת מן מעי אמי לקושט
שציבת

---

71. Ibid., 115.
72. Ibid., 115, italics original.
73. Poulssen, "Time and Place in Genesis 5," 30.
74. Dimant, "Noah," 125.
75. Ibid., 126.

(and in the womb of her who bore me I came out for uprightness; and when I came forth from my mother's womb, I was planted for uprightness).[76]

Noah's "planting" metaphor echoes *Bat Enosh's* entreaty to Lamech earlier in *1Q20* that:

ומשך נצבת פריא[דן

(and from you the planting of this fruit . . .).[77]

This section of *1Q20* is "inspired by Gen. 6:9, which reports that in his generation Noah was איש צדיק 'a righteous/upright man,' the account repeatedly refers to Noah's קושט 'uprightness,' six times in the first six lines [of *1Q20* and appears] to be poetically structured and to describe Noah's birth . . . [in] מעי 'the womb' of his mother" *Bat Enosh*.[78] And thus the idea of "planting" is a "development from the *Book of Watchers* [in *1 Enoch*], in which Noah is the one *from which* a plant (נעבה) would be planted that would be established (קום) forever."[79] Noah's identification as the "righteous remnant" does not negate his angelic status. It merely confirms his moral stature: Noah is aligned with Yhwh.

Some scholars have noted that "after the rebellion of Adam and Eve and the degeneration of their progeny up to the rebellion of the 'sons of God' (Gen. 6:1–8), the redemptive story unfolds where Noah is seen to be in some sense a redeemer of creation . . ."[80] Some scholars have observed that "Noah is presented as a type of Adam" and that Noah (following his Mesopotamian counterpart Utnapishtim in the Epic of Gilgamesh) serves not only as a savior of humanity, but as the first priest and sacrificer of animals in Genesis 8:20.[81]

With the converging traditions of Noah now firmly ensconced within Genesis, the remaining Hebrew scripture continues to develop the pattern which will influence later canonical and extracanonical concepts associated with the son of man long into the first century C.E. The

---

76. Fitzmyer, *Genesis Apocryphon*, 77.
77. Ibid., 69.
78. Loader, *Dead Sea Scrolls on Sexuality*, 291.
79. Peters, *Noah Traditions*, 109, italics original.
80. Stanton, "Asking Questions," 164. It is also interesting that in the Epic of Gilgamesh, Gilgamesh is given the "plant" of immortality by Utnapishtim, Noah's counterpart in the Mesopotamian flood story.
81. Rendsburg, "Biblical Flood Story," 117ff.

character of Noah found in Genesis and in the extracanonical material is the first Son of Man who incorporates the consequences of the "yahwist version of Genesis" which portrays the "gods trying to cross the barrier from their side."[82]

THE BIBLICAL BIRTH NARRATIVE

I have argued elsewhere that the biblical birth narrative is a particular genre in both the Hebrew Scriptures and the Gospels which describe how human women interact with the divine in a prescribed pattern in order to produce promised sons.[83] There are nine such "birth narratives" that include 1) description of a woman's "mother status," that is, a statement identifying the woman as barren or virgin/maiden; 2) an initial protest made by the woman or her surrogate; 3) an offer made by Yhwh or an angelic ambassador concerning the terms of the "contract"; 4) the divine forecast of the promised son's future; 5) the "naming" of Yhwh by the woman or her surrogate; 6) the acceptance of the divine contractual terms by the woman or her surrogate; and, finally (in three instances), a poem or song of celebration.[84]

Feminist scholars have noted that the narrative of Genesis is replete with examples of women's procreative activity. Indeed, the entire continuation of Yhwh's promise of covenant with Abraham hinges on the production of a son. So it is imperative that Yhwh develop and maintain relationships with women in order to guarantee the patriarchs' progeny. Thus, the women in the birth narratives found in Genesis (and in later books as well) become the nexus mediating the sanctioned intercourse between human and divine. But since the earlier chapters of Genesis focus on the misappropriation of that intercourse between the divine (the sons of God) and the human (daughters of men), the compilers and redactors of Genesis must formulate a circumscribed tradition to insure the divinely sanctioned creation of promised sons for the continuation of God's covenant. The first woman to inaugurate the pattern is Hagar, the handmaid of Sarah. It is Yhwh's contractual connection with Hagar, created in Genesis 16:7–15 that serves as the foundation and prototype for all potential child-bearing women in Scripture and that eventually

82. Forsyth, *Old Enemy*, 155.
83. Jarrell, "Birth Narrative."
84. Ibid., 5.

culminates in the New Testament pericope of the impregnation of Mary, the mother of Jesus. In this way, the birth narrative becomes a female counterpart to "covenant," specifically formulated by the compilers and redactors of Genesis for the purposes of superseding women's past associations with fallen angels and temporarily raising their theological status. Hagar is the first among other future "chosen" childless women to transcend her female cultic (priestly) limitations in order to interact with Yhwh on a basis equal to that of Abraham.

The theophany of Hagar occurs in Genesis 16:7–15:

> The angel of the Lord found her by a spring of water in the wilderness, the spring on the way to Shur. And he said, "Hagar, slave-girl of Sarai, where have you come from and where are you going?" She said, "I am running away from my mistress Sarai." The angel of the Lord said to her, "Return to your mistress, and submit to her." The angel of the Lord also said to her, "I will so greatly multiply your offspring that they cannot be counted for multitude." And the angel of the Lord said to her, "Now you have conceived and shall bear a son; you shall call him Ishmael, for the Lord has given heed to your affliction. He shall be a wild ass of a man, with his hand against everyone, and everyone's hand against him; and he shall live at odds with all his kin." So she named the Lord who spoke to her, "You are El-roi"; for she said, "Have I really seen God and remained alive after seeing him?" Therefore the well was called Beer-lahai-roi; it lies between Kadesh and Bered.[85]

In the MT, Hagar's status as "handmaid" is described by the Hebrew term *shifhah* (שפחה). In addition to the usual meaning of "maid-servant" ("slave-girl" in the NRSV translation), the biblical Yahwist author uses the term *shifhah* in relation to women who conceive and become pregnant.[86] In the LXX, Hagar is called παιδίσκη, a term that can mean a young girl or maiden, which is similar to the term specified by Mary, the mother of Jesus, who also identifies herself as ἡ δούλη κυρίου (handmaiden/servant of the Lord).[87] Indeed, both Hagar and Mary (the only "chosen women" in Scripture who are unmarried and not barren) are situated along a

---

85. NRSV online: http://bible.oremus.org/?passage=Genesis+16.

86. Teubal, *Hagar the Egyptian*.

87. The importance of these terms for women who are not barren will be more fully discussed in chapter 5.

Fallen Angels and Fallen Women

biblical trajectory which defines how a particular woman engages in a powerful relationship with divinity.

Evidence for Hagar's powerful status is first given in Genesis 16 in the narrative report of her "calling" the name of Yhwh. This astounding instance is the only act of naming by a human (and a woman!) to a deity in the entire Hebrew Bible. The use of the verb קרא used to connote the act of naming without an intervening preposition occurs approximately 110 times in Genesis alone.[88] But in the case of Hagar, the act of "calling" represents a significant parallel to Yhwh's revelation of the divine name to Moses in Exodus 33:19.[89] Further evidence of Hagar's powerful status is noted by Nancy Jay who observes that Hagar is the only woman who receives a promise from Yhwh in Genesis 16:10 concerning her זרע ("seed").[90] As Jay points out, when Yhwh says to Hagar in the wilderness, "'I will so greatly multiply your offspring that they cannot be counted for multitude' in the 'J' [Yahwist] version of the story, it is too much for the [Elohist redactor]. His version cleans things up patrilineally: God said to Abraham, 'I will make a nation of the son of the slave woman also, because he is your seed' (Genesis 21:13)."[91]

Although the text of Genesis 16:13, 14 presents some difficulties in translation, the theme of sight and seeing are clearly established when Hagar "names" Yhwh the "Yhwh who sees me" and adds further, "truly I have seen Yhwh after he has seen me." The linguistic play between the location of the theophany (a "spring") with Hagar's and Yhwh's "seeing" are apparent in the use of עין (spring/eye) for both concepts.[92] The term also serves to indicate that the messenger of Yhwh (מלאך יהוה) could also be considered a potentially threatening עירין or Watcher, terms found in *1 Enoch* and *1Q20* that also allude to the "sons of God" in Genesis 6:2. It seems that the lingering association between the messengers of Yhwh with fallen the sons of God (or Watchers) never completely disappears from the canonical material and remains mythological present, even if only in the background. Moreover, the compliers of Genesis must reconcile the rules of androcentric covenant making to the biological fact that women possess the essential procreative power needed to fulfill and

88. Whitaker, *Eerdmans Analytical Concordance*, 144 s.v. 'קרא.'
89. Janzen, "Hagar in Paul's Eyes."
90. Jay, *Throughout*.
91. Ibid., 102.
92. Alter points out that "betrothal type-scenes" in the Hebrew Bible "often serve as meeting grounds for women and their bethrothed" (*Art of Biblical*, 53).

perpetuate Yhwh's own covenant previously ratified with Abram in the earlier scene of Genesis 15:18. These two competing factors (the necessity of women for the production of Yhwh's promised sons and the threat of paternity originating from fallen angels) remain in tension throughout the rest of Genesis and into the New Testament.

We have seen how the extracanonical book of *Jubilees* "rewrites" the story of Genesis, and in so doing, grants the women more status especially as it relates to the importance of their inclusion within the community of Israel and more specifically within the ancient Israelite priestly class. Some scholars argue that the purpose of *Jubilees* is to, like the canonical Ezra, warn against the dangers of the defilement of the priesthood through the intermarriage of foreign women.[93] Scholars trace such a supposed "transformation" from the lesser theological status of the women in Genesis to the more powerful females in *Jubilees*. But the original passage found in Genesis 16:7–14 containing the "dialogue between Hagar and the angel of Yhwh" has been omitted in *Jubliees*.[94] Through this omission, "everything that raises the status of Hagar [in Genesis] is also omitted . . . her direct communication with the angel about her son (a sort of birth report), which elsewhere in Genesis is reserved only for the patriarchs, not for women, let alone a slave woman . . ."[95]

The birth narrative obtains its proper form in Genesis 16, but the concept of birth narrative may be prefigured in the story of Eve and the birth of Cain in 4:1:

וְהָאָדָם יָדַע אֶת־חַוָּה אִשְׁתּוֹ וַתַּהַר וַתֵּלֶד אֶת־קַיִן וַתֹּאמֶר קָנִיתִי אִישׁ אֶת־יְהוָה:

"Now Adam had known his wife Eve and she conceived and bore Cain, saying, 'I have acquired a man with Yhwh'"(NASB).

In the MT, the pun for the name of Eve's son (קָנִיתִי) "I have acquired" underscores her powerful relationship to Yhwh. The same verb

---

93. Halpern-Amaru, *Empowerment of Women*. This also represents the argument that the "sons of God" were foreign kings or princes instead of angelic beings. See, for example Kline, "Divine Kingship" and Gilboa, "Who 'Fell Down'?"

94. In Goodman, *Abraham, the Nations*, 125.

95. In Goodman, *Abraham, the Nations*, 125. And J. van Ruiten also comments that "in Gen 16:13 Hagar seems to suggest that she has seen God: 'So she called the name of Yhwh who spoke to her: 'You are a God of seeing': for she said: 'Have I really seen God and remained alive after seeing him?' She would have been the only woman in Genesis and Exodus who had encountered God, and this was probably too much honour accorded to a slave woman," in Goodman, *Abraham, the Nations*, 125.

Fallen Angels and Fallen Women

can also mean "to purchase, or to redeem" as in the case of the ransom paid to free slaves.[96] This concept is also connected to other promised sons (see below). By calling Cain a "*man/ish* . . . [Eve] puts him into close relationship to God: *a man created with God*, or even a *man-with-God* (like, e.g., Enoch in 5:22.)"[97] Rashi states, however that Eve's proclamation simply means that "When [God] created me and my husband, He created us by Himself, but in the birth of this child, we are partners with [God]."[98] The LXX also carries the same sense of collaborating agency between Yhwh and Eve:

Αδαμ δὲ ἔγνω Ευαν τὴν γυναῖκα αὐτοῦ καὶ συλλαβοῦσα ἔτεκεν τὸν Καιν καὶ εἶπεν ἐκτησάμην ἄνθρωπον διὰ τοῦ θεοῦ.

Clearly, Eve creates Cain through the powerful association with, or by the means of Yhwh. This passage must prefigure the birth narrative of Genesis 16 since Eve's procreative abilities are a direct result of her sexual awakening that cause the first couple to be exiled from the garden and denied immortality. What cannot be known (and is scarcely asked) is whether Yhwh originally intends Adam and Eve to procreate (in the second Genesis story) as Yhwh clearly intends with animals. The dependence of Yhwh on the procreative ability of women is a fundamental issue which paradoxically traces its origin to Eve's sexual awakening. Eve's ability to procreate is a direct result of her "fall" and is oddly contingent with her relationship to males, one divine and one human. In Genesis 4:1, when Eve "creates a man," she does so ambiguously. It remains unclear whether the father of Cain is Yhwh or Adam.

The LXX also preserves the term "man/ איש / ἄνθρωπον causing Kahl to notice that "nowhere else in the Bible is a newborn baby called *ish, a man*."[99] She alludes to the "linkage between [Genesis] 4:1 and [Lamech's] song in 4:23–24 which takes up the key terms *man-woman-child (yeled)* . . . now confronting two mothers who had given birth (*yalud*—4:20, 22) like Eve (4:1) with a proud male statement on the counter-generative power to kill 'man' (*ish*) and 'child' (*yeled*)."[100] Such a description of the generative power of women (especially Eve and then

---

96. Kahl also notes that the name can mean "I have created" See ("She Called His Name Seth," 24).

97. Ibid., 24.

98. Rashi, *Rashi 'al ha-Torah*, 41.

99. Kahl, "She Called His Name Seth," 24.

100. Ibid., 224n8.

Hagar) to produce promised sons by divine agency parallels the trajectory whereby Yhwh's promised sons are marked for both exaltation and sacrifice as a "son of man."

Susan Ackerman focuses on the story of the wife of Manoah in Judges 13 as the template for "the story of a barren woman whose tragic fate is reversed by the miraculous acts of a merciful God" that occurs six times in the Hebrew Bible, and connects the promised son to a miraculous birth, a "motif" of the son's "near-death" or (in its place) a "consecration to divine service under the terms of a Nazirite vow."[101] Jon Levenson, however, more completely traces the development of the death and resurrection of the beloved son in his work.[102]

Levenson contends that the ancient Israelite requirement that the firstborn be given to God (Exod 22:28–29) is a primordial pagan remnant of an actual practice in child sacrifice that was later transformed into "a foundational story of Judaism: the first-born [who]belongs to God, the beloved son—generally not the first-born—is chosen by the father for suffering and exaltation (i.e., death or near death or symbolic death followed by eventual elevation to the status of ruler)."[103] According to Levenson's thesis, "this transformation [from actual sacrifice to symbolic action] takes the form of both narrative and ritual: [and examples include] the link between Moriah and the Temple Cult (2 Chronicles 3:1); [substituting] the Pascal lamb in lieu of the first-born (Exodus 12:21–23); Levitical service (Numbers 8:16–19); the institution of the Nazirite (Numbers 6:1–21) and circumcision (Exodus 4:24–26, Genesis 17:2)."[104] But more importantly, Levenson underscores the gendered relationship of Yhwh to specific women who are chosen to bear the promised sons by providing an example through Yhwh's command found in Exodus 34:19: "All that opens the womb is mine."[105] The womb opened by Yhwh presumably referred originally to the animal womb, but after the exile from the garden, it included the human female womb as well.

Levenson argues that "the impulse to sacrifice the first-born son never died in ancient Israel . . . [it] was only transformed . . . [since] the special status of the oldest boy continued to be a point of great significance

---

101. Ackerman, *Warrior, Dancer, Seductress*, 185. She also points out the parallels with the virgin birth in the New Testament.

102. Levenson, *Death and Resurrection of the Beloved Son*.

103. Fuchs-Kreimer, "Sibling Rivals," 49.

104. Ibid.

105. Levenson, *Death and Resurrection of the Beloved Son*, 7.

in the society and of noteworthy resonance in its law."[106] Levenson cites the law of primogeniture in Deuteronomy 21:15–17 as further proof for the potentially powerful role of women in the divinely sanctioned procreative process and remarks that "the intention of this law is to prevent the status of a man's wives from impairing the claim of the husband's firstborn as chief heir to his father's estate. That the scenario it envisions was not hypothetical is suggested by narratives in which a father prefers the late-born son of a favored wife over the first-born of an unfavored one."[107] It is through Sarah's insistence that Abraham expels his firstborn Ishmael so that he would not have a share in the younger son Isaac's inheritance.

Levenson also notes that "a father's preference for a late-born son over his first-born may, at one stage in the evolution of law and custom, have violated the principle of primogeniture less than seems the case at first glance. For Isaac and Joseph were both first-born sons not of their fathers but of their mothers . . . that Israelite primogeniture may at some point have involved matrilineal factors is perhaps to be inferred from a few biblical texts that equate 'the first-born male' (*bekor*) with 'the first issue of the womb' (*peter rehem*)" found in Numbers 3:11–13.[108] Levenson observes that "when Ezekiel addresses child sacrifice, he speaks only of 'every first issue of the womb' (*kol peter raham*) and never the first-born son (*bekor*)—as if it is maternal primogeniture that identifies the child to be sacrificed (Ezekiel 20:25–26)."[109] Such practice clearly connects the patriarchal women/wives to their essential and even acknowledged power directly to Yhwh.

With similar ambiguous tensions the creation and presentation of the biblical birth narrative is an attempt to theologically regulate Yhwh's interaction with potential mothers. Levenson also notices that "the way rabbinic tradition handles the ambiguity between 'the first issue of the womb,' with its maternal orientation, and the 'first-born [son],' with its paternal reference means that in the Mishnah, early attempts are made to categorize classes of sons in order to differentiate the "*bekor lannabala*, the son who may claim the double portion, and the *bekor lakkoben*, the

---

106. Ibid., 55.
107. Ibid.
108. Ibid., 56.
109. Ibid.

son who must be redeemed by payment to the priest for five shekels, the latter being determined by reference to the mother."[110]

While "in the case of animals ... the firstling is to be donated to God by sacrifice," the redeeming of the firstborn "is necessary because the first-born belongs to Yhwh and can be gotten back only through substitution ... the underlying theology of the redemption of the first-born son is that, even more so than in the case of other human beings, the life of the son in question is not by right, but by gift. He is alive only by virtue of a legal fiction, one of the several rituals that Israelite religion evolved as a substitute for the literal sacrifice of the son who belongs to God rather than to his mortal father."[111] But the promised son is also only alive through the mother's agreement to the birth contract.

In the biblical birth narrative, therefore, the firstborn's connection to his mother is crucial. The same kind of legal fiction that raises the non-cultic status of potential mothers to almost Levitical proportion is nearly identical to the same type of legal fiction that perceives the firstborn son as belonging to Yhwh. In both cases, it is the maternal primogeniture (at least historically) that designates the son for sacrifice. In the patriarchal narratives of Genesis the question concerning who may be assigned the role "beloved son" must also take into consideration the structure and trajectory of the biblical birth narrative vis-à-vis women who are the mothers of those sons. The ongoing relationship between patriarch and beloved son progresses in parallel symbiosis with the evolving trajectory of the biblical birth narrative that eventually includes the ongoing relationship between Yhwh and his son of man. The structure solidified within the story of God's interaction with Hagar and Ishmael shares antecedents with the story of Eve and Cain and *Bat Enosh* mentioned above. But it is in Genesis 16 that the genre of the birth narrative begins its trajectory which will merge with the concept of the Biblical "son of man" most profoundly inside the New Testament.

---

110. Ibid., 57.
111. Ibid., 59.

Chapter Four

THE BIBLICAL BIRTH NARRATIVE AND THE SON OF MAN

IN THE PREVIOUS CHAPTER, we outlined the genre of the biblical birth narrative and its importance to the concept of the Son of Man. This chapter will focus on the foundational birth narrative which is expanded by the Son of Man mythology is creative ways. The chart below combines the elements of the biblical birth narrative with Levenson's five "transformational points" (see above) stemming from earlier vestiges of the "sacrifice" or near sacrifice of the beloved son.[1]

---

1. See Fuchs-Kreimer, "Sibling Rivals."

Chapter Four

Citation	Biblical Birth-Narrative Son	Announced By	Divine narrative	Biblical 'Son of Man'	Mother Status	"wife" order	Birth Order	Extra-Canonical 'Son of Man'	Associated Mother
Gen 4	Cain	Eve	"acquired a man" (named by mother)		Virgin	First	First		Eve
Gen 6	Noah	Lamech	"relief from cursed ground"		Virgin	First	First	Noah	Bat Enosh
Gen 16	Ishmael	Angel *			Virgin	Second	First		Hagar
Gen 18	Isaac	Angel			Barren	First	First		Sarah
Gen 25	Jacob	Yhwh	Elohim "opened her womb."		Barren	First	Second		Rebekah
Gen 30	Joseph		(named by mother)		Barren	Second	First		Rachel
Judges 13	Samson	Angel * (nazir)	(named by mother)		Barren	First	First		Manoah's Wife
1 Samuel	Samuel	Eli (prophet) (nazir)	Yhwh "remembered her." (named by mother)		Barren	Second	First		Hannah
2 Kings 4	Shunammite son	Elisha (prophet)			Barren (?)	First	First		Shunammite Woman
Ezekiel				Ezekiel					Rahab (?)
Daniel				Daniel (1)					(?)

Fallen Angels and Fallen Women

Luke	John Baptizer	Gabriel (prophet) (nazir)	(named by mother)	Barren					Elizabeth
Luke		Gabriel*	(named by mother)	Jesus	Virgin	First	First		
								Elijah (Apoc. of Elijah)	
								Daniel (2) (Susanna and the Elders)	
								Enoch (Book of Enoch)	'son of the mother of the living'

As the chart indicates, the biblical birth narratives contain only three instances (*) where the themes of women and sexual awareness (or procreative potential) and the transmission of (divine) knowledge intersect. In the case of these narratives, a woman as potential mother comes within the presence of an angel who converses directly with her concerning the promised son. These three narratives provide evidence that the biblical birth narrative genre begun in Genesis 16 and ending in Luke 1:29 incorporate concepts found both within canonical and also extracanonical ideology regarding the son of man.

The story of Samson in Judges 13 provides the transitional "hinge" bridging the birth narrative genre to the son of man ideology. Since this narrative is crucial to providing evidence for the requirements for a promised son's status as a Son of Man, it is reproduced below in full:

> There was a certain man of Zorah, of the family of the Danites, whose name was Manoah; and his wife was barren and had borne no children. Then the angel of the LORD appeared to the woman and said to her, "Behold now, you are barren and have borne no children, but you shall conceive and give birth to a son. Now therefore, be careful not to drink wine or strong drink, nor eat any unclean thing. For behold, you shall conceive and give birth to a son, and no razor shall come upon his head, for the boy shall be a Nazirite to God from the womb; and he shall begin to deliver Israel from the hands of the Philistines." Then the woman came and told her husband, saying, "A man of God came to me and his appearance was like the appearance of the angel of God, very awesome. And I did not ask him where he *came* from, nor did he tell me his name. But he said to me, 'Behold, you shall conceive and give birth to a son, and now you shall not drink wine or strong drink nor eat any unclean thing, for the boy shall be a Nazirite to God from the womb to the day of his death.'" Then Manoah entreated the LORD and said, "O Lord, please let the man of God whom You have sent come to us again that he may teach us what to do for the boy who is to be born." God listened to the voice of Manoah; and the angel of God came again to the woman as she was sitting in the field, but Manoah her husband was not with her. So the woman ran quickly and told her husband, "Behold, the man who came the *other* day has appeared to me." Then Manoah arose and followed his wife, and when he came to the man he said to him, "Are you the man who spoke to the woman?" And he said, "I am." Manoah said, "Now when your words come *to pass*, what

shall be the boy's mode of life and his vocation?" So the angel of the LORD said to Manoah, "Let the woman pay attention to all that I said. She should not eat anything that comes from the vine nor drink wine or strong drink, nor eat any unclean thing; let her observe all that I commanded." Then Manoah said to the angel of the LORD, "Please let us detain you so that we may prepare a young goat for you." The angel of the LORD said to Manoah, "Though you detain me, I will not eat your food, but if you prepare a burnt offering, *then* offer it to the LORD." For Manoah did not know that he was the angel of the LORD. Manoah said to the angel of the LORD, "What is your name, so that when your words come *to pass*, we may honor you?" But the angel of the LORD said to him, "Why do you ask my name, seeing it is wonderful?" So Manoah took the young goat with the grain offering and offered it on the rock to the LORD, and He performed wonders while Manoah and his wife looked on. For it came about when the flame went up from the altar toward heaven, that the angel of the LORD ascended in the flame of the altar. When Manoah and his wife saw *this*, they fell on their faces to the ground. Now the angel of the LORD did not appear to Manoah or his wife again. Then Manoah knew that he was the angel of the LORD. So Manoah said to his wife, "We will surely die, for we have seen God." But his wife said to him, "If the LORD had desired to kill us, He would not have accepted a burnt offering and a grain offering from our hands, nor would He have shown us all these things, nor would He have let us hear *things* like this at this time." Then the woman gave birth to a son and named him Samson; and the child grew up and the LORD blessed him. And the Spirit of the LORD began to stir him in Mahaneh-dan, between Zorah and Eshtaol (NASB).

The story of Samson's birth "conforms to the norms of biblical narrative" within type-scenes of other annunciations.[2] While the birth-narrative structure in Judges 13 is similar to others in the genre it is "most striking . . . that the protagonist, the barren woman to whom the angel appears, is not named."[3] The book of Judges also provides two other examples of unnamed women "Jephthah's daughter (Judg. 11) and the Levite's concubine (Judg. 19) . . . [but] neither is the principal protagonist of the story in which she figures."[4] Because there is a "dissonance

2. Reinhartz, "Samson's Mother," 26.
3. Ibid.
4. Ibid., 27.

between the centrality of Samson's mother, Manoah's wife, on the one hand, and her anonymity on the other" some scholars conclude that "the literary function of the woman's anonymity in [the story of Judges 13] is to emphasize her relationship with, and similarities to, the angel."[5] I argue, however, that it is not the woman's similarity to the angel that is striking but her intimate (and implied sexual) association with the angel. Scholars have noted that "there is no positive indication . . . that Samson is the natural son of Manoah" and in fact there are two indications in the text which indicate "the angel may have had some more direct role in the conception of this child than merely announcing it."[6]

During the first appearance of the angel in 13:3, as the angel reiterates the woman's barrenness, the angel uses the verb והרית ("and you will conceive") indicating action that is to take place in the future. Then "in v. 5, the prophecy is repeated . . . [with] the verb in the perfect tense: 'for behold, you have conceived [*hara* הרה] and will bear a son.'"[7] Some scholars believe that "the second verb, in the perfect tense, should be understood as meaning that the woman became pregnant during the encounter with the angel."[8] The wording of the passage contains "the suggestion of a sexual relationship between the angel and the woman [which] is strengthened by her report in v. 6 that the angel *ba' 'elay*, בא אלי . . ."[9] While this phrase "can simply mean, as the RSV translates it, 'he came to me,' it can also mean, 'he came in unto me,' a common biblical way of referring to sexual intercourse."[10] What is noteworthy for our purposes is that the angel comes to the woman the second time while she is sitting alone in a field and might "easily call to the mind of a reader familiar with the legal texts . . . [especially] Deut. 22.25 [where] sexual accounts in fields were not unheard of, though a woman could not be punished in the circumstances under the assumption that her protests would have gone unheard."[11] It is likely the text does not "suggest that Manoah's wife was raped by the angel" but the mere suggestion of rape in combination with a visitation from a divine being would also recall to readers familiar

5. Ibid.
6. Ibid., 33. See also Chisholm, "Identity Crisis," 149ff.
7. Reinhartz, "Samson's Mother," 34.
8. Ibid.
9. Ibid.
10. Ibid.
11. Ibid., 35.

Fallen Angels and Fallen Women

with Genesis 6:4 the entire myth of the fallen angels (the sons of God) and uses the same sexual euphemism found in Judges 13 to describe how they "came in to the daughters of men, and they bore children to them" (אֲשֶׁר יָבֹאוּ בְּנֵי הָאֱלֹהִים אֶל־בְּנוֹת הָאָדָם וְיָלְדוּ לָהֶם).

Returning to the question of the woman's curious state of anonymity, I argue that the wife of Manoah is not anonymous in the least. She is always "referred to by the narrator . . . by the angel . . . and even by her husband . . . as 'the woman.'"[12] A reading of the text reveals the way Manoah's wife is designated and by whom reveals an interesting point:

Citation (NASB)	Term used	Spoken by	Translated as	Direct Speech
13:2	אשתו	Narrator	Wife	No
13:3	האשה	Angel	The Woman	Yes (to Woman)
13:6	האשה	Narrator	The Woman	No (about Angel)
13:9	האשה	Narrator	The Woman	No (Angel present)
13:10	האשה	Narrator	The Woman	No (about Angel)
13:11	אשתו	Narrator	Wife	No
13:11	האשה	Manoah	The Woman	Yes
13:13	האשה	Angel	The Woman	Yes (to Manoah)
13:19	אשתו	Narrator	Wife	No
13:20	אשתו	Narrator	Wife	No
13:21	אשתו	Narrator	Wife	No
13:22	אשתו	Manoah	Wife	Yes
13:23	אשתו	Narrator	Wife	Yes
13:24	האשה	Narrator	The Woman	No (gives birth to Samson)

As the chart indicates, when the terms for the anonymous woman are analyzed together with the speaker employing those terms, several factors concerning the identity of Manoah's wife emerge. The narrator in the story uses the term "wife" six times and the term "the woman" four times. While the same Hebrew term can be translated both "wife" as well as "woman" (see Genesis 2 and 3 above), it is instructive to notice how it has been historically translated in conjunction with the speaker using the term.

12. Ibid., 40.

When the narrator uses the term "the woman" for Manoah's wife, it is either when the angel is present in the story or Manoah's wife is relating to Manoah past facts concerning the presence of the angel when Manoah is not with her. The last time the narrator uses "the woman" for Manoah's wife, it is to report the birth of Samson (as the angel has foreseen and/or caused). Manoah/narrator uses the term "wife" once in 13:22, but in the presence of the angel, Manoah refers to his wife as "the woman." Most importantly, it is the angel who calls Manoah's wife "the woman," once during his first appearance to her and again in repeating his initial instructions to her for the benefit of Manoah.

This analysis suggests that Manoah's wife has one clear designation and that is the term "the woman." This title places Manoah's wife first in the category of those same daughters of men who became sexually aware by the agency of the sons of God, but more importantly places Manoah's wife in the direct lineage of the first woman whose revelation of sexual knowledge brought about the expulsion from the garden of Eden.

Judges 13 also has parallels with Genesis 18, 16, and 2 and 3. Scholars note that the woman's encounters "with and knowledge of a divine being . . . are far superior in quantity and quality to that between her . . . very human spouse."[13] As we have seen in previous examples given in Genesis, the woman's knowledge of the angel cannot be isolated from the mythological antecedents of sexual awareness excerpted from the "daughters of men," and from the first woman's original sexual awareness which now manifests itself in the promise of a son.

JUDGES 13, GENESIS 18, AND JUDGES 6

The particular term angel of God (as Yhwh) (מלאך יהוה) occurs "fifty-eight times in the Hebrew Bible" whereas the other corresponding designation for angel of God (as Elohim) (מלאך האלהים) has only "thirteen occurrences."[14] Only two passages, both in Judges (6:20 and 13:6) "mix the designations of מלאך האלהים and מלאך יהוה."[15] There is every reason to infer that the two terms are combined deliberately by the author/compiler since both passages are also thematically related and contain "the appearance of the angel, the appointment/announcement of a saviour,

---

13. Ibid., 36.

14. Eynikel, "Angel in Samson's Birth," 118.

15. Ibid. Judges 6:20 reports the angel's announcement that Gideon will overcome the Midianites.

the sacrifice on the rock and consum[ation] by fire followed by the sudden disappearance of the angel."[16] But the designation for the angel used by Manoah's wife is instructive. In relating her experience of the encounter, Manoah's wife reports that:

אִישׁ הָאֱלֹהִים בָּא אֵלַי וּמַרְאֵהוּ כְּמַרְאֵה מַלְאַךְ הָאֱלֹהִים

"A man of *Elohim* came to me and his appearance was like the appearance of the angel of *Elohim*."

Manoah's wife's identification of the angel as *elohim* only serves to connect the angel to the בְּנֵי־הָאֱלֹהִים (sons of *Elohim*) found in Genesis 6:2.[17] Manoah's wife calls the angel "a *man* of *Elohim*" which underscores both aspects of the angel: he is a heavenly being who is also a male capable of inseminating a human woman and producing offspring.

The concept of angels being portrayed as "men" has a long history not only within the canonical scripture, but also within the extracanonical material as well.[18] In Genesis 18, for example, the angels who appear to Abraham to announce the birth of Isaac to Sarah are also referred to as "men." These "men"/angels are offered food that they consume before they give the announcement concerning Isaac's future birth. The thematic similarities and differences are worth noting:

Genesis 18	Judges 6	Judges 13
Lord appears by an Oak	Angel of the Lord appears by Oak	
Lord and *Men*	Lord and Angel of the Lord	Angel of the Lord and *Man*
	Angel sends flame under the Oak and does not eat	Angel performs flame "wonders" and does not eat
The *Men* eat under the Oak	Sacrifice of food	Sacrifice of food
No sacrifice of food	Rock under oak sacrifice	Rock becomes Altar
Men turn and depart	Angel disappears	Angel ascends in flame
	Seeing Angel face to face	Seeing Angel face to face
	Lord tells Gideon he will not die	Manoah's wife tells Manoah they will not die
Food offered:		
Bread cakes, choice calf Curds and milk	Kid, unleavened bread, broth	Kid

16. Ibid., 119.

17. The term "Elohim" may also be translated in the plural as "gods" as in the case of the Canaanite pantheon "sons of El."

18. See especially Barker, *Great Angel*.

Other scholars have noticed "a literary dependency between Judg 13 and Judg 6" but when these two passages are compared against the entire genre of the birth narrative, a larger and more complicated pattern emerges.[19] The Lord/"men" in Genesis 18 eat the food prepared for them, and no sacrifice is offered. In Judges 6, Gideon asks the Lord/Angel of the Lord to remain while he prepares the sacrifice that is then burnt as an offering. In Judges 13, Manoah, mistaking the "man" for a human, repeats the actions of Abraham in offering the angel food, which the angel then refuses. The angel commands Manoah to offer the food as an offering on the "altar" (no such designation is used in Judges 6). This thematic trajectory follows the pattern recognized by both Ackerman and Levenson. The point of sacrifice in each passage from Judges reveals the relationship between the messenger sent by the Deity and the promised son. In Genesis 18, no sacrifice is required until the Aqedah when the promised son Isaac is nearly sacrificed. In Judges 6, Gideon's offering is required by covenantal law and is not for purposes of identifying a promised son. In Judges 13, however, both themes of Genesis 18 and Judges 6 are combined: the man originally believed to be human is now perceived through his performing "wonders" as a messenger of the Deity who may also be the father of the promised son. It is this same promised son Samson, who will be "sacrificed" at the end of his life during his destruction of the Temple of Dagon in Judges 16:28ff.

JUDGES 13 AND GENESIS 16

The birth narrative genre in Genesis 16 continues to develop and expand to include the canonical ideas concerning the son of man but is also influenced by extracanonical material. The biblical birth narrative of Hagar in Genesis 16 describes a young woman who is not considered barren. In the case of Judges 13, the woman is announced as barren by the angel who proceeds to reveal the birth of a promised son. However, in stark contrast to other barren women in the birth narratives, Manaoh's wife never asks God to "deliver her from her barren condition," nor does her husband Manoah seek God's help in order to "open her womb."[20] When the Genesis 16 and Judges 13 are compared, we may see how the combination of barren/unexpected birth in Judges 13 serves to create further

---

19. Eynikel, "Angel in Samson's Birth," 179.
20. Chisholm, "Identity Crisis," 152.

evidence that the story of Samson is a fulcrum joining the trajectory of the birth narrative to concepts related to the son of man:

Genesis 16	Judges 13
Now the angel of the LORD found her	Then the angel of the LORD appeared to the woman and said to her, "Behold now, you are barren and have borne no children, but you shall conceive and give birth to a son.
Then the angel of the Lord said to her, "Return to your mistress, and submit yourself to her authority."	Now therefore, be careful not to drink wine or strong drink, nor eat any unclean thing.
Moreover, the angel of the LORD said to her, "I will greatly multiply your descendants so that they will be too many to count."	
The angel of the Lord said to her further, Behold, you are with child and you will bear a son;	For behold, you shall conceive and give birth to a son
	and no razor shall come upon his head, for the boy shall be a Nazirite to God from the womb;
And you shall call his name Ishmael, because the Lord has given heed to your affliction.	and he shall begin to deliver Israel from the hands of the Philistines."
	And the woman came and told her husband saying, "A man of God came to me and his appearance was like the appearance of the angel of God, very awesome.
	But he said to me, 'Behold, you shall conceive and give birth to a son, and now you shall not drink wine or strong drink nor eat any unclean thing, for the boy shall be a Nazirite to God from the womb to the day of his death.'"
Then she called the name of the LORD who spoke to her, "You are a God who sees";	

	So the angel of the LORD said to Manoah, "Let the woman pay attention to all that I said. She should not eat anything that comes from the vine nor drink wine nor strong drink, no eat any unclean thing; let her observe all that I commanded."
	So Manoah said to his wife, "We will surely die, for we have seen God."
For she said, "Have I even remained alive here after seeing Him?"	But his wife said to him, "If the Lord had desired to kill us, He would not have accepted a burnt offering and a grain offering from our hands, nor would He have shown us all these things, nor would He have let us hear things like this at this time."
So Hagar bore Abram a son; and Abram called the name of his son, whom Hagar bore, Ishmael. (NASB)	And the woman gave birth to a son and named him Samson.

The angel in both narratives gives an injunction to the woman that she subsequently follows. In Genesis 16, the angel's annunciation to Hagar is a pronouncement that she is already pregnant. Judges 13 uses the birth narrative to highlight elements of Genesis 6:4. The angel is one of the sons of God who is either the father of the child, or suspected of being the father. Just as *Bat Enosh* is suspected by Lamech of having been impregnated by an angel, Manoah's wife will be considered sexually suspect by readers. Both narratives give the forecast of the son's future (Hagar is given naming instructions). In both narratives, the recipients of the angel's words express concern that looking upon the face of the angel, or seeing God will constitute death. Both narratives end with the report of the birth of the son—in Genesis 16 Abram names Ishmael, but in Judges 13, it is the woman who names Samson.

JUDGES 13 AND GENESIS 2 AND 3

The following chart indicates the differences and similarities between the angel's injunction to Manoah's wife, and her report of the angel's annunciation to Manoah:

Angel	Manoah's wife's report
Behold now … but **you shall Conceive and give birth to a son.**	Behold, you shall Conceive and give birth to a son,
Now therefore, be careful Not to **drink wine or strong drink,** Nor eat any unclean thing.	And now You shall not drink wine or strong drink Nor eat any unclean thing,
For behold, you shall conceive and give birth to a son,	
and no razor shall come upon his head,	
for the boy shall be a Nazirite to God from the womb;	For the boy shall be A Nazirite to God from the womb to the day of his death.
Let the woman pay attention to all that I said.	
She should not eat anything that comes from the vine	
nor drink wine or strong drink, nor eat any unclean thing;	
let her observe all that I commanded.	

The bold font indicates agreements in the words of the angel with the words of Manoah's wife. But Judges 13 also shares similarities with Genesis 3. Just as the conversation between Eve and the serpent is not heard by Adam, Manoah's wife is alone with the angel when the announcement of her promised son is given. And as Yhwh's first words to Adam are given as a commandment (וַיְצַו) not to eat from the Tree of the Knowledge of Good and Evil, the angel advises Manoah's wife to take the vow of a *nazir* during her pregnancy and "observe all that I commanded (her)" (צִוִּיתִיהָ). Just as Eve makes certain emendations to the injunctions given to her by Yhwh in her report to the serpent, Manoah's wife makes a surprising addition to the angel's future forecast given to her son. Samson's mother adds to the admonitions given to her by the angel by mentioning the death of her son. While the angel's pronouncement regarding Samson's forecasted *nazir* status will deviate significantly from what actually occurs later in the narrative, the mother's prophecy is fulfilled. In no other birth narrative is the death of the promised son mentioned or foretold by the mother and in no other canonical or extracanonical scripture up to the time of the New Testament and Gospels is a promised son (and later son of man) killed or sacrificed.

SAMSON AS הַגִּבֹּרִים (HA-GIBBORIM)

Finally, Samson's similarity to the *gibborim* in Genesis 6:4 completes the bridge between earlier forms of the promised-son birth narrative and later concepts associated with the son of man. According to scholars, "the word *gibbor* describes a man who performs feats of extraordinary strength ... this is the meaning the word has elsewhere in the rabbinic literature when it refers to such heroes as Samson, Abner, and Joab."[21] So by this later rabbinic terminology, Samson certainly qualifies as a *gibbor*. We have already analyzed the term *ha-gibborim* associated with Genesis 6:4 as the qualifying reason Yhwh sends the flood. Because the offspring of the sons of God and the daughters of men wreak so much violence on earth, they must be destroyed. And in *1 Enoch* 10:9, we read:

> [God said] "Go, Gabriel to the bastards, to the half-breeds, to the sons of miscegenation; and destroy the sons of the watchers from among the sons of men; send them against one another in a war of destruction. Length of days they will not have; and no petition will be (granted) to their fathers in their behalf, that they should expect to live an everlasting life, nor even that each of them should live for five hundred years."[22]

While the rabbinical view associates Samson with the *gibborim* because of his extraordinary strength, earlier canonical and extracanonical literature connects Samson to the *gibborim* because of his mother's associations with an angel and his own potentially angelic paternity.[23] Samson's misuse of his great strength echoes the use of violence by the *gibborim* in both Genesis 6:4 and in *1 Enoch* and *Jubilees*. The excessive sexual appetite and violent nature of Samson also certainly displays a common theme with the *gibborim* in Genesis 6:4, for as the sons of God

---

21. Marks, "Dangerous Hero," 182.
22. Nickelsburg, *1 Enoch: A New Translation*, 29.
23. According to Marks, "the word *gibbor* has other meanings in rabbinic usage. It can specify a particular type of soldier, such as a knight on horseback or a veteran soldier of high rank" ("Dangerous Hero," 182).

pursue and mate with human women, so the *gibborim* also follow in the examples of their fathers.²⁴

One scholar has asked, "Is Noah of pure human stock, the legitimate seed of Lamech, or is he in actuality one of the famous גיבורים, that bastard race of 'Giants?'"²⁵ In the previous chapter, we attempted to answer the question, "why does Lamech suspect his wife of adulterous behavior?"²⁶ We have argued that it is precisely Noah's questionable paternity stemming from one of the "sons of God/Watchers" that gives him the status to be considered a son of man. Samson's own questionable connection to a potentially fallen angel fulfills the requirement for his status as a Son of Man, but it is his combined role as a promised son that moves the birth narrative trajectory in closer alignment to first-century-Palestinian ideas associated with the son of man.

NOAH AND SAMSON

In the previous chapter, we outlined and explained the variables contributing to the qualities of the son of man in both canonical and extracanonical sources who we identified as Noah. We are now in a position to analyze the factors that place Samson in the role of mythological link that binds both the birth narrative genre with the "beloved son" motif and later conceptions of the son of man.

Previously, I have argued that the first criterion to be fulfilled in order for a promised son to be considered a son of man focuses on the centrality of his mother, whose name or identity must ultimately connect her to the first woman, Eve. As we have demonstrated above, the "lack" of a proper name for Manoah's wife ("the woman"), rather than proving her complete anonymity, serves to underscore her connection to Eve. The second criteria for the mother of a son of man concerns her association to the "daughters of men," in Genesis 6 who experience sexual awareness and whose angelic partners concomitantly bestow some kind of wisdom or other type of knowledge upon their wives. In the case of Manoah's wife, the ambiguity of Samson's paternity and the possibility that the angel is

---

24. None of the half-breeds produced by the sons of God with the daughters of men are ever female, providing a clear and unmistakable connection between sons of God, the *Nephilim* and the *Gibborim*.

25. Reeves, "Utnapishtim in the Book of Giants," 110.

26. Ibid. Contrast with Huggins, "Noah and the Giants."

the father of Samson indicate that the compilers of Judges allow for such an association to be made by the reader. The angel fulfills the criterion for conferring wisdom to Manoah's wife by imparting divine knowledge concerning her vows as a *nazir* as well as those required of her son.

Noah's questionable paternity is not mentioned in the canonical scripture, but is contained within the mythology *in 1Q20, 1 Enoch* and *Jubilees* (see above). The biblical development of the promised son concedes as its initial foundation the story of the Aqedah and alleges that the "binding" of Isaac which "licenses the ritual substitution of the animal for the 'favored' son."[27] Thus, circumcision, naziritehood, and Levitical priesthood all become substitutions for the near sacrifice of the original Aqedah. The story of Noah, however, precedes the formation of such a substitution ritual for a promised son and is the original type for the son of man whose themes are combined with the later substitution ritual(s). And since Noah and his family are never in any danger of succumbing to the flood, it cannot be the case that during his experience on the ark he was "near death."

But the institution by Yhwh of the Noahic covenant has clear parallels with Levenson's sacrificial system. Contained within the recapitulation of the creation story ("be fruitful and multiply"), it is likely that "Noah provided compensation for the disobedience of Adam" not only through his role as the first viticulturalist, but also in the specific section of the Noahide laws pertaining to "life blood:"[28]

> Every moving thing that is alive shall be food for you; I give all to you, as I gave the green plant. Only you shall not eat flesh with its life, that is, its blood. Surely I will require your lifeblood; from every beast I will require it. And from every man, from every man's brother I will require the life of man. "Whoever sheds man's blood, by man his blood shall be shed, for in the image of God He made man" (NASB).

Further criteria required by the promised son in order to be considered a son of man is clear evidence of God's favor. In the case of Samson, as noted above, his tremendous physical strength places him in the category of *gibborim*, not only in the eyes of later rabbinic tradition, but through the biblical tradition found within Genesis 6. Finally, while two canonical examples of promised sons with the title "son of man" (Noah and Jesus)

---

27. Levenson, *Death and Resurrection of the Beloved Son*, 112.
28. Ibid., 80.

are focused on themes of cosmic judgment with salvific emphasis, it is Samson who becomes the chief judge of Israel and rules peacefully for twenty years.

According to some scholars "the sheer number of strikingly similar events in Samson's and Jesus' lives strongly suggest that there is a typological connection between them, even if it is not explicitly stated as such in the New Testament."[29] There are some nineteen "significant points of comparison" between Samson and Jesus including their birth announcements, role as judge, and sacrificial death.[30] While I would not argue that Samson is a "type" or "foil" preceding Christ, the thematic similarities between Samson and Jesus reveal an underlying structure in the development of the honorific title "Son of Man."

Finally, it is Samson's role as *nazir* that serves as the nexus along the trajectory between Noah (as the first son of man) and Jesus (as the final son of man). Two of these "sons of men" have intimate and somewhat inappropriate (if not seemingly heretical) associations with wine. Noah is the first viticulturalist whose actions while drunk cause his son Canaan to "cover the nakedness of their father" and be cursed. Jesus identifies "eating and drinking" (wine) as a particular characteristic of the "Son of Man" in Luke 7:33. In the Judges narrative, Samson comes near "a vineyard (14:5)" and holds a "a seven-day wedding banquet ... where wine and beer would have abounded (14:10–18) ... [and thus places himself in] an environment where his Nazirite status could be easily compromised."[31]

EZEKIEL

In his essay on the evolution of the expression "The Son of Man," Sabino Chialà divides the ongoing problem in the scholarly classification of the phrase "into two general categories."[32] In the first category, the phrase is used as a "Christological title, the fruit of a particular interpretation of the book of Daniel or another text."[33] In the second category, the phrase is "a redundant substitute for a personal pronoun or for the noun

---

29. Ashmon, "Sampson and Christ," 16.
30. Ibid., 15ff.
31. Chisholm, "Identity Crisis," 157.
32. Chialà, "Son of Man," 153.
33. Ibid.

'man.'"[34] Chialà begins his analysis by reviewing a brief chronology of the texts in which the phrase is used to show how the texts "placed side by side" reveal "an evolutionary parabola with two key phrases, or levels of reinterpretation."[35] We will concern ourselves in this chapter with the "evolutionary parabola" outlined by Chialà as it is found within the Hebrew Bible.

In the texts of Jeremiah, Isaiah, Psalms, Numbers, and Job, the expression "'son of man' ... appears in a sentence composed of two parts: in the first part the subject is 'man,' or a similar noun, and in the second part the subject is 'son of man.'"[36] Thus in these texts, the expression is a Semitic linguistic practice for conveying the term "human being." The same may be said for the plural, "sons of men." In contrast, I have argued that both the singular "daughter of man" and the plural "daughters of men" are never used to denote a generic "human being" or even a generic female human, but are always used when the referent is a specific human woman (sexually) engaged with an angel.

In the book of Ezekiel, however, not only is the term "son of man" used "amply," but the term "is no longer a simple linguistic device used to emphasize the fragility of human nature" but instead has been textually transformed into a term that will be used to "represent a particular function."[37] Evidence that the term is used more than a generic "vocative formula," is that in Ezekiel "only God or his messengers" use the phrase "and it is always addressed exclusively to Ezekiel."[38]

Unfortunately, we are in no position to argue (except tangentially and by thematic association) that Ezekiel (as son of man) follows the paradigm we have been outlining above, since there are no canonical or extracanonical texts to provide evidence for the role of Ezekiel's female progenitor in the life of the prophet. It is interesting, however, that rabbinical tradition assigns the role of Ezekiel's foremother to Rahab.[39]

Rahab is a major character in the second chapter of the book of Joshua. When Joshua as successor to Moses attempts to take over the

---

34. Ibid. Evidence of the scholarly debate between these two particular meanings is legion. For the most recent forays, see Vermìs, "Son of Man Debate Revisited"; Casey, "Aramaic Idiom"; Olson, "'Enoch and the Son of Man."

35. Chialà, "Son of Man,," 154.

36. Ibid., 155.

37. Ibid.

38. Ibid., 156.

39. See Meg. 14b and Sifri, Num. 78.

city of Jericho, Rahab shelters two of his spies in her home along the wall of the city from Jericho's king, thus insuring that the Israelite attack is a success. Rahab is clearly identified as אשה זונה a term that means "prostitute." Despite attempts "beginning with Josephus . . . to soften Rahab's characterization as a 'prostitute' (זונה), arguing that she is merely an innkeeper," her status as prostitute is unmistakable.[40] Indeed, in chapter 2 of the book of Joshua, "the spies are dispatched from Shittim, where in Num. 25.1 the Israelites had sexual relations with Moabite women and were enticed into apostasy. Again, the narrator selects terminology (e.g. בוא , vv.1,3–4; שכב, v.1; ידע, v.4) that can function as common Hebrew sexual euphemisms. Even Rahab's name (related to רחב, 'to open wide/stretch out') might be an instance of paronomasia, a name appropriate for a prostitute."[41] Some scholars also argue that "in relating the story of Rahab and the spies, the narrator appropriates language from the story of Lot and his angelic visitors in Genesis 19."[42]

This parallel is striking because it emphasizes the relationship between the sexual aggression of the "sons of God" (as angels) in Genesis 6 to daughters of Lot who function as the "daughters of men" in the story and who are offered to the human men in place of the visiting angels desired by the crowd in Genesis 19. Thus, in Joshua, Rahab the harlot becomes a possible sexual aggressor to the spies (angels), thereby providing a connection between Rahab and the "angels." As Rahab refuses to allow the spies to be surrendered to the king of Jericho, so Lot refuses to allow the angels to be given over to the human men.

It cannot be proven that the relationship between angels and human men and "daughters" in Genesis 19 is based upon Genesis 6, but it is curious that Lot possibly understands, not the immorality of "sodomy" in general, but the danger of overturning the previously fixed paradigm established between angels and humans. He thus acts to prevent human

---

40. Sherwood, "Leader's Misleading," 47. And S. Gillmayr-Bucher (quoting Phyllis Bird) notes that "the association of prostitutes with taverns or beer houses is well attested in Mesopotamian texts" Gillmayr-Bucher, "She Came to Test Him," 142ff. See also Bernard Robinson, who argues, contra Bird, that Rahab cannot be a sacred prositute (despite associations of the city of Jericho with a sanctuary of Astarte) since if "Rahab is sleeping with her Israelite guests in her own home, the presumption must surely be that she is being portrayed as a secular, not a sacral, whore" Robinson, "Rahab of Canaan," 265.

41. Sherwood, "Leader's Misleading," 50. We have seen such an example, e.g., the meaning of the name "Shamhat" in the Epic of Gilgamesh.

42. Sherwood, "Leader's Misleading," 52.

males from engaging sexually with the angels (sons of God). The fact that Lot so quickly suggests the human men "have relations" with his daughters instead of the angels indicates that the author of Genesis 19 was aware that (in Genesis 6) "the sons of God saw that the daughters of man were fair" and hoped to preempt such a dangerous reoccurrence of the angelic/human interaction that brought about the deluge.

Finally, at least according to Josephus, "Rahab was seen as a sort of prophetess . . . [who foresees] the coming victory of the Israelites by the signs given to her by God . . ."[43] Some scholars allow that "Rahab is portrayed as a wise woman in the tradition of the capable woman of Proverbs 31:10–31."[44] And thus her connection to knowledge and wisdom contains echoes of the capable and wise tavern keeper, Shiduri. While a proper historical connection between Ezekiel and Rahab is tenuous at best, there is a fulsome amount of mythological evidence to suggest a thematic continuity associating the canonical prophet Ezekiel who is referred to "ben 'adam . . . [son of man] almost a hundred times" to the traditions of his foremother Rahab is within the pattern we have been exploring.[45]

DANIEL

The use of the "Aramaic plural bene 'anasha, which appears twice (Dan 2:38; 5:21), and the Hebrew bene 'adam, which appears once (10:16), are simple synonyms for 'men' . . .'"[46] But Chialà argues that "in 8:17, on the other hand, the Hebrew singular ben 'adam recalls the book of Ezekiel: God's messenger, Gabriel, speaks to Daniel the visionary, calling him 'son of man.'"[47] While "in the book of Daniel there is no trace of a particular figure with the functions that later texts were to attribute to him . . . nevertheless, the book contains the basic imagistic repertoire that was taken up and elaborated in the centuries that followed . . ."[48]

Chialà makes a sharp distinction between the figures Daniel sees in his visions. They are of "a higher, probably angelic nature . . . who belong to a higher order than that of the prophet" whereas Daniel himself is

---

43. Robinson, "Rahab of Canaan," 258.
44. Lockwood, "Rahab," 45.
45. Chialà, "Son of Man," 155.
46. Ibid., 156.
47. Ibid.
48. Ibid.

functioning in the role of a son of man.[49] Why, then, does Gabriel address Daniel as "son of man"? According to Chialà, it in only in the much later extracanonical *1 Enoch* that role of the son of man found in the book of Daniel comes fully into being. As he explains it, "[In *1 Enoch*] it is no longer the Son of Man who is called into the presence of the Beginning of Days, But Enoch himself" and clearly Daniel, while addressed as "Son of Man" by Gabriel, is not called into the presence of the Ancient of Days.[50] Daniel only witnesses the actions of a figure that is compared to (said to be "like") "a Son of Man."[51]

Aside from the title given to him by the angel Gabriel, we have no annunciation scene nor any maternal identification that would place the historical Daniel within the purview of our paradigm. Chialà identifies the shift from the metaphorical nature of the term "son of man" (i.e., although "in human form" but with an "angelic nature")[52] taking place in the extracanonical *1 Enoch* where Daniel's metaphor becomes a real persona or "character."[53] He claims that the salvific role of the son of man (contra Levenson, see above) "which he carries out by sacrificing his life" is a Christian addition "absent from both Daniel and the Parables [of *1 Enoch*]."[54] But as we have shown from the example given by Samson, this cannot be the case. We will argue this point more fully in the next chapter.

PAUL

In tracing the mythological development of the term "Son of Man," we continue to examine the mythological antecedents in the characteristics of the son of man paradigm in the writings of the apostle Paul. Most biblical scholars agree that the Pauline epistles, written by the man who was originally known as Saul of Tarsus predate the Gospels by some twenty or thirty years.[55] In the following pages, we briefly analyze Paul's concept of

49. Ibid., 158.
50. Ibid., 161.
51. Ibid.
52. Ibid., 158.
53. Ibid., 160.
54. Ibid., 164.
55. Some scholars maintain that the Gospels are earlier than Paul and were written by actual eyewitnesses who followed Jesus throughout his ministry, among them see

messianism and explore the possible evolution of his ideas and how they might have contributed to the shape of the son of man mythology found in the Gospels.

We will focus primarily on three particular areas of Pauline theology: his employment of the allegory of Hagar used in Galatians and his understanding of the canonical biblical birth narrative; his admonition concerning the veiling of women as it pertains to "the angels" used in 1 Corinthians; and finally, (utilizing the "beloved son" theories of Levenson), Paul's contribution to the trajectory of the concept of the Son of Man as it culminates in the gospels in the person of Jesus.

PAUL AND HAGAR (GALATIANS 4:21-31)

We previously surveyed the character of Hagar found in Genesis, *Jubilees*, and *1Q20* (see above). Paul's contemporary, Philo of Alexandria, although "not entirely unacquainted with referring to Hagar in a literal sense ... [often uses] Hagar frequently ... as trope, most often representing lower learning or even ignorance and lack of discipline."[56] Paul's employment of the story of Hagar is "in line with the Philonic allegorical tradition ... [but] while the focus of Philo and Paul's allegories differ ... they both employ the same form and they both have contemporary contexts to which each is applied."[57]

In Galatians, Paul (as does the author of *Jubilees*) omits using "any of the particulars in the Genesis tradition (particularly Genesis 16) that negatively characterize the figure of Sarah."[58] This omission by Paul indicates, correspondingly, that Paul ignores the original biblical birth narrative and concomitant covenant-status and theophany given to Hagar by the angel (and by proxy, Yhwh). This rhetorical move by Paul is interesting, for previously in Galatians 3, he makes an astonishing claim concerning the seed (Hebrew זרע/Greek σπέρμα) of Abraham with brilliant midrashic aplomb. According to Levenson, "Paul's midrash in v 16 turns upon his morphologically singular collective noun *ulezar aka* (Greek,

---

Bauckham, *Jesus and the Eyewitnesses*. Arguments concerning the authorship questions of the disputed letters need not concern us here.

56. Busch, "Figure of Eve," 147.

57. Ibid., 149.

58. Ibid., 150. For a detailed explanation of Hagar's reduced theological status by the omission of her theophany, see Ruiten, "Hagar in the Book of Jubilees."

kai to spermati sou) in Genesis 13:15 and 17:8 as therefore semantically singular as well: not 'to your offspring' in the sense of many people but 'to your *one* offspring,' whom Paul identifies as the Christ."[59] This singularizing of the term "seed" allows Paul to include gentiles in the nascent Jewish/Christian movement. Unnoticed by Levenson (and may be a polemic by Paul against Hagar) is that in Genesis 16:10 Hagar receives the same promise of "seed" and "multitude" from the מַלְאַךְ יְהוָה (the angel of Yhwh) as do Abraham, Isaac, and Jacob in Genesis from Yhwh himself.[60]

PAUL'S USE OF "SON OF MAN"

There is no use of the term "Son of Man" in any of the undisputed letters of Paul. While the scholarly arguments concerning the authorship of the pseudepigraphal letters need not concern us, the only example of the term "son of man" found in a (possible) Pauline pseudepigraphal work is used in Hebrews 2:6, which quotes Psalm 8:5–7: "But one has testified somewhere, saying, "What is man, that Thou rememberest him? Or the son of man, that Thou art concerned about him?" (NASB).[61] As we have noted previously, that particular type of two-part usage ("man" paired with "son of man") is consistent with the Semitic narrative device that signifies "'man,' 'human being,' and in most cases" this use of the linguistic phrase connotes merely the "fragile and mortal nature of humanity."[62] This conventional usage is the most original and prototypical form for the eventual honorific title "Son of Man" whose trajectory we are tracing.[63]

PAUL AND THE ANGELS

An in-depth analysis of the theological significance of Paul's angelology found in his "undisputed" letters is beyond the scope of this chapter. We are concerned, however, with the significance of Paul's use of "angel"

59. Levenson, *Death and Resurrection of the Beloved Son*, 210.

60. The instances of the combination of "seed" and "multitude" or "many" reported by Yhwh or his angel are found in 13:6; 15:5; 16:10; 22:17; 26:4; and 28:14.

61. On the question of the authorship of Hebrews, see especially Thompson, "Epistle to the Hebrews."

62. Chialà, "Son of Man," 155.

63. The curious fact that Pauline literature is not acquainted with this term when every evangelist employs the title with subtle theological differences is beyond the scope of this inquiry.

terminology as it pertains specifically to the son of man trajectory found in the Hebrew Bible and in the extracanonical material. Paul, in his undisputed letters, uses the generic term "angel" in several passages—all of which presuppose a generic understanding of the beings created by God for the purposes of divine communication. First Corinthians, for example, uses the term to address the priority of love ("If I speak with the tongues of men and of angels, but do not have love . . ."). And in 4:9, Paul uses the term to describe the general created order: "God has exhibited us apostles last of all, as men condemned to death; because we have become a spectacle to the world, both to angels and to men." There are other passages, however, to suggest Paul has specific theological concepts concerning the role of angels which may indicate his theoretical understanding of the term "Son of Man."

In Galatians 3:19, after making his theological argument for the "singularity" of the word "seed" in making the case for believing in Christ as means for providing Gentiles direct ancestry to Abraham, Paul, in arguing for the origin of "the Law" (Torah/νόμος), says:

> Τί οὖν ὁ νόμος τῶν παραβάσεων χάριν προσετέθη ἄχρις ἂν ἔλθῃ τὸ σπέρμα ᾧ ἐπήγγελται διαταγεὶς δι' ἀγγέλων ἐν χειρὶ μεσίτου.
>
> Why the Law, then? It was added because of transgressions, having been ordained through angels by the agency of a mediator, until the seed should come to whom the promise had been made (NASB).

This same idea is also expressed in the letter to the Hebrews (9:15) where the "mediator" is assumed to be Christ: "And for this reason He is the mediator of a new covenant in order that since a death has taken place for the redemption of the transgressions that were committed under the first covenant, those who have been called may receive the promise of the eternal in heritance" (NASB). Noticeably absent is the idea in Hebrews concerning the giving of the law by angels.[64] In Galatians 3:19–22, "Paul entertains the idea that demonic figures had a role in promulgating the law. There Paul argues . . . that (evil) angels gave the law precisely in order

---

64. Unless Christ himself is the angel substitute (as a heavenly and not fallen angel). See Barker, *Great Angel*. Thompson argues that "we have no compelling reason to consider the author of Hebrews a student of Paul or to place the homily within the reception of Pauline theology. Nevertheless, the cumulative effect of the topics shared by the two authors suggests that a synchronous relationship may exist between parallel theological movements that existed in proximity to one another" ("Epistle to the Hebrews," 205 ff.).

to provoke transgressions . . . even though the divine intention of the law itself was to bring life."[65] Some scholars connect the (demonic) giving of the law in Galatians to Romans 7 where "Paul equates sin with the mythological serpent who brings Eve the commandment in Genesis 3 and, on analogy, with the evil angels that promulgate the law in Gal. 19–20."[66] Thus Paul's entire debate connects the "original sin" of Eve to the identification of the serpent as "an angelic Satan."[67] The correlation between Eve's sexual awareness and the concept of "original sin," especially in its nonsexual (i.e., moral and ethical dimensions) is beyond the scope of this work, but Paul's association of Eve with demonic angels and the giving of the law is instructive. Few scholars trace the Pauline phrase that the law was added "because of transgressions, having been ordained by angels" to the book of *Jubilees*. It has been suggested that Paul understands from Deuteronomy (LXX) 33:2 that the law has been "promulgated through angels, [with] Moses acting as an intermediary . . . [and] representing not a single person but a plurality [of] (the angels)."[68] But in *Jubilees*, the good (or heavenly) angels give the law to Adam and Eve (1.29) before the serpent engages Eve and the couple are expelled from paradise prior to the actions of the fallen "angels of God" who take "wives" and produce the giants.[69]

We cannot know if Paul drew upon any extracanonical sources such as *Jubilees* in his midrash on the law but it is probable that Paul is "taking advantage of two ideas which were commonly accepted in contemporary Judaism, the role of the angels at the giving of the Law and the superiority of oneness to plurality" and "thus Paul repudiates his adversaries [using his midrash] by means of conceptions which they had previously accepted."[70] Yet in his retelling of the Sarah/Hagar analogy, Paul also completely omits any details from Genesis 16 which in addition parallels the literary treatment of Hagar in *Jubilees* (see above). It is Paul's contemporary Philo whose views concerning the interpretation of

---

65. Busch, "Figure of Eve," 20.

66. Ibid. According to Benoit, "Paul takes over the Jewish tradition on evil Spirits, opposed to the salvation of men, without asking questions on the origin of the angelic evil" ("Pauline Angelology," 5).

67. Busch, "Figure in Eve," 20.

68. Riesenfeld, *Misinterpreted Mediator in Gal 3:19–20*, 408. Riesenfeld also mentions *Jubliees* 1.29 but does not elaborate.

69. *Jubilees* 5.1–2. Charles, *Book of Jubilees*, 43.

70. Riesenfeld, "Misinterpreted Mediator," 409.

Genesis 6:1–4 found especially in *De Gigantibus, Quod Deus immutabilis sit*, and *Quaestiones et Solutiones in Genesin* that indicate that "Philo had knowledge of some form of the Watcher tradition [found in 1 Enoch]."[71]

Finally, there is an enigmatic and puzzling admonition from Paul to the women of Corinth suggesting that the women cover their heads "on account of the angels" in 1 Corinthians 11:10. Susan Calef and Ronald Simkins have written an insightful analysis of the passage from an anthropological and sociological "honor/shame" perspective which connects the veiling of women with procreation and to social boundaries within the culture. Especially germane to our analysis, however, is the "mysterious reference 'because of the angels.'"[72] Using the honor/shame model, it may be the case that "the identity and role of the angels in relation to veiling must have something to do with the belief that woman is 'from man and for man' (vv. 7–9); that is, the angels must have something to do with the sexual, procreative order established at creation."[73]

It may be more likely that the entire process of Eve's sexual awareness beginning in Genesis 3 is the motivation underlying Paul's theological understanding of the "sexual, procreative order."[74] Yet Calef asserts that "since the subtext of Paul's argument is the creation narrative, the identity of the angels of v. 10 . . . is a reference to Genesis 6:1–4, where the sons of God, angelic beings, upon eyeing the beautiful daughters of men, take them as wives, who then bear them children" who are then responsible for the resulting flood.[75]

Calef asserts that Paul is not concerned with an actual "sexual assault by angels" upon women since such angels "would feature more prominently in his argument."[76] However, Paul does attribute possible

---

71. Wright, "Some Observation," 471.

72. Calef, "*Kephale*," 38.

73. Ibid. I find Stuckenbruck's argument that the problem of Paul's phrase in question "lies less in the sorts of angels being referred to than in the assumption of sexual vulnerabilty of women to pollution" making it "unneccesary to consider whether 'the angels' are good or bad" much less persuasive. His conclusion, however, that the Corinithan women's veil "is protective on two fronts: on the one hand it protects the woman against inadmissible invasions from the outside and, on the other hand, protects those on the outside" (so, from the male point of view!) "against the vulnerability to evil that the woman represents" is in alignment with Calef's basic argument. See Stuckenbruck, "Why Should Women Cover Their Heads?," 232.

74. Calef, "*Kephale*," 38.

75. Ibid.

76. Ibid.

demonic capabilities, at least in the historical past, to angels in Galatians 3:19–22.[77] Calef's conclusion is worth quoting in full:

> Paul alludes to the well-known story of a "fall for women" as a kind of biblical exemplum to warn of the cosmic disorder that can result when women, whose erotic appeal attracted even the gaze of heavenly beings, are not covered by the veil that signals the boundaries of the marital relationship to which they belong. Unsurprisingly, the story to which Paul refers here reflects one of the fundamental assumptions of the veiling ideologies in the Mediterranean ... that women are notorious confounders of the boundaries of order. Rhetorically, the allusion to this story allows Paul to add still more scriptural weight to his argument from the order of creation.[78]

Some scholars suggest that knowledge of the angel mythology prevalent during Paul's writings "was apparently wide-spread" and that "as a result of [the angels] lusting after human women ... the alleged result of their fall was moral disorder and bloodshed."[79] And thus, "at least in [the extracanonical Testament of Reuben] the women are blamed with causing the trouble, because they were continually visible to the Watchers."[80] The reason Paul connects women to the fallen angels is to strengthen his argument "in favour of a hierarchic relationship between man and woman ... out of fear for cosmic disorder ... [since] in Paul's perception the great change of the aeons his generation was witnessing may have revived the dangers of primordial times."[81]

As for the Pauline connection between veiled women, "original sin," and angelic threat, it is passing strange that Paul never mentions the mother of Jesus by name, even through allegory or anecdote, but says merely in Galatians 4:4 that:

> ὅτε δὲ ἦλθεν τὸ πλήρωμα τοῦ χρόνου, ἐξαπέστειλεν ὁ θεὸς τὸν υἱὸν αὐτοῦ, γενόμενον ἐκ γυναικός, γενόμενον ὑπὸ νόμον . . .
>
> But when the fullness of time came, god sent forth His Son, born of a woman, born under the Law . . . (NASB).

---

77. And in 2 Corinthians, Paul connects "Satan" with angels in 11:14 and 12:7.
78. Calef, "*Kephale*," 39.
79. Peerbolte, "Man, Woman, and the Angels," 90.
80. Ibid.
81. Ibid., 92.

Chapter Four

In this passage "Paul speaks of God sending his son (implicitly, into the world) in order to effect salvation. The same stereotyped expression for God sending his son is frequent in the Johannine literature"[82] This type of sending expression "can be seen to have clear links with Wisdom tradition . . . also closely related to the kind of tradition represented by Wisd 9.10, which has the specific phrase 'send forth (wisdom).' . . . specifically from heaven."[83] Perhaps Paul employs a type of collapsed messianic birth narrative that removes the mother of Jesus from any direct involvement or agency in the incarnation since in his "choice of verb for Jesus' birth in Galatians 4.4, Romans 1.3, and Philippians 2.7" is not some form of the more commonly used γεννάω but γένομενον—a form of the verb "to be" or "to come into being," "to happen."[84]

However, this "sending forth" passage connects Paul "in relation to angelological traditions . . . (simply the sending of the angel/messenger does already itself suggest a point of contact), and the significance of this usage may be correspondingly enhanced."[85] We may conclude that Paul may have been ignorant of some of the angelological traditions connected to the birth narrative found in Scripture but more probably omitted or at least obfuscated concepts that would not give weight to his theological arguments. It is difficult not to conclude that Paul either did not know about the historical and mythological role of mothers in the begetting of a "son of man," or chose to reshape those concepts for his own theological agenda.

---

82. Chester, "Jewish Messianic Expectations," 72.
83. Ibid., 73.
84. Matlock, "Birth of Jesus," 50.
85. Chester, "Jewish Messianic Expectations," 73.

Chapter Five

THE FINAL MYTHOLOGICAL DAUGHTER of Man is found within the New Testament. Mary the mother of Jesus is mentioned in the three Synoptic Gospels and the Gospel of John, but her status as a "daughter of man" is most notably expressed in the first chapter of the Gospel of Luke. We will begin our analysis with the Gospels of Matthew and Luke—the only two gospels that mention Mary by name in their account of the extraordinary conception of Jesus.

Any study of Mary in the New Testament must include an overview of recent scholarly developments in the social-scientific aspects of the "honor/shame" code found in first-century Palestinian culture. Susan Calef summarizes the pioneering work of Carol Delaney in her work on the enigmatic Pauline angel ideology as it pertains to women (see above) and in so doing, highlights the ways in which women and their sexual/procreative roles are embedded within the honor/shame complex.[1]

In this system, women's procreative process is viewed culturally in terms of "seed and soil," which Delaney terms "'monogenic' because it assumes that there is only one principle of generation, the male seed . . . in which resides the life, the fetus, the child" for whom the mother provides the "soil" for growth.[2] Through this type of cultural construction "men give life; women give birth. Men are sowers of seed; women are fields for the man's sowing; hence, men are potent or impotent, women are fertile or barren . . . men author life; women receive life from the authors."[3]

---

1. Calef, "*Kephale*," 23ff. See also Delaney, *Seed and the Soil*; Hanson, "Herodians and Mediterranean"; Sawicki, *Crossing Galilee*; Horsley, *Message and the Kingdom*; Malina, *Social-Science Commentary*.

2. Calef, "*Kephale*," 24.

3. Ibid.

This particular procreative ideology gives rise to the concept of honor and shame characteristic in Mediterranean cultures and is the means by which men and women are defined: "honor is gendered masculine, the prerogative of the male; shame is gendered feminine . . . men embody honor, women . . . embody shame."[4] Women, then, are seen as "fields" whose boundaries are to be protected and thus "a woman's value depends not so much on her fertility, which is presumed of her until proven otherwise, but on her purity . . . [it is] her ability to guarantee the security of a man's seed that makes her valuable, hence, the emphasis [is] placed on her virginity before marriage and her fidelity after marriage, both of which require specific social measures aimed at boundary maintenance."[5]

A woman's reputation in this culture depends directly upon the reputation of the patriarch, "a woman or girl conducts herself with reserve, modesty, guardedness . . . in so doing, she embodies shame, that is, concern for and sensitivity to reputation" that is directly connected to the reputation of the patriarch (i.e., the woman's husband or father).[6] Any interest in the woman by a male outside the family is considered problematic. The male gaze, the "eye of desire, if not deflected, is thought to penetrate the woman, defiling her, and she will be blamed for having received and accepted it . . . there must be no doubt . . . about a man's authority in relation to his 'fields,' a girl or woman's body must be closed and covered, for her reputation reflects the honor on her husband or shames him in the public eye. Male honor, then requires female shame . . ."[7]

Viewed by the writers of the Gospels Matthew and Luke in terms of the honor/shame complex, the role of Mary as the terminus "Daughter of Man" who gives birth to the promised son/messiah/Son of Man assumes a multivalent and complicated tapestry of ideological and mythological strands that we will, in this chapter, explore.

MARY IN THE GOSPEL OF MATTHEW

Only in the Gospels of Matthew and Luke do we find any type of narrative concerning the conception and birth of Jesus with information pertaining to Mary his mother. Matthew probably drew most of his material from

4. Ibid.
5. Ibid., 25.
6. Ibid.
7. Ibid.

Mark and from the primitive "sayings gospel" known as "Q."[8] According to Barker, "Matthew tells the story [of the conception and birth of Jesus] in terms of the three dreams" in which Joseph is given information that Mary had conceived by the Holy Spirit, that he was to take his family to Egypt, and finally that he was to bring them back to the land of Israel.[9]

Matthew's version is fairly concise:

> Now the birth of Jesus Christ was as follows: when His mother Mary had been betrothed to Joseph, before they came together she was found to be with child by the Holy Spirit. And Joseph her husband, being a righteous man and not wanting to disgrace her, planned to send her away secretly. But when he had considered this, behold, an angel of the Lord appeared to him in a dream, saying, "Joseph, son of David, do not be afraid to take Mary as your wife; for the Child who has been conceived in her is of the Holy Spirit. She will bear a Son; and you shall call His name Jesus, for He will save His people from their sins." Now all this took place to fulfill what was spoken by the Lord through the prophet: "Behold, the virgin shall be with child and shall bear a son, and they shall call his name Immanuel," which translated means, "God with us." And Joseph awoke from his sleep and did as the angel of the Lord commanded him, and took Mary as his wife, but kept her a virgin until she gave birth to a Son; and he called His name Jesus (NASB).

Raymond Brown's influential theory concerning the inclusion of the four women in Matthew's genealogy maintains that it provides the most probable solution to the puzzling characteristics found in each of the women. He argues that it is both "the combination of the scandalous or irregular [martial] unions and of divine intervention through the woman" that provides the commonality. But his thesis is untenable since there is nothing "scandalous or unusual" in the begetting of Jesse by Ruth.[10] But it is the case, as I will argue below, that while Mary does have the other qualities found in each Matthew's four women (her marital union with Joseph will be undoubtedly viewed as highly suspect in first-century Palestine and she is the actual end point for the Davidic Messiah), she never engages in any sexual activities in producing Jesus.

---

8. "Q" for the abbreviated "Quelle" or source (in German) Gospel.
9. Barker, *Christmas*, 94.
10. Hutchison, "Women, Gentiles," 160.

Matthew never uses the term παρθένον in his description of Mary except within his recitation of Isaiah's prophecy (7:14) or in his account of her impregnation by the Holy Spirit. In the Matthean version, Mary is simply "found to be with child" (εὑρέθη ἐν γαστρὶ ἔχουσα) without any mention or hint of sexual intercourse or any sort of discourse with angels. Only an unidentified angel is mentioned in connection to Joseph that, as we have already noted, is a common component in other literary strategies found within birth narratives. Brown suggests that usually the angel's "revelation to the visionary tells what was not already known; and the more obvious meaning here is that Joseph did not know the origins of Mary's pregnancy."[11] The fact that Joseph was not aware of the origin of Mary's pregnancy also presumes that it was noticeable and also scandalous—he was about to "put her away secretly." The only admission to any sexual activity occurs in Matthew 1:25 when Joseph "takes Mary as his wife" (καὶ παρέλαβεν τὴν γυναῖκα αὐτοῦ). Matthew alerts the reader to Mary's later sexual activity by using the standard phrase common in Hebrew scripture telling the reader that Joseph "did not know her" (καὶ οὐκ ἐγίνωσκεν αὐτὴν) until after the birth of Jesus.

Since Matthew uses the birth narrative trope in the angelic discourse with Joseph, we may presume that he did have some knowledge of previous birth narratives. The question is whether we may ascertain if Matthew connected the coming of the Messiah as a promised son to the mythological background of the "fallen angels" in Genesis 6. Mythological antecedents to the Joseph story in Genesis are apparent in Matthew's gospel through the similarity of the dream "appearances to Joseph in 1:20–21, 24–25; 2:13–15a; 2:19–21" that echo the account of the man who was considered "'the master of dreams' in Genesis 37:19."[12] And the Joseph of Genesis 37 has earlier antecedents to Ishmael in Genesis 16 and 22. Ishmael's descendants are later described as "caravan traders, to whom Joseph is sold" when he is taken as a slave to Egypt.[13] It is possible that Matthew intends to draw a specific narrative parallel between the adoptive father of Jesus and the Joseph of the Hebrew scriptures since only Matthew's gospel has the flight to Egypt in which the infant Jesus and his family escape the retribution from the power-threatened King Herod. As Barker suggests, Matthew's inclusion of the four women in

---

11. Brown, *Mary in the New Testament*, 85.
12. Ibid., 87–88.
13. Goodman, *Abraham, the Nations*, 33.

Hebrew scripture who in some way rescue the messianic line (Tamar, Rahab, Ruth, and Bathsheba) could "have been answering the critics who said that Jesus was born of fornication" since the remark recorded in Matthew by John "'We were not born of fornication' shows that this was an early slander."[14]

It is indeed possible that Matthew, knowing the connection between "daughters of men" who are impregnated by "sons of God" (i.e., "fallen" angels), either borrowed the concept of Mary's virginity or invented it completely for the distinct purpose of severing the mythological link between women and angels that historically brought stigma upon the impregnated women.

At the time the Gospels were compiled, the concepts surrounding the birth of the promised son undergo a transformation. Now the Gospel writers are working within the dual trajectory describing the coming of a messiah who will not be merely *a* son of man but who is *the* Son of Man. Their attempt to coalesce the prevailing historical and mythological ideas create a significant tension, especially as it concerns Mary's role as "virgin."

There are at least three layers which underlie the rationale beneath the Gospel writers Matthew and Luke in creating the status of "virgin" for the mother of Jesus. First, in order to be the bearer of a son of man, Mary would naturally have been associated with those "daughters of men" who mated with "fallen" angels in Genesis 6. Since mythologically it would have been impossible to prevent readers from making these strong associations historically embedded in the culture and sacred texts, the Gospel writer Matthew strives to mitigate the loss of Mary's status (as suspected consort of a fallen angel) by removing any hint of sexual activity on her part, or on the part of anyone capable of impregnating her. Matthew achieves this goal by never referring to Mary even as a potential *parthenos* (i.e., an unmarried woman who is expected to marry and engage in sexual relations) and by having the angel appear to Joseph only. Second, Matthew's use of the passive voice to describe the state of Mary's pregnancy (i.e., that she "was found to be with child") is a narrative hinge that establishes the subsequent layer and defines her status as "virgin." The impregnation of Mary will not accomplished by an fallen angel, nor even by (a supposedly male) God, but through the agency of the Holy Spirit.

---

14. Barker, *Christmas*, 99. Barker's comment that "Jesus was sometimes known, unusually, as the son of his mother not his father" does not necessarily mean that he was considered illegitimate. See Ilan, "Man Born of Woman."

Third, the final layer of Mary's status as "virgin" is connected to the view of Mary as a woman in a perpetual nonsexual state for the purposes of "minimizing the degree to which [she is] female, that is, connected to material through reproduction" such that she does not "engage in activities which expressed the difference between the sexes."[15] This type of asceticism is present in Christian apocryphal texts, but it is also evident in the behavior of many women who are the followers of Jesus such as Mary Magdalene and will greatly influence how women's sexuality is seen historically throughout the rest of Christian tradition.

THE SOCIAL-SCIENCE VIEW OF MARY

In addition to briefly surveying the impact of the honor/shame code in first-century Palestinian culture on the role of Mary as the mother of Jesus, Marianne Sawicki relates the importance of cultural as well as historic events that transpired around the time of the birth of Jesus that undoubtedly influenced the birth narratives of Matthew and Luke.

In Luke's gospel, Mary's home Nazareth is the setting for the annunciation. Nazareth's more famous neighboring city, Sepphoris, is a mere four miles distant. There is textual evidence suggesting "that Sepphoris in early Roman times was home to families who married their daughters into priestly lineages, with alliances enduring for many generations. In several places the Palestinian Talmud mentions that Sepphorean women were exceptionally devoted to the Temple," which could remain in operation as long as it was maintained by "pure lineages of priests."[16] Because priests were not allowed to marry "non-Jews, Jews of doubtful parentage, widows, divorced women, or victims of violence" it was vitally important to keep accurate records. These records were maintained because "Sepphoris archived its marriage contracts so that bridal pedigrees could be thoroughly researched."[17]

During the time of Herod the Great's death in 4 BCE (and also approximately the time of Jesus' birth), Josephus records that large-scale revolts occurred throughout Israel to the extent that the Syrian governor Varus required four entire legions to quell the uprising. At Sepphoris "according to Josephus's *Jewish War*, a rebel named Judas 'broke open

---

15. Stefaniw, "Becoming Men, Staying Women," 352.
16. Sawicki, *Crossing Galilee*, 125.
17. Ibid.

the royal arsenals, and, having armed his companions, attacked the other aspirants to power,'" which prompted Varus to send "a detachment of his army into the region of Galilee adjoining Ptolemais, under the command of his friend Gaius; the latter routed all who opposed him, captured and burnt the city of Sepphoris and reduced its inhabitants to slavery."[18] Although accounts of the devastation at Sepphoris were not recorded, similar circumstances of siege recorded by Josephus may provide comparison to Sepphoris in the account of Vespasian in 67–68 CE when "on the other side of the Jordan from Sepphoris Lucius Annius 'put to the sword a thousand of the youth, who had not already escaped, made prisoners of women and children, gave his soldiers license to plunder the property, and then set fire to the houses and advanced against the surrounding villages.'"[19] Nazareth and the surrounding towns of the Galilee could have been similarly affected. There is evidence from the Mishnah that "preserves a ruling that, when a town falls to a siege, all its women are rendered ineligible to marry priests (Ket 2:9)."[20] Consequently, "Sepphoris would have lost its bride crop once, in 4 BCE when Varus took the city."[21] It is probable that, given Nazareth's proximity to Sepphoris Mary would have been thus threatened by the invading army since "the archeological evidence of the siege of Sepphoris confirms at least one event during which Roman soldiers combed through Mary's neighborhood and, following their standard procedure, raped whomever they could catch."[22]

MARY IN THE GOSPEL OF LUKE

We turn now to an analysis of the portrayal of Mary in Luke's gospel using the various mythological as well as social-scientific lenses previously discussed. There are two types of narrative in Luke's gospel "pertinent to a study of Mary: *first*, an extensive set of references to Mary in the . . . narratives of chaps. 1–2, where she has an important role in the annunciation, the visitation, the birth at Bethlehem . . . [and] *second*, four relatively brief passages in the narrative of Jesus' public ministry."[23] It is certainly

---

18. Crossan, *God and Empire*, 109.
19. Ibid., 110.
20. Sawicki, *Crossing Galilee*, 125.
21. Ibid.
22. Ibid., 192.
23. Brown, *Mary in the New Testament*, 105, italics original.

true that "the Lucan Marian material is more abundant that that of any other [New Testament] writer" but I will argue that the Lucan Marian material, especially as it pertains to Mary as the last "Daughter of Man" is far more extensive in its mythological scope and more theologically sophisticated than previously realized.

Earlier scholarship maintains that Luke was a gentile writing for a gentile audience. But his intricate knowledge of Torah as well as his thoughtful attention to extracanonical texts (as we shall see) are woven throughout his work and indicate his intimate associations with Judaism.[24] The most pertinent section of Lucan Marian material is Luke 1:26–38:

> 26 Ἐν δὲ τῷ μηνὶ τῷ ἕκτῳ ἀπεστάλη ὁ ἄγγελος Γαβριὴλ ἀπὸ τοῦ θεοῦ εἰς πόλιν τῆς Γαλιλαίας ᾗ ὄνομα Ναζαρὲθ 27 πρὸς παρθένον ἐμνηστευμένην ἀνδρὶ ᾧ ὄνομα Ἰωσὴφ ἐξ οἴκου Δαυίδ, καὶ τὸ ὄνομα τῆς παρθένου Μαριάμ. 28 καὶ εἰσελθὼν πρὸς αὐτὴν εἶπεν· Χαῖρε, κεχαριτωμένη, ὁ κύριος μετὰ σοῦ. 29 ἡ δὲ ἐπὶ τῷ λόγῳ διεταράχθη καὶ διελογίζετο ποταπὸς εἴη ὁ ἀσπασμὸς οὗτος. 30 καὶ εἶπεν ὁ ἄγγελος αὐτῇ· Μὴ φοβοῦ, Μαριάμ, εὗρες γὰρ χάριν παρὰ τῷ θεῷ· 31 καὶ ἰδοὺ συλλήμψῃ ἐν γαστρὶ καὶ τέξῃ υἱόν, καὶ καλέσεις τὸ ὄνομα αὐτοῦ Ἰησοῦν. 32 οὗτος ἔσται μέγας καὶ υἱὸς Ὑψίστου κληθήσεται, καὶ δώσει αὐτῷ κύριος ὁ θεὸς τὸν θρόνον Δαυὶδ τοῦ πατρὸς αὐτοῦ, 33 καὶ βασιλεύσει ἐπὶ τὸν οἶκον Ἰακὼβ εἰς τοὺς αἰῶνας, καὶ τῆς βασιλείας αὐτοῦ οὐκ ἔσται τέλος. 34 εἶπεν δὲ Μαριὰμ πρὸς τὸν ἄγγελον· Πῶς ἔσται τοῦτο, ἐπεὶ ἄνδρα οὐ γινώσκω; 35 καὶ ἀποκριθεὶς ὁ ἄγγελος εἶπεν αὐτῇ· Πνεῦμα ἅγιον ἐπελεύσεται ἐπὶ σέ, καὶ δύναμις Ὑψίστου ἐπισκιάσει σοι· διὸ καὶ τὸ γεννώμενον ἅγιον κληθήσεται, υἱὸς θεοῦ· 36 καὶ ἰδοὺ Ἐλισάβετ ἡ συγγενίς σου καὶ αὐτὴ συνείληφεν υἱὸν ἐν γήρει αὐτῆς, καὶ οὗτος μὴν ἕκτος ἐστὶν αὐτῇ τῇ καλουμένῃ στείρᾳ· 37 ὅτι οὐκ ἀδυνατήσει παρὰ τοῦ θεοῦ πᾶν ῥῆμα. 38 εἶπεν δὲ Μαριάμ· Ἰδοὺ ἡ δούλη κυρίου· γένοιτό μοι κατὰ τὸ ῥῆμά σου. καὶ ἀπῆλθεν ἀπ᾽ αὐτῆς ὁ ἄγγελος (SBL Greek version).

> Now in the sixth month the angel Gabriel was sent from God to a city in Galilee called Nazareth, to a virgin engaged to a man whose name was Joseph, of the descendants of David; and the virgin's name was Mary. And coming in, he said to her,

---

24. Barker, *Christmas*, 52 ff. Barker also points out that the knowledge of "good Greek" was also typical of Paul, who was a Jew. Further, she argues that Luke's "sequence of ten hymns" (the Magnificat among them) found in his narrative have their parallel in the Qumran materials and indicate Luke's understanding of the First Temple cult.

"Greetings, favored one! The Lord is with you." But she was very perplexed at this statement, and kept pondering what kind of salutation this was. The angel said to her, "Do not be afraid, Mary; for you have found favor with God. And behold, you will conceive in your womb and bear a son, and you shall name Him Jesus. He will be great and will be called the Son of the Most High; and the Lord God will give Him the throne of His father David; and He will reign over the house of Jacob forever, and His kingdom will have no end." Mary said to the angel, "How can this be, since I am a virgin?" The angel answered and said to her, "The Holy Spirit will come upon you, and the power of the Most High will overshadow you; and for that reason the holy Child shall be called the Son of God. And behold, even your relative Elizabeth has also conceived a son in her old age; and she who was called barren is now in her sixth month. For nothing will be impossible with God." And Mary said, "Behold, the bondslave of the Lord; may it be done to me according to your word." And the angel departed from her (NASB).

As I have argued elsewhere, it is clear that Luke models the telling of this birth narrative upon the biblical birth-narrative pattern originating in Genesis 16.[25] Luke's use of the term παρθένον serves several functions. First, "Mary is not named immediately, but is referred to twice by the narrator as 'a virgin' (παρθένος)."[26] Such emphatic usage underscores Mary's kinship with her mythological ancestor Hagar and signals Mary's status as unmarried woman who is not barren, unlike her cousin Elizabeth. Hagar is the origin for this type of narrative pattern and now Luke portrays Mary is the *terminus*. Both are the only two women in the biblical birth-narrative continuum who are also identified by "servant" metaphors. Hagar is identified by the Yahwist writer in Genesis as "*shifhah*" and by the writer of the LXX as παιδίσκη, both terms that mean unmarried woman and also slave/servant. Mary will identify herself with the same servant language when she agrees to become the mother of the promised son and tells the angel "I am a servant of the Lord" (Ἰδοὺ ἡ δούλη κυρίου). Finally, the term παρθένος will be shaped by Luke to erase any indication or hint that Mary will engage in any sexual activity or be suspected in engaging in such activity (to use Paul's phrasing) "on account of the (fallen) angels."

25. Jarrell, "Birth Narrative."
26. Coleridge, *Birth of the Lukan Narrative*, 54.

Brown is not the first to ponder the strange marriage of the "christology of divine sonship" which "has been attached to the conception of Jesus *by a virgin.*"²⁷ Whether or not Luke originated the concept of the virginal conception of Jesus, he skillfully uses literary technique, designs a forceful theological construct, and displays cogent mythological understanding in his portrayal of Mary as Daughter of Man.

There is never any question in Luke's narration that the promised son Jesus will be conceived through Mary's engagement in sexual activity with a human male. The visitation by the angel Gabriel removes that possibility by coming into contact with Mary before she is (as in Matthew) "found to be with child." Luke is bound by mythology to follow accurately the paradigm of birth narrative and thus it is the angel of God who must give the annunciation announcement. "Gabriel is named not simply as 'Gabriel,'" he is identified as "the angel Gabriel."²⁸ In order to disrupt the association between women and fallen angels, Gabriel is commissioned by Luke to appear to Mary. Gabriel is one of the only named angels found in Scripture and is the same named angel who in Daniel 8:17 calls the prophet "son of man." Because Gabriel possesses the authority in the prophetic writings to identify and designate the "son of man," he is now employed by Luke to carry the message to Mary and to identify the promised son about to be conceived. Since it is also Gabriel who is commissioned by God in *1 Enoch* to destroy the Giants, Luke erases any mythological traces of any potential involvement between an angel who might be perceived as fallen and a human woman (Mary) by using the name "Gabriel" and thus recalling that scene:

> "Go, Gabriel, to the bastards, to the half-breeds, to the sons of miscegenation; and destroy the sons of the watchers from among the sons of men . . ."²⁹

Also in his narrative, Luke "names God immediately and explicitly as prime mover: 'the angel Gabriel was sent from God.'"³⁰ There can be no doubt in Luke's annunciation that Gabriel could be the (male) source of Mary's pregnancy.

According to Brown, "in accepting the thesis that Luke did intend a virginal conception in 1:34–35 . . . what is being described is not a *hieros*

27. Brown, *Mary in the New Testament*, 120, italics original.
28. Coleridge, *Birth of the Lukan Narrative*, 52.
29. Nickelsburg, *1 Enoch: A New translation*, 29.
30. Coleridge, *Birth of the Lukan Narrative*, 53.

gamos, a 'sacred marriage' or mating between a god and a mortal."³¹ But Luke's annunciation has an ancient and complicated history that has been established in ancient Mesopotamia and been molded through centuries by his own tradition. The complexity has also arisen due to the influence of monotheism. As some scholars have noted, "In monotheistic religions, there is not a god and goddess whose sacred marriage brings forth the world. There is, rather, only one God, who is without divine partner; and that One God, Creator of all is male. Divinity itself is creativity and potency and is defined as masculine. The feminine element is subordinated and becomes symbolically equated with what is created (the world) rather than with the divine creative power."³² However, as this work has been trying to establish, even within the monotheistic religion of Judaism, strictly defined categories between (male) divine and (female) human are more nuanced and occasionally the role of the feminine is granted powerful status.

Luke attempts to lessen the reader's concern that there is any possibility the promised son will be conceived through the sexual agency of (a male) God in a deft theological move by allowing Mary herself to ask the angel the question that will burn in minds for thousands of years: Πῶς ἔσται τοῦτο, ἐπεὶ ἄνδρα οὐ γινώσκω; (How will this be possible, since I do not know a man?) The question is as starkly erotic as Mary will ever be permitted. She uses the Semitic "know" as a euphemism for sexual activity recalling the sexual agency and awareness of Eve but without the concomitant gaining of knowledge. Mary is (unlike her counterpart Hagar who "sees" and "names" God) not given any sort of divine wisdom or knowledge from her encounter with the angel except that which pertains to her promised son and the fact of her pregnancy. Mary's exemption from any sexual activity is evidence that she will not be the recipient of wisdom.

Mary's acceptance of her fate begins with her statement Ἰδοὺ ἡ δούλη κυρίου ("Behold, [I am] the handmaiden of the Lord"). The once powerful association made by Hagar's status as *shifhah* is sandwiched between two sets of rhetorical phrases that both mirror God. These utterances between Mary and the angel are "a paradoxical blend of the passive and active" and reflect the narrator's attempt to have Mary "seem wholly passive before the divine initiative . . . but [also] a collaborator in the unfolding

---

31. Brown, *Mary in the New Testament*, 121.

32. Calef, "*Kephale*," 26. I leave aside for this topic the possibility that Yhwh did have a consort.

revelation."³³ To a certain extent, Mary's agency is not diminished, but her sexual agency is completely absent. The angel's words "ὅτι οὐκ ἀδυνατήσει παρὰ τοῦ θεοῦ πᾶν ῥῆμα," that "nothing is impossible through God's word" are acknowledged by Mary with her assent that γένοιτό μοι κατὰ τὸ ῥῆμά σου—"let it happen to be according to your word." The two phrases effectively place God's active creative power within the same theological space as the discourse from the angel and serve as a reminder to the reader that while it is the angel "who promises a child, predicts his birth, and foretells his way of life or future acts is always, without exception, a *god*" it is now the Deity and not the angel who is "the father of the child."³⁴

While Mary is given no additional wisdom or knowledge except that which pertains directly to her son, she does question the angel once but asks nothing about the details of the divine plan. Some scholars have argued that this lack of inquiry indicates Mary "presumes a knowledge of Scripture . . . she knows not only who God is, but also . . . knows of the divine promise to David and his dynasty, and how this relates to the house of Jacob."³⁵ But this form of knowledge is not something imparted directly by angels and in no way enhances Mary's agency in the rest of Luke's gospel. There is also a strange dichotomy between Luke's parallel annunciation accounts where Zechariah is punished by the angel for his doubtful response and Mary's doubtful response ("how can this be?") is answered without rebuke. In terms of such Lucan narrative logic, "there must be a reason that Zechariah is punished and Mary is not. The only possible reason is that Mary is told she will conceive as a virgin. Zechariah can fairly be punished because there is precedent for his situation. This has happened before in the OT . . . on the other hand, there is no OT precedent for a virginal conception . . . the uniqueness of a virginal conception would give her an excuse, but without it she has no excuse and she seemingly is the beneficiary of an unfair double standard."³⁶ Mary's question, then, arises because she cannot fathom a precedent for such an event as Gabriel describes.

---

33. Coleridge, *Birth of the Lukan Narrative*, 63.

34. Irvin, *Mytharion*, 100–1.

35. Coleridge, *Birth of the Lukan Narrative*, 65n1.

36. Landry's whole argument is to refute the hypothesis by Jane Schaberg that Mary leaves open by her question the possibility that she will be raped by a human male and thus the conception is not miraculous or "virginal" ("Narrative Logic," 76). For Schaberg's entire argument, see *Illegitimacy of Jesus*.

Fallen Angels and Fallen Women

Because it is impossible to remove entirely the concept of God's creative (male) potency from the birth narrative, Luke follows Matthew by positing the work of the Holy Spirit in the conception of the promised son. But again, the Lucan use of the words to describe the process of impregnation are employed over and against any suggestion or even euphemistic intention that Mary's role is erotic or even remotely sexual. The word used to describe the process is "overshadow": "(ἐπισκιάζειν) is thus the opposite of human pro-creation . . . it must be emphasized that in religious sources the word is never a *terminus technicus* nor even a euphemism for sexual intercourse."[37] Even the Holy Spirit's action of "coming upon" (ἐπέρχεθαι) Mary carries no hint of sexual activity.[38] In the description of the actions of the Holy Spirit, even "the Syriac versions chose to translate ἐπισκιάσει in the annunciation narrative of Lk. 1:35 by *naggen ʿal* (*afʿel* of *gnn*, 'cover over,' 'overshadow'). That verb was already established at a very early date in Syriac tradition as a technical term for a specific type of salvific activity on the part of God is shown by the fact that it is used in a number of other important New Testament passages, translating quite different Greek verbs . . ."[39] Accordingly, "the earliest translators of the Syriac New Testament evidently took over the word from Jewish Aramaic where it had already become something of a technical term for divine action."[40]

Another aspect of the role of the Holy Spirit in the conception of Jesus is the aural nature of the meeting between Gabriel and Mary. In Luke's narrative, we are never told that Mary actually sees the angel—the focus is on the Mary's *hearing* and may be a Lucan literary homage to the customary way God communicates to his people and how the people of Israel respond: "Hear O Israel, the Lord is our God, the Lord is One" (Deuteronomy 6:4). The aural account of conception is also the focus of the early church. Accordingly, "Ephrem's allusion to the characteristically Syriac idea of conception through the ear perhaps reflects an early polemic against the supposition that Mary was inseminated by the Holy Spirit (feminine in early Syriac literature), a polemic that is already found in a second-century document with a Syrian background, the Gospel of

37. Kittel, *Theological Dictionary of the New Testament*, 400.

38. "Neither of the verbs here, ἐπέρχομαι ("come upon") or ἐπισκιάζω ("overshadow") has in itself any connotation of conception" (quoted in Landry, "Narrative Logic").

39. Brock, "Passover," 224.

40. Ibid.

Philip (§ 17): Some have said that Mary conceived of the Holy Spirit. They are wrong, and they do not realize what they are saying, for when did a woman ever conceive of a woman?"[41] The motivating idea is, however, that the role of the Holy Spirit was never intended by Luke to be that of Mary's inseminator. Gabriel's vague account of the mechanics of the conception is purposefully ambiguous since Luke's theological objective is to remove Mary completely from any act that could be remotely considered sexual. We have observed how Mary's question to the angel Gabriel serves as a foil linking her theoretical potential sexual activity to the "daughters of men" in Genesis 6 and also to Eve in Genesis 3. Thus, underlying the angel Gabriel's almost inchoate explanation of the process of Mary's virginal conception, we uncover another attempt by Luke to completely dissociate Mary from her sexually active mythological ancestors.

Luke employs that narrative device in 1:42 when he uses in Elizabeth's greeting of Mary "Blessed are you among women and blessed in the fruit of your womb," which is "reminiscent of the prophet Deborah's praise of Jael, 'Blessed is Jael among women . . . among tent-dwelling women most blessed' and of Uzziah's praise of Judith, 'Blessed are you, daughter, by the Most High God above all women on earth.'"[42] Thus, some scholars have argued that Mary foreshadows "the life and death of her son, Jesus . . . who overcomes violence through peace . . . Mary ushers in a new age, in which women are called most blessed for their acts of peace rather than violence."[43] But both accounts of violence exhibited by Jael and by Judith (the latter being modeled on the former) are charged with graphic sexual allusions and metaphors. In the case of Jael's execution of Sisera:

> . . . the poetic language used in describing his death is full of sexual overtones. The principal clue is the appearance of the word *feet* (NRSV; Hebrew *raglaim*) in 5:27. The NRSV translation pictures Sisera on the ground at Jael's *feet* (literally). But the Hebrew certainly knows an alternative, euphemistic meaning of the word *feet* as genitals. And the Hebrew word can also mean *legs*. Hence Niditch, Wansbrough, and others translate *between her legs* (with clear sexual overtones) rather than *at her feet*.

---

41. Ibid., 227.
42. Wilson, "Pugnacious," 436.
43. Ibid.

> Niditch renders the key verse as follows: Between her legs he knelt, he fell, he lay
> > Between her legs he knelt, he fell
> > Where he knelt, there he fell, despoiled.[44]

By using the phrase "blessed are," Luke definitely recalls Jael and Judith's violent acts and it is possible that Luke wishes to contrast the violence of the women in the Hebrew scriptures with the nonviolence of both Elizabeth and especially Mary. Yet, after the birth of Jesus, Mary is "never mentioned by name in the Lucan account of Jesus' ministry, death, and resurrection," a silence that is "startling, granted the great interest Luke has shown in Mary in the infancy narrative."[45] Brown reports that such silence towards Mary by Luke is understandable "once we realize that such interest was not primarily in Mary as a person but in Mary as symbol of discipleship."[46] But the Lucan concept of what discipleship means, first as it applies to Mary and then to all women followers of Christ, is discipleship without sexual activity. By employing the disjunctive scriptural echoes of Judith and Jael, Luke is drawing the parallel between those women who engage in violence (especially violence against men) and women's sexual natures. Mary is a disciple of peace, but only because she has not engaged in sexual activity that would normally be the case had not God intervened to provide a promised son without the benefit of a male partner. Since it is always the case that sexual behavior for women is connected to reproduction in all the Hebrew scriptures surveyed thus far, it would be premature to conclude that Luke does not envision the absence of sexual behavior for all women as a specific criterion for discipleship.

The Christian evolution of the concept of Mary as mother and continued (chaste) virgin is beyond the scope of our inquiry. Yet there are traces in Luke's later narrative that indicate Mary's virginal status was not only preferential for Mary, but also for other female followers and disciples of Jesus as well. "The Lucan representation of Mary do not merely contribute to positive images of particular female actors on the stage of his narrative, but ultimately beckon certain types of female hearers in the implied audience to a life of spiritual adventure, to a socio-religious experiment of fashioning themselves in accordance with

---

44. Sakenfeld, "Deborah, Jael, and Sisera's Mother," 20, italics original.
45. Brown, *Mary in the New Testament*, 162.
46. Ibid.

unconventional modes of existence and action that were anything but uncontroversial in Luke's cultural milieu."[47] Presumably such a reference to discipleship for women would be considered in stark contrast to the previously historic religious mandate to "be fruitful and multiply"; for without the burden of reproduction, women would be free to engage in other spiritual activities. It seems clear, however, that ultimately the Lucan birth narrative of Jesus especially as it pertains to Mary makes the attempt to link women's role in "hearing the word of God" to one without the benefit of sexual expression.

There is an odd "incompatibility between the idea of a virgin conception and the Jewish genealogy" in the Christian birth narratives.[48] One purpose of the Matthean and Lucan genealogy and birth narratives may be to disrupt the "the Jewish conception of paternity which until that time had been figured through the male line."[49] It may be the case that "it is no accident that Matthew recorded the genealogy first and then appended the story of the virgin birth subsequently. In ordering things this way, the virgin birth story would have shocked Jewish readers into rethinking what the genealogy meant."[50] This whole ideology effectively dismisses "descent through the male line as central to Jesus' status" and makes Jesus the son of David and Abraham only through spiritual means. This thesis is similar to Levenson's account of Paul's rationale whereby he provides a theological context of "adoption" that makes it possible to include gentiles among the followers of the Jewish Jesus.

However, the criteria for a Son of Man requires not only divine male paternity, but also a human mother who traces her lineage, her female line, back to the first woman. At the time it occurred, the first woman's discovery and expression of sexuality was in no way connected to reproduction. According to the compilers of Genesis, the causal relationship between sexual expression and reproduction exists as Yhwh's punishment for the original couple's acquisition of sexual awareness/wisdom. It is far from clear in Genesis how reproduction might have been factored into the originally conceived immortal lives of Adam and Eve. In Genesis, loss of immortality brings with it painful birth for all women. Even though in the narrative they require Mary to be inseminated through the means of

---

47. Klutz, "Value of Being Virginal," 81.
48. Eilberg-Schwartz, *God's Phallus*, 226.
49. Ibid., 233.
50. Ibid., 232.

the Holy Spirit, neither Matthew nor Luke are able to repair the painful birth curse of Yhwh. The Gospel writer's use of the concept of "virginal conception" only serves to eliminate the sexual awareness and knowledge that was originally forbidden by Yhwh from the beginning. Jesus' status as Son of Man depends upon his dual lineage—one divine and one human. We now turn our focus to that Son of Man as he is portrayed in the Gospels.

JESUS AS THE LAST SON OF MAN

Margaret Barker has argued persuasively that the Gospel writer's understanding of Jesus' nature as divine son "indicates that pre-Christian Judaism was not monotheistic in the sense that we use that word. The roots of Christian trinitarian theology lie in pre-Christian Palestinian beliefs about the angels. There were many in first-century Palestine who still retained a world-view derived from the more ancient religion of Israel in which there was a High God and several Sons of God, one of whom was Yahweh, the Holy One of Israel."[51] Thus, Jesus' status as divine son is based upon an important distinction between the two different words for God. First, "there are [those sons] of El Elyon, sons of El or Elohim [who are] all clearly heavenly beings, and there are those called sons of Yahweh or the Holy One who are human. This distinction is important for at least two reasons; Yahweh was one of the sons of El Elyon [in the Canaanite pantheon], and Jesus in the Gospels was described as a Son of El Elyon, God Most High" in the Lucan annunciation narrative.[52] Barker traces the origin of the "sons of Elohim" in Genesis 6:4 but does not mention the possibility that the moral intention of those same "sons of Elohim" could be nefarious, or discuss their interaction with human women.

THE SON OF MAN AND THE GOSPEL OF MARK

The narrator's multivalent use of ἄγγελόν at the beginning of the Gospel indicates the narrator of Mark is well versed in the son of man mythology we have been tracing and is cognizant of the pejorative status associated

---

51. Barker, *Great Angel*, 3.

52. Ibid., 4. Barker argues that "after the reforms of the exilic period . . . Yahweh was fused with El-Elyon" and also brilliantly traces the development of the Enochic "two powers" concept as it was assimilated into Christianity.

with a promised son with an angelic heritage. It is clear that one of his narrative missions is to distinguish Jesus from those fallen angels of Genesis 6:4 whose descendants are in first-century Palestine culture considered to be the demons and evil spirits in league with Satan. Throughout the Gospel, the narrator wrestles with Jesus' angelic heritage in order to theologically assert that Jesus as the Son of Man, while certainly displaying angelic properties, has no such associations with fallen angels.

Beginning with the introduction, the narrator encapsulates his own particular version of what may be considered an entire "infancy" narrative by designating "Jesus Christ, Son of God." The narrator quotes from Isaiah's prophecy in 40:3 which signals the people of Israel to the revelation of God's glory inside two quotations (Exodus 23:20 and Malachi 3:1) and refers to angels (ἄγγελόν) who are specifically sent from God. Thus the reader is alerted not only to Jesus' angelic status, but made aware that his angelic status is one that is sanctioned by God.

Immediately after his baptism, Jesus is expelled into the wilderness where among the wild animals he is ministered to by (holy) angels. The narrator's use of the prophet Isaiah's "verbal collocation of 'the way [of holiness],' 'the wilderness,' and 'the wild beasts' is too strong to ignore . . . [since] the point of the Isaiah text is to portray the absence of evil from the 'way of holiness'" and thus underscores the mention of wild beasts (θηρίων) which are set "over against the angels."[53] In this way, the narrator draws a sharp distinction between the wild beasts whose ruler is Satan and the holy angels who are in the wilderness to prepare and provide for Jesus before his temptation.

According to scholars, the "earliest stratum of New Testament miracle stories—the exorcisms—belongs not to the Hellenistic wonder-worker tradition so much as to the demonology characteristic of apocalyptic Judaism," which the narrator of Mark's gospel depends upon in order to focus on what he perceives as the problem of Jesus' angelic identity.[54] In 1:32, the narrator proposes this conundrum by having Jesus silence the demons "because they knew who he was."[55] It cannot be the case that the demons recognize Jesus because they are also descended from angels,

---

53. Caneday, "Mark's Provocative," 32–33.

54. Forsyth, *Old Enemy*, 287.

55. Forsyth points out that "recognition as a phenomenon takes up a good deal of Mark's gospel. The paradox is that the devils and unclean spirits recognize Jesus instantly, while many others, including often the disciples themselves, do not" (*Old Enemy*, 290).

although the earlier mythology certainly supports this view.⁵⁶ But this same Pharisaic position (that Jesus is only able to drive out the demons because he is one of them) is untenable for the narrator who confronts it on two levels. First, in 3:11, we read:

> καὶ τὰ πνεύματα τὰ ἀκάθαρτα ὅταν αὐτὸν ἐθεώρουν προσέπιπτον αὐτῷ καὶ ἔκραζον λέγοντα, ὅτι Σὺ εἶ ὁ υἱὸς τοῦ θεοῦ.
>
> And whenever the unclean spirits beheld Him, they would fall down before Him and cry out, saying, "You are the Son of God!" (NASB).

The narrator creates a stark separation between Jesus and the "unclean spirits" who are descendants of the fallen angels by having them "fall down" once again, not from heaven in the mythological past, but in recognition and worship of Jesus as God's son. In this way the demons acknowledge that not only is Jesus unrelated to them, he is holy. The narrator's wording of the Greek is emphatic: *you* are the Son, not of Man, but of God.

The narrator's argument continues in 3:23 where Jesus answers the charge that his angelic heritage is derivative from the leader of the fallen angels by using a parable which asserts the same logic: "Πῶς δύναται Σατανᾶς Σατανᾶν ἐκβάλλειν? (How is it possible for Satan to cast out Satan?) In this parable, Jesus remarks:

> καὶ εἰ ὁ Σατανᾶς ἀνέστη ἐφ᾽ ἑαυτὸν καὶ ἐμερίσθη οὐ δύναται στῆναι ἀλλὰ τέλος ἔχει ἀλλ᾽ οὐ δύναται οὐδεὶς εἰς τὴν οἰκίαν τοῦ ἰσχυροῦ εἰσελθὼν τὰ σκεύη αὐτοῦ διαρπάσαι ἐὰν μὴ πρῶτον τὸν ἰσχυρὸν δήσῃ καὶ τότε τὴν οἰκίαν αὐτοῦ διαρπάσει
>
> And if Satan has risen up against himself and is divided, he cannot stand, but he is finished! But no one can enter the strong man's house and plunder his property unless he first binds the strong man, and then he will plunder his house (NASB).

Supposedly, "the audience of Mark knows from 1:7–8 that Jesus is the 'stronger one' (ἰσχυρότερος) to come after John and baptize with the Holy Spirit. As the 'stronger one,' Jesus has 'bound' Satan, the 'strong one,' when he withstood with the help of God's angels the testing of Satan in the wilderness that included his being with wild animals (1:13). Rather

---

56. According to Heil, the demons in 1:32 "know the more profound identity of Jesus . . . because Jesus overcame his testing by Satan, leader of the unclean spirits," which is entirely possible were it not for the "Son of Man" angelic connections ("Jesus With the Wild Animals," 77).

than driving out demons by the power of Satan, then, Jesus drives them out by the power of the Spirit given him as God's beloved Servant and Son (1:11–12)."[57] Unfortunately, this excellent theological argument ignores the angel mythology prevalent in the minds of first-century Palestinians. There is also canonical evidence to suggest that it is Jesus himself who is the "binder" of the angels in the New Testament letter to Jude (who actually quotes *1 Enoch* in verse 14) and compares Jesus to God's avenging angel in 1:6:

> ἀγγέλους τε τοὺς μὴ τηρήσαντας τὴν ἑαυτῶν ἀρχὴν ἀλλὰ ἀπολιπόντας τὸ ἴδιον οἰκητήριον εἰς κρίσιν μεγάλης ἡμέρας δεσμοῖς ἀϊδίοις ὑπὸ ζόφον τετήρηκεν
>
> And angels who did not keep their own domain, but abandoned their proper abode, He has kept in eternal bonds under darkness for the judgment of the great day (NASB).

It seems that "in Jude [there] is also a clear example of how Jesus could be credited with a divine act which had already been attributed by Jews to the principal angel. Verse 6 says that Jesus is detaining the fallen angels, by whom we are to understand the 'sons of God,' who—according to Gen. 6:1–4—formed unions with the 'daughters of men.'"[58] Certainly the baptism of Jesus distinguishes the previous life of the Son of Man from his final destiny, but his status as "binder of angels" has been implicitly inferred since his conception.

The evolution of the term "Son of Man" in the Gospel of Mark includes his role both as savior, "which he carries out by sacrificing his life" and by his eschatological role that includes coming "in the glory of His Father with the holy angels."[59] Thus, in Mark's gospel, the reader is continually reminded by the narrator's reference to the "Son of Man" in connection with his "holy angels" that Jesus' angelic heritage can in no way be associated with those angels who are fallen.

THE SON OF MAN IN THE GOSPEL OF LUKE

Both the authors of Mark and Luke compete with the dilemma of Jesus' angelic heritage. We have already reviewed how Luke embellishes

---

57. Heil, "Jesus With the Wild Animals," 76.
58. Fossum, "Jewish-Christian Christology," 230.
59. Chialà, "Son of Man," 164.

Matthew's concept of the virgin birth in order to dismantle the existing mythology that allows the (male) divine to impregnate a human woman. Like Mark, who wrestles with Jesus' status as Son of Man through the proclamations from the demons, so Luke also contends with the ancient mythology that might potential taint the divinity of Jesus.

It is entirely possible that the parable of the Prodigal Son which appears only in Luke (15:11–32) contains traces of angel mythology and can be viewed from a more cosmic standpoint. From this perspective, "the father in the narrative should not be seen as an earthly father but as an image of God himself."[60] Many scholars have asserted that the two sons are neither to be considered role models since "one squanders away all his worldly goods in the company of prostitutes, whereas the other clings desperately to his property."[61] It is possible that the characters of the two sons are to be considered foils to represent in parabolic form the charges against Jesus by his spiritual detractors. In the narrative, the argument given by the Pharisees claims that Jesus is profligate with himself and all he owns, while they perceived themselves as valuable stewards of God's gifts. Thus, in the parable the older brother's defense to his father is "symptomatic of evil: to keep to himself what has been given to him, desperately as if it were plunder; not to be able to join in others' pleasure; never to be able to temper justice with mercy."[62] Because he displays these characteristics, the image of the older brother "must be one of the New Testament's Satan images . . . [since in the parable he is] the one who takes great care with what he has, and prefers to hoard assets rather than throw them away in festivities" unlike the younger brother (Jesus) who "squanders away everything."[63] This reading of the narrative clearly reveals the author's thorough knowledge of the ancient Son of Man mythology and offers another literary opportunity to express on a more sophisticated level the problem of Jesus' angelic heritage. Luke understands that both the sons of God in Genesis 6 (one of whom, now fallen, is Satan) as well as Jesus have the same authority to call God, "father."[64]

60. Nielsen, *Satan the Prodigal Son?*, 135.
61. Ibid.
62. Ibid., 139.
63. Ibid.
64. It is also possible that Luke is making reference to *1 Enoch* in 10:18 when Jesus declares, "I was watching Satan fall from heaven like lightning." The name of one of the head fallen "watchers," and also the name of the father of *Bat Enosh* is "*Baraki'il,*" which can be translated "lightning." Possibly the preexistant and angelic Jesus means

Chapter Five

COMPARISONS OF JESUS IN THE GOSPELS TO OTHER "SONS OF MEN"

Jesus as Noah

In the Gospels of Matthew (24:37–38) and especially Luke (17:27–30), reference is made to previous canonical "sons of men" in connection to Jesus as the final Son of Man.

> And just as it happened in the days of Noah, so it shall be also in the days of the Son of Man: they were eating, they were drinking, they were marrying, they were being given in marriage, until the day that Noah entered the ark, and the flood came and destroyed them all. It was the same as happened in the days of Lot: they were eating, they were drinking, they were buying, they were selling, they were planting, they were building; but on the day that Lot went out from Sodom it rained fire and brimstone from heaven and destroyed them all. It will be just the same on the day that the Son of Man is revealed (NASB).

Eschatological information is described in this narrative which associates the coming of the Son of Man with two episodes recounted in Genesis where destruction followed the sexual progress of the fallen angels. Presumably, in the narrative "they" must refer to both the sons of God (who are "marrying," i.e., engaging in sexual activity) as well their offspring the giants whose violent behavior is the reason for the flood. It is interesting to note the inclusion of Genesis 19 here in the Gospel. We have discussed (see above) the possibility that even though the angels sent to Sodom may not have been considered fallen, the writer/compiler of Genesis 19 might have also understood the danger in the pairing of any type of angel with human (male or especially female). By joining the story of the flood to the scene featuring Lot's daughters, the narrator recalls the entire mythological construct that links the final Son of Man, Jesus, to the first son of man, Noah, whose salvific qualities may also be compared to those found in the person of Jesus.

---

to say that he observed the orignal descent of the fallen angels and by making this statement, he distinguishes himself from Satan.

Jesus as Samson

Accordingly, "what is unique to Matthew can be found essentially in the four passages that describe the Son of Man as judge."[65] This theme, while also found in Mark, is further developed in Luke. We have already discussed the significant points of comparison between Samson and Jesus since "if Samson is a type of Christ, it becomes easier to see how Samson is God's called servant from conception to death . . . we can also see more clearly, in Samson's light, how Jesus is God's judge."[66] It is Matthew's dependence upon the extracanonical "Book of Parables" that explains the canonical evolution of the concept of the Son of Man since it contains "the first element [of the Son of Man] in Matthew that is totally foreign to the Enochic tradition [which] is the series of sayings about how the Son of Man must die."[67] But within the Son of Man tradition associated with Samson, we find canonical evidence to suggest a development toward the expected death of a Son of Man. As previously discussed, the theme of the promised son's near death has robust origins that logically and theologically predict that in order for the promise son to fulfill his salvific obligations as the Son of Man, he must die.

Jesus as Ezekiel

We have already discussed how the Son of Man's mythological trajectory includes Ezekiel as a son of man. In all the Gospels (most notably in John),[68] there is thematic evidence to suggest that the compilers intended to draw specific parallels between Jesus and Ezekiel. While "the dependence is not quotational . . . the influence of Ezekiel on the portrait and mind of Jesus as presented in the gospels can easily be detected."[69] Both Ezekiel and Jesus are known as prophets and there may also be a connection between the "thirtieth year" of Ezekiel's prophetic inauguration and Luke's careful "mention that Jesus was baptized when he was 'about

---

65. Chialà, "Son of Man," 167.

66. Ashmon, "Sampson and Christ," 16. For another comparison between Samson and Jesus on the topic of violence, see Bowman, "Samson and the Son of God."

67. Chialà, "Son of Man," 168.

68. For a more extensive list of parallels between Ezekiel and John's gospel, see Vawter, "Ezekiel and John."

69. Bullock, "Ezekiel," 23.

thirty years of age.'"⁷⁰ Both prophets utilized parable "and the audiences of both seemed to have been offended by it."⁷¹ Both display an intimate knowledge of God, have a "zeal for a purified temple," and share their prophetic witness by means of resurrection themes. "Just as in Matt 27:51 an earthquake is followed by the opening of the tombs (v. 52), likewise in Ezek 37:7 there is an earthquake at the voice of the prophecy, and in v 12 the Lord says, 'Behold I am opening your tombs' [and] the opening of the graves is then succeeded by the divine impartation of the Spirit (37:14)."⁷²

Like the comparisons between Noah and Samson, with the use of material from the prophet Ezekiel, the compilers of the Gospels confirm that Jesus is indeed intended by God to be the final Son of Man. "Only with difficulty can we write off the affinities of Ezekiel with the life and work of Jesus. While [Ezekiel] was not *the* Son of Man, he was indeed oriented toward his appearance . . . Ezekiel builds a prophetic bridge between the testaments . . ."⁷³

JESUS AS BOTH THE BINDER OF AZAZEL AND AS THE "SCAPEGOAT."

Jesus as the final Son of Man and the promised Son of God takes the ritual of the scapegoat to its perfectly logical conclusion and thereby becomes the substitute for the scapegoat on the Day of Atonement. "The correspondences between the Passion [narrative in the New Testament] and the [Day of Atonement] scapegoat ceremony are too often underutilized" especially as they pertain to the Son of Man mythology.⁷⁴ "In the Christian tradition [the myth of the sin offering] has been extended by the story of a descent from the heavenly world of a 'son of God' who

---

70. Ibid., 24.

71. Ibid., 26.

72. Ibid., 30. Bullock also comments that "it may not be without signficance in this regard that in John 20:22 we see the risen Christ who 'breathed' upon the disciples and said, 'Receive the Holy Spirit.' The Lord's instructions to the prophet Ezekiel were: 'Propesy to the spirit, prophesy, son of man, and say to the to the spirit, Thus says the LORD God: Come from the four winds, O spirit, and breathe upon these slain that they may live (37:9). So we may suggest that Jesus, by his resurrection and the attendant revivification of many of the dead saints (Matt 27:52), inaugurated the eschatalogical era that Ezekiel predicted" ("Ezekiel," 30).

73. Ibid., 31.

74. Davies, "Women, Men, Gods," 201n1.

reverses the pattern of the original descent myth [found in Genesis 6:4 and in 1 Enoch] by suffering violence and offers, instead of Azazel, a means for humans to avoid the due punishment for their own sins."[75] It has been argued that the extracanonical stories of descent by the fallen angels were devised in part for the purpose of removing the onus of blame for the "sin" of human rebellion against God from humans and transferring that fault to the fallen angels who mate with human women. The debate concerning the origin of evil and the particular role of fallen angels in theodicy is beyond the scope of our inquiry. But that the Day of Atonement ritual may have specific associations to Son of Man mythology is worth considering since it connects Jesus as the Son of Man to a ritual that involves (possibly only in name) the leader of the fallen angels found mentioned in the *Book of Giants* and in *1 Enoch* 10:8. It is "open to speculation that the New Testament story of an incarnated heavenly saviour owes its formation as much to the myth of the heavenly descent of the 'sons of God' which early Christians could have read (and surely did) in the books of 1 Enoch and of Jubilees . . . read from this point of view, the mixing of divine and human natures is no startling innovation, Jesus is no second Adam, but an anti-Azazel . . ."[76]

Indeed, Jesus becomes the perfect sin offering because as he is portrayed in the Gospels and New Testament, he is the binder of the fallen angels (Jude 6). Mythologically, he shares the same angelic qualities as the rebellious angel(s) (now Satan and demons) who are responsible for the origination of sin. As the promised son/Son of Man, Jesus is destined to become the very sacrifice itself—the culmination and fruition of the Aqedah never completed in Genesis, concluding the need for any and all further ritual sacrifices, which according to Levenson only came into existence as a substitution for actual human sacrifice. If Levenson's theory is correct, the death of Jesus becomes the actual realization of the ancient cultic practice.

One scholar contends that the scapegoat ritual "is a purely native, Israelite invention, not a modification of pre-Israelite, Near Eastern rites."[77] The ritual may be traced to the account found in the book of *Jubilees* that recounts the story of Joseph in Genesis. Thus, in the scapegoat ritual, "the issue the [biblical lawgiver] focused on is the occasion when Joseph's

75. Ibid., 201.

76. Ibid.

77. Carmichael, "Origin," 182. For another approach to the ritual, see Tawil, "Azazel."

brothers seek forgiveness for their offense against Joseph . . . [which] involved the killing of a goat to suggest an evil beast had slain Joseph, thereby transferring to the beast their own wrongdoing."[78] Viewed from this perspective, "the legislation concerning the forgiveness of sins on the Day of Atonement is illuminated once we see that it harks back to the first occurrence in the history of the nation when forgiveness is sought for an act of wrongdoing."[79] Both the Day of Atonement and the forgiveness of Joseph's brothers are concerned with the first instance of national "concealed offenses" which "the later descendants of Israel are not to conceal" but instead to confess openly and publicly.[80] The argument can be made that "the ritual is commemorative is [shown by] its sheer impracticality. How does one cause a goat to go off into the wilderness?" an action which may reflect "the fact that the [Joseph] story does not single out any one brother as coming up with the idea of killing the goat and saying that a wild beast had killed Joseph."[81]

Possibly the scapegoat ritual reverberates even further into the story of Genesis when one considers that Joseph is sold by his brothers to the descendants of Ishmael who "are pictured as caravan traders . . . and as Bedouin raiders interchangeable with the Midianites . . ."[82] Ishmael, a promised son, also nearly perishes in the wilderness which is also the location of the pit inhabited by Joseph before he is sold and the Day of Atonement. Both Isaac and Ishmael escape their respective Aqedahs. But Jesus, after he is tested in the same wilderness and temporarily escapes his demise by wild beasts, is later sacrificed like the scapegoat on the Day of Atonement.[83]

SON OF MAN JESUS AND THE EPIC OF GILGAMESH

Since we began our inquiry into the mythology concerning the Son of Man with an examination of the Epic of Gilgamesh, it might be instructive

---

78. Carmichael, "Origin," 182.
79. Ibid., 179.
80. Ibid.
81. Ibid., 180.
82. Noort, "Created," 33.
83. Jewish rabbinic developments included the inclusion of angels before the Aqedah of Isaac. See Bernstein, "Angels at the Aqedah."

to return to the Epic in light of the association made by the Gospel writers between Jesus and John the Baptist. Two of the promised sons in the Hebrew Scriptures have associations with wilderness themes. Clearly Ishmael (who is a promised son, but not a Son of Man) is connected to the wilderness. Samson (who is both a promised son and a Son of Man) also shares some affinity to the wilderness. For example, "Samson's hair, uncut since birth, is his signal trait . . . [he] sleeps in a rock crevice (Judg 15:8), and he eats wild honey (Judg 14:9–10)."[84] Samson's relationship to the wilderness, however, is secondary to his status as a Son of Man.

Obviously we cannot make reference to any direct literary dependence between the Epic of Gilgamesh and the narratives of the Gospels, but the larger mythological associations are undoubtedly present. John the Baptist shares many similarities with the "wild man" Enkidu. John the Baptist "lives in the wilderness, eats a primitive diet, wears animal skins, dies though the agency of a woman, and above all, functions as the secondary, wild counterpart to the primary hero . . ."[85] According to Luke's infancy narrative, John the Baptist is made a promised son but not a Son of Man. While Enkidu is created by the Goddess Aruru to be the counterpart of Gilgamesh, he is not partially divine like the hero. John is a promised son who is destined to be a great prophet, but it is Jesus alone who is partially divine.

Enkidu is created expressly for the purpose of making Gilgamesh a more noble ruler. Without John's baptism, Jesus would not be able to fulfill the sacred role destined for him. Just as Enkidu's death prompts Gilgamesh toward a journey in search of immortality, so does John's death enable Jesus to begin his earthly ministry and later heavenly pilgrimage to immortality. And as Enkidu's death is brought about through the civilizing agency of the harlot Shamhat, John's death occurs through the agency of Salome, whose sexual behavior (dancing during Herod Antipas' symposium) permits her mother to demand the death of the prophet—the same prophet who previously condemned her marriage to Antipas (and by extension her sexual behavior) as sinful.[86]

The sexual influence of Salome (who is not named in any Gospel narrative, but is generally believed to be the daughter of Herodias)[87] on

---

84. Mobley, "Wild Man," 229.
85. Ibid., 228.
86. There are slight parallels here to Enkidu's cursing of Shamhat.
87. Hanson, *Palestine in the Time of Jesus*.

John the Baptist, unlike the civilizing influence of Shamhat on Enkidu by means of sexual engagement, is devoid of any actual physical contact with the prophet, since by now the trajectory of women's association between sexual enactment and the giving of wisdom has been disconnected. What remains from the three original mythological outcomes of women's sexual engagement and awareness (sexual awareness, wisdom, mortality) in the Synoptic Gospels is represented only by the shadow or potential for sexual engagement. Salome's dancing is distanced from the prophet and enacted only by proxy and the result is John's mortality.

With the death of John the Baptist (Enkidu), Jesus, as a distant representative of Gilgamesh, is now free to begin his pilgrimage to Jerusalem where he will be made (as Gilgamesh was in the final stages of the mythology of the Epic) king of the underworld for a time before his resurrection and ascension. However, before Jesus is allowed to finish the final stages of his journey he must meet with his representative Shamhat/Shiduri, which he does at the garden of Gethsemane in the Gospel of John.

THE SON OF MAN JESUS IN THE GOSPEL OF JOHN

In the Gospel of John, "the Son of Man is clearly a being who has an unusual relationship with heaven: angels ascend and descend upon him, and he himself came down from heaven and must return to heaven."[88] Whereas in the Synoptic Gospels, even though the angelic nature of Jesus is important, it is never made as explicit as in John's gospel. But a significant aspect of John's mythological treatment of his understanding of Jesus as the Son of Man is revealed though the reference "to the Son of Man being lifted up or glorified (John 3:14; 8:28; 12:23; 13:31), an event which corresponds to the passion-resurrection in the Gospel."[89] Charlesworth has argued, I believe convincingly, that John 3:14 provides a profound example of serpent symbolism that is crucial for determining how the Fourth Evangelist characterizes Jesus as the final Son of Man. According to Charlesworth, the narrator of John 3:14 "uses a simile; Jesus is like the serpent raised up by Moses, at God's command, in the wilderness."[90] Charlesworth reminds us that "the symbol of the serpent most often represents life . . . but is also symbolized eternal life . . . the Fourth Evangelist

88. Chialà, "Son of Man," 169.
89. Ibid.
90. Charlesworth, *Good and Evil Serpent*, 403.

Fallen Angels and Fallen Women

[in 3:14] put the accent on the symbolism of eternal life; that is, Jesus is raised up symbolically like Moses' serpent. And while Moses' serpent gave life, Jesus guarantees eternal life for those who believe."[91]

Indeed, as Charlesworth rightly observes, in the Gospel of John, "the end of salvation of history [is] mirrored in the beginning of history."[92] Charlesworth's brilliant exegesis of John 20:11–18 also serves as the foundation for understanding the complex relationship between the resurrection scene of Jesus and Genesis 3.

> Μαρία δὲ εἱστήκει πρὸς τῷ μνημείῳ ἔξω κλαίουσα. ὡς οὖν ἔκλαιεν παρέκυψεν εἰς τὸ μνημεῖον, καὶ θεωρεῖ δύο ἀγγέλους ἐν λευκοῖς καθεζομένους, ἕνα πρὸς τῇ κεφαλῇ καὶ ἕνα πρὸς τοῖς ποσίν, ὅπου ἔκειτο τὸ σῶμα τοῦ Ἰησοῦ. καὶ λέγουσιν αὐτῇ ἐκεῖνοι· Γύναι, τί κλαίεις; λέγει αὐτοῖς ὅτι Ἦραν τὸν κύριόν μου, καὶ οὐκ οἶδα ποῦ ἔθηκαν αὐτόν. ταῦτα
> εἰποῦσα ἐστράφη εἰς τὰ ὀπίσω, καὶ θεωρεῖ τὸν Ἰησοῦν ἑστῶτα, καὶ οὐκ ᾔδει ὅτι Ἰησοῦς ἐστιν. λέγει αὐτῇ Ἰησοῦς· Γύναι, τί κλαίεις; τίνα ζητεῖς; ἐκείνη δοκοῦσα ὅτι ὁ κηπουρός ἐστιν λέγει αὐτῷ· Κύριε, εἰ σὺ ἐβάστασας αὐτόν, εἰπέ μοι ποῦ ἔθηκας αὐτόν, κἀγὼ αὐτὸν ἀρῶ. λέγει αὐτῇ Ἰησοῦς· Μαριάμ. στραφεῖσα ἐκείνη λέγει αὐτῷ Ἑβραϊστί· Ραββουνι (ὃ λέγεται Διδάσκαλε). λέγει αὐτῇ Ἰησοῦς· Μή μου ἅπτου, οὔπω γὰρ ἀναβέβηκα πρὸς τὸν πατέρα· πορεύου δὲ πρὸς τοὺς ἀδελφούς μου καὶ εἰπὲ αὐτοῖς· Ἀναβαίνω πρὸς τὸν πατέρα μου καὶ πατέρα ὑμῶν καὶ θεόν μου καὶ θεὸν ὑμῶν. ἔρχεται Μαριὰμ ἡ Μαγδαληνὴ ἀγγέλλουσα τοῖς μαθηταῖς ὅτι Ἑώρακα τὸν κύριον καὶ ταῦτα εἶπεν αὐτῇ.

But Mary was standing outside the tomb weeping; and so, as she wept, she stooped and looked into the tomb; and she saw two angels in white sitting, one at the head and one at the feet, where the body of Jesus had been lying. And they said to her, "Woman, why are you weeping?" She said to them, "Because they have taken away my Lord, and I do not know where they have laid Him." When she had said this, she turned around and saw Jesus standing there, and did not know that it was Jesus. Jesus said to her, "Woman, why are you weeping? Whom are you seeking?" Supposing Him to be the gardener, she said to Him, "Sir, if you have carried Him away, tell me where you have laid Him, and I will take Him away." Jesus said to her, "Mary!" She turned and said to Him in Hebrew, "Rabboni!" (which means, Teacher). Jesus said to her, "Stop clinging to Me, for I have not

---

91. Ibid., 394.
92. Ibid., 401.

Chapter Five

yet ascended to the Father; but go to My brethren and say to them, 'I ascend to My Father and your Father, and My God and your God.'" Mary Magdalene came, announcing to the disciples, "I have seen the Lord," and that He had said these things to her (NASB).

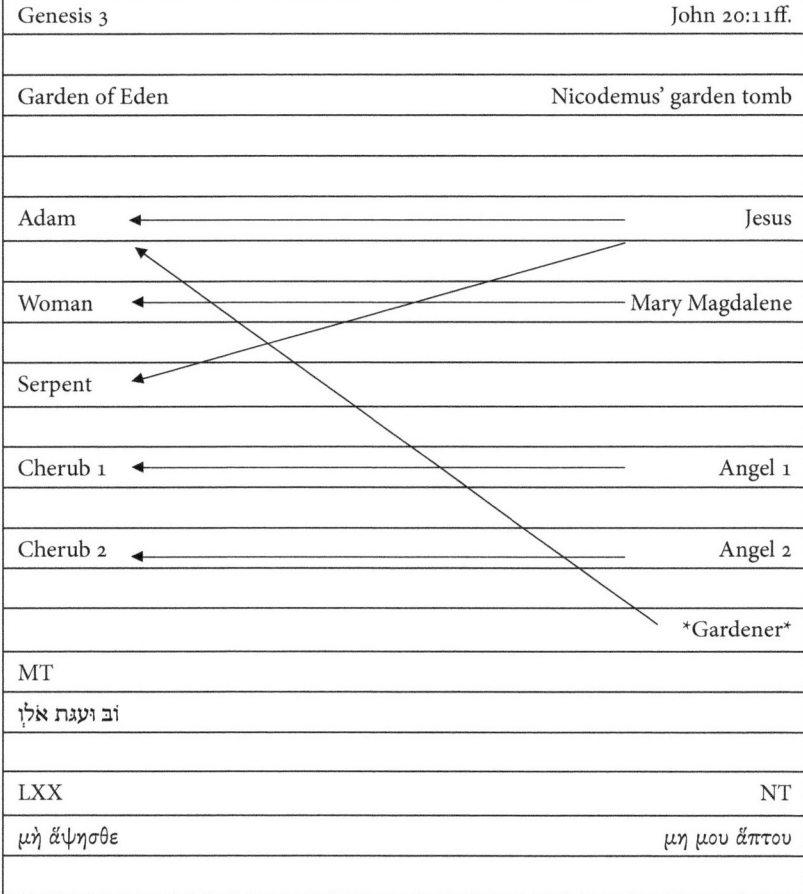

As Charlesworth notes, "only the Fourth Evangelist stages the first resurrection appearance of Jesus in a garden."[93] The garden tomb setting prepares the reader to recall the garden of Eden where sin first entered the world. Mary Magdalene enters the tomb of Jesus and is identified by both angels as "Γύναι" (woman) a title that serves to connect her to the long list of her female spiritual ancestors: among them, the "woman," wife

93. Ibid.

of Manoah and ultimately the first woman, Eve. The two angels represent the two cherubim who in Genesis 3 escort Eve and Adam from paradise—in the midst of the New Eden, the angels represent the return to paradise that has been transformed by the resurrection. Now that Jesus has been resurrected, the tomb is no longer a place of death, and Eden is again habitable.

Jesus, like the angels, identifies Mary as "woman," which serves the dual function of associating Mary not just with the first woman, but with the first woman who was created to be the nonsexualized spouse of Adam. Mary identifies Jesus first as the "gardener," that is, the Adam originally created by Yhwh to cultivate the garden of Eden, and then as a rabbi ("my teacher") who is placed in an authoritative position relative to Mary. This is the first stage of the Fourth Evangelist's portrayal of the nonsexual marriage between Jesus and Mary that will become the new paradigm for future female followers of Jesus; the words and actions of the resurrected Jesus in the garden repair the fateful mistake of Eve's original sexual awareness and (re)create the original pairing desired by Yhwh since the beginning.

The command of Jesus to Mary, "Μή μου ἅπτου," (do not touch me) recalls the first woman's own addition to Yhwh's original command given to the serpent concerning the fruit of the Tree of the Knowledge of Good and Evil. Charlesworth remarks that Jesus' command to Mary "is an echo of what the first woman added to God's command when she tells the Nachash: 'And you must not touch it' (Gen 3:3)."[94] This command of Jesus also places him in the role of the creator God since the first words Yhwh speaks to his creation is a command not to eat from the fruit of the Tree of Good and Evil and gain sexual awareness. By employing the words of the first woman's response to the serpent and placing the prohibition upon himself, Jesus combines two originally competing roles. First, he is now the New Serpent—not the replica of the original tempter in the garden, but the One who, like the healing symbol in the wilderness in Numbers 21:4–9 has been lifted up thrice: by his crucifixion, by his resurrection, and soon by his ascension. He is also the new Adam who has swallowed up the original bringer of death and has restored the first couple to their respective nonsexual relationship. The disastrous sexual touch of the fruit from the Tree of the Knowledge of Good and Evil by the first woman and the resulting fall into death is completely nullified by Jesus' com-

---

94. Ibid.

mand to his new Eve. Jesus has been made the fruit of the original Tree of the Knowledge of Good and Evil, Sophia (Wisdom) incarnate, whose purpose is to grant eternal life without sexual knowledge and thus, he does not allow Mary to touch him.

Eilberg-Schwartz contends that the theory behind the creation of the virgin birth was to remove the concept of paternal lineage from the criteria for being a Jew and thus open the new religion of Christianity to gentiles.[95] But as we have explored here, inside the concept of the virgin birth is an entire ideology that promotes not just the end of associating religiosity with paternity, but with maternity as well.[96] Eilberg-Schwartz makes the point that with the virgin birth of Jesus "since masculinity was no longer defined in terms of procreation, it did not matter that Christ had no consort."[97] But I argue that the sexuality and procreative capacity of Jesus is of the utmost importance in terms of the new religion of Christianity. Jesus only becomes salvific through his nonsexual conception that allows the final dismantling of the original sexual sin. The evidence for the proliferation of beliefs concerning abstinence and chastity beginning as early as the book of Acts attest to this fact.[98]

And thus it is not Mary the mother of Jesus who is the new Eve, but the redeemed and chaste Mary Magdalene, who is sent by Jesus to announce (ἀγγέλλουσα) to the other disciples the first words spoken by a human female—words that reverberate from Genesis. In John's garden, the first woman's mistake has been nullified: Mary Magdalene has not touched! The curse has been reversed because Mary has instead only "seen the Lord."

---

95. Eilberg-Schwartz, *God's Phallus*, 223ff. See also Levenson, *Death and Resurrection of the Beloved Son*.

96. C.f. Luke 14:26 "If anyone comes to me and does not hate his own father and mother and wife and children . . ."

97. Eilberg-Schwartz, *God's Phallus*, 236. If Sawicki's thesis is to be trusted, Jesus' status as the son of Mary would have precluded him from ever expecting to marry.

98. Klutz, "Value of Being Virginal."

Bibliography

Abusch, Tzvi. "The Courtesan, the Wild Man, and the Hunter: Studies in the Literary History of the Epic of Gilgamesh." In *An Experienced Scribe Who Neglects Nothing: Ancient Near Eastern Studies in Honor of Jacob Klein*, edited by Jacob Klein and Yitzhak Sefati, 413–33. Bethesda, MD: CDL Press, 2005.

———. "The Development and Meaning of the Epic of Gilgamesh: An Interpretive Essay." *Journal of the American Oriental Society* 121/4 (October–December 2001): 614–22.

———. "Gilgamesh's Request and Siduri's Denial, Part I: The Meaning of the Dialogue and its Implications for the History of the Epic." In *The Tablet and the Scroll*, edited by Mark E. Cohen et al., 1–14. Bethesda, MD: CDL Press, 1993.

———. "Gilgamesh's Request and Siduri's Denial, Part II: An Analysis and Interpretation of an Old Babylonian Fragment about Mourning and Celebration." *Journal of the Ancient Near Eastern Society* 22 (1993): 3–17.

———. "Ishtar's Proposal and Gilgamesh's Refusal: An Interpretation of the Gilgamesh Epic, Tablet 6, Lines 1–79." *History of Religions* 26/2 (November 1986): 143–87.

Ackerman, Susan. *Warrior, Dancer, Seductress, Queen: Women in Judges and Biblical Israel*. New York: Doubleday, 1998.

———. *When Heroes Love: The Ambiguity of Eros in the Stories of Gilgamesh and David*. Gender, Theory, and Religion. New York: Columbia University Press, 2005.

Albright, W. F. "The Goddess of Life and Wisdom." *The American Journal of Semitic Languages and Literatures* 36/4 (July 1920): 258–94.

Allen, David Lewis. "The Authorship of Hebrews: Historical Survey of the Lukan Theory." *Criswell Theological Review* 8/2 (March 2011): 3–18.

Alster, Bendt. "Enki and Ninhursag: The Creation of the First Woman." *Ugarit-Forschungen* 10 (1979): 15–27.

———. "Lugalbanda and the Early Epic Tradition in Mesopotamia." In *Lingering Over Words*, edited by Tzvi Abusch et al., 59–72. Atlanta: Scholar's, 1990.

Alter, Robert. *The Art of Biblical Narrative*. New York: Basic, 1981.

Amaru, Betsy Halpern. "The First Woman, Wives, and Mothers in Jubilees." *Journal of Biblical Literature* 113/4 (December 1994): 609–26.

Ashmon, Scott A. "Sampson and Christ, Type and Antitype." *Lutheran Forum* 42/3 (September 2008): 15–17.

Ataç, Mehmet-Ali. "'Angelology' in the Epic of Gilgamesh." *Journal of Ancient Near Eastern Religions* 4/1 (January 2004): 3–27.

Bibliography

Auffarth, Christoph, and Loren T. Stuckenbruck, eds. *The Fall of the Angels*. Themes in Biblical Narrative 6. Leiden: Brill, 2004.

Azize, Joseph, and Noel Weeks, eds. *Gilgamesh and the World of Assyria: Proceedings of the Conference Held at the Mandelbaum House, the University of Sydney, 21–23 July, 2004*. Ancient Near Eastern Studies Supplement Series 21. Leuven: Peeters, 2007.

Bahrani, Zainab. *Women of Babylon: Gender and Representation in Mesopotamia*. New York: Routledge, 2001.

Bailey, John A. "Initiation and the Primal Woman in Gilgamesh and Genesis 2–3." *Journal of Biblical Literature* 89/2 (June 1970): 137–50.

Barker, Margaret. *Christmas: The Original Story*. London: SPCK, 2008.

———. *The Great Angel: A Study of Israel's Second God*. Louisville: John Knox, 1992.

———. "The Life-Bearing Spring." In *Origins of the Cult of the Virgin Mary*, edited by Chris Maunder, 127–35. New York: Burns & Oates, 2008.

Barringer, Judith M., Jeffrey M. Hurwit, eds. *Periklean Athens and Its Legacy: Problems and Perspectives*. Austin: University of Texas Press, 2005.

Barton, George A. "A Sumerian Source of the Fourth and Fifth Chapters of Genesis." *Journal of Biblical Literature* 34/ 1/4 (1915): 1–9.

Bauckham, Richard. *Jesus and the Eyewitnesses: The Gospels as Eyewitness Testimony*. Grand Rapids: Eerdmans, 2006.

———. "Jesus and the Wild Animals (Mark 1:13): A Christological Image for an Ecological Age." In *Jesus of Nazareth, Lord and Christ: Essays on the Historical Jesus and the New Testament Christ*, edited by Joel B. Green and Max Turner, 3–21. Grand Rapids: Eerdmans, 1994.

Bell, Lanny. "Luxor Temple and the Cult of the Royal Ka." *Journal of Near Eastern Studies* 44/4 (October 1985): 251–94.

Benoit, Pierre. "Pauline Angelology and Demonology: Reflexions on Designations of Heavenly Powers and on Origin of Angelic Evil According to Paul." *Religious Studies Bulletin* 3/1 (January 1983): 1–18.

Bernstein, Moshe J. "Angels at the Aqedah: A Study in the Development of a Midrashic Motif." *Dead Sea Discoveries* 7/3 (January 2000): 263–91.

Black, Jeremy A., Anthony Green, and Tessa Rickards. *Gods, Demons, and Symbols of Ancient Mesopotamia: An Illustrated Dictionary*. Austin: University of Texas Press, 1992.

Boccaccini, Gabriele. "Finding a Place for the Parables of Enoch within Second Temple Jewish Literature." In *Enoch and the Messiah Son of Man: Revisiting the Book of Parables*, edited by Gabriele Boccaccini, 263–89. Grand Rapids: Eerdmans, 2007.

Boomershine, Thomas E. "The Structure of Narrative Rhetoric in Genesis 2–3." *Semeia* 18 (January 1980): 113–29.

Bottéro, Jean. *Religion in Ancient Mesopotamia*. Translated by Teresa Lavender Fagan. Chicago: University of Chicago Press, 2001.

Bowman, Richard G., and Richard W. Swanson. "Samson and the Son of God Or Dead Heroes and Dead Goats: Ethical Readings of Narrative Violence in Judges and Matthew." *Semeia* 77 (January 1997): 59–73.

Bremmer, Jan N. *Greek Religion and Culture, the Bible, and the Ancient Near East*. Jerusalem Studies in Religion and Culture 8. Leiden: Brill, 2008.

———. "Pandora Or the Creation of a Greek Eve." In *The Creation of Man and Woman: Interpretations of the Biblical Narratives in Jewish and Christian Traditions*, edited by Gerard P. Luttikhuizen, 19–33. Leiden: Brill, 2000.

Brenner, Athalya. "The Tree of Life as a Female Symbol?" In *Genesis*, edited by Athalya Brenner, Archie Chi Chung Lee, and Gale A. Yee, 35–42. Minneapolis: Fortress, 2010.

Brock, Sebastian P. "Passover, Annunciation and Epiclesis: Some Remarks on the Term *Aggen* in the Syriac Versions of Lk 1:35." *Novum Testamentum* 24/3 (July 1982): 222–33.

Brown, A. S. "Aphrodite and the Pandora Complex." *The Classical Quarterly* 47/1 (1997): 26–47.

Brown, Raymond Edward. *The Birth of the Messiah: A Commentary on the Infancy Narratives in the Gospels of Matthew and Luke*. Anchor Bible Reference Library. New York: Doubleday, 1993.

———, et al., eds. *Mary in the New Testament: A Collaborative Assessment by Protestant and Roman Catholic Scholars*. Philadelphia: Fortress, 1978.

Bryan, David T. "A Reevaluation of Gen 4 and 5 in Light of Recent Studies in Genealogical Fluidity." *Zeitschrift Für Die Alttestamentliche Wissenschaft* 99/2 (October 2009): 180–88.

Bullock, C. H. "Ezekiel, Bridge between the Testaments." *Journal of the Evangelical Theological Society* 25/1 (March 1982): 23–31.

Busch, Austin. "The Figure of Eve in Romans 7:5–25." *Biblical Interpretation* 12/1 (January 2004): 1–36.

Calef, Susan A. "Kephalē, Coverings, and Cosmology: The Impenetrable 'Logic' of 1 Corinthians 11:2–16." *Journal of Religion & Society Supplemental Series* 5 (2009): 21–44.

Caneday, Ardel B. "Mark's Provocative Use of Scripture in Narration: 'He Was with the Wild Animals and Angels Ministered to Him.'" *Bulletin for Biblical Research* 9 (1999): 19–36.

Carmichael, Calum M. "The Origin of the Scapegoat Ritual." *Vetus Testamentum* 50/2 (April 2000): 167–82.

Casey, Maurice. "Aramaic Idiom and the Son of Man Problem: A Response to Owen and Shepherd." *Journal for the Study of the New Testament* 25/1 (September 2002): 3–32.

Cassuto, Umberto. *The Documentary Hypothesis and the Composition of the Pentateuch: Eight Lectures*. Jerusalem: Shalem, 2006.

Charles, R. H. *The Book of Jubilees Or the Little Genesis*. Translations of Early Documents Series 1, Palestinian Jewish Texts (Pre-Rabbinic). London: 1917.

Charlesworth, James H. *The Good and Evil Serpent: How a Universal Symbol Became Christianized*. Anchor Yale Bible Reference Library. New Haven, CT: Yale University Press, 2010.

Chester, Andrew. "Jewish Messianic Expectations and Mediatorial Figures and Pauline Christology." In *Paulus Und Das Antike Judentum: Tubingen-Durham-Symposium im Gedenken an den 50. Todestag Adolf Schlatters (19. Mai 1938)*, edited by Martin Hengel and Ulrich Heckel, 17–89. Tübingen: Mohr, 1991.

Chialà, Sabino. "The Son of Man: The Evolution of an Expression." In *Enoch and the Messiah Son of Man: Revisiting the Book of Parables*, edited by Gabriele Boccaccini, 153–78. Grand Rapids: Eerdmans, 2007.

Bibliography

Chisholm, Robert B., Jr. "Identity Crisis: Assessing Samson's Birth and Career." *Bibliotheca Sacra* 166/662 (April 2009): 147–62.

Clay, Jenny Strauss. *Hesiod's Cosmos*. Cambridge: Cambridge University Press, 2003.

Clifford, Richard J. "Cosmogonies in the Ugaritic Texts and in the Bible." *Orientalia* 53/2 (1984): 183–201.

Clines, David J. A. "Tree of Knowledge and the Law of Yahweh, Psalm 19." *Vetus Testamentum* 24/1 (1974): 8–14.

Coleran, James E. "The Sons of God in Genesis 6:2." *Theological Studies* 2/4 (December 1941): 487–509.

Coleridge, Mark. *The Birth of the Lukan Narrative: Narrative as Christology in Luke 1–2*. Journal for the Study of the New Testament, Supplement Series 88. Sheffield, UK: JSOT, 1993.

Colless, Brian E. "Ba'al's Relations with Canaanite Goddesses." In *Religion in the Ancient World: New Themes and Approaches*, edited by Matthew Dillon, 79–89. Amsterdam: Hakkert, 1996.

Crossan, John Dominic. *God and Empire: Jesus Against Rome, Then and Now*. 1st ed. San Francisco: Harper, 2007.

Daise, Michael A. "Biblical Creation Motifs in the Qumran Hodayot." In *The Dead Sea Scrolls Fifty Years After Their Discovery*, edited by L. Schiffman et al., 293–305. Jerusalem: Israel Exploration Society, 2000.

Dalley, Stephanie, ed. and trans. *Myths from Mesopotamia: Creation, the Flood, Gilgamesh, and Others*. Oxford: Oxford University Press, 1989.

Davies, Philip R. "Women, Men, Gods, Sex and Power: The Birth of a Biblical Myth." In *Feminist Companion to Genesis*, edited by Athalya Brenner, 194–201. Sheffield, UK: Sheffield Academic Press, 1993.

Day, Peggy L. "Anat: Ugarit's 'Mistress of Animals.'" *Journal of Near Eastern Studies* 51/3 (July 1992): 181–90.

Delaney, Carol Lowery. *The Seed and the Soil: Gender and Cosmology in Turkish Village Society*. Comparative Studies on Muslim Societies 11. Berkeley: University of California Press, 1991.

Di Luccio, Pino. "Son of Man, Sons of the Woman, and Teachers of the Law: Eschatological Features of the Gospel Beatitudes, with a Selected Bibliography on the 'Son of Man.'" *Estudios Eclesiásticos* 84/329 (April 2009): 337–53.

Dickson, Keith M. "Enki and Ninhursag: The Trickster in Paradise." *Journal of Near Eastern Studies* 66/1 (January 2007): 1–32.

———. "Looking at the Other in Gilgamesh." *Journal of the American Oriental Society* 127/2 (April 2007): 171–82.

Dimant, Devorah. "Noah in Early Jewish Literature." In *Biblical Figures Outside the Bible*, edited by Michael E. Stone and Theodore A. Bergren, 123–50. Harrisburg, PA: Trinity, 1998.

Dobbs-Allsopp, F. "The Syntagma of Bat Followed by a Geographical Name in the Hebrew Bible: A Reconsideration of its Meaning and Grammar." *Catholic Biblical Quarterly* 57/3 (July 1995): 451–70.

Dunand, Françoise, and Christiane Zivie-Coche. *Gods and Men in Egypt: 3000 BCE to 395 CE*. Ithaca: Cornell University Press, 2004.

Eastman, Susan Grove. "Whose Apocalypse? The Identity of the Sons of God in Romans 8:19." *Journal of Biblical Literature* 121/2 (June 2002): 263–77.

Eilberg-Schwartz, Howard. *God's Phallus and Other Problems for Men and Monotheism.* Boston: Beacon, 1994.

Eiselen, Frederick Carl. "'The Tree of the Knowledge of Good and Evil.'" *The Biblical World* 36/2 (August 1910): 101–12.

Ellens, Deborah L. *Women in the Sex Texts of Leviticus and Deuteronomy: A Comparative Conceptual Analysis.* New York: T & T Clark, 2008.

Eynikel, Erik. "The Angel in Samson's Birth Narrative: Judg 13." In *Angels: The Concepts of Celestial Beings,* edited by Friedrich V. Reiterer et al., 109–23. Berlin: Walter de Gruyter, 2007.

Falk, Daniel K., et al., eds. *Qumran Cave 1 Revisited: Texts from Cave 1 Sixty Years After their Discovery: Proceedings of the Sixth Meeting of the IOQS in Ljubljana.* Studies on the Texts of the Desert of Judah 91. Leiden: Brill, 2010.

Fitzmyer, Joseph A. *The Genesis Apocryphon of Qumran Cave 1: A Commentary.* 3rd rev ed. Rome: Editrice Pontificio Biblico, 2004.

Fockner, Sven. "Reopening the Discussion: Another Contextual Look at the Sons of God." *Journal for the Study of the Old Testament* 32/4 (June 2008): 435–56.

Forsyth, Neil. *The Old Enemy: Satan and the Combat Myth.* Princeton, NJ: Princeton University Press, 1987.

Fossum, Jarl. "Jewish-Christian Christology and Jewish Mysticism." *Vigiliae Christianae* 37/3 (September 1983): 260–87.

Foster, Benjamin. "Gilgamesh: Sex, Love and the Ascent of Knowledge." In *Love and Death in the Ancient Near East: Essays in Honor of Marvin H. Pope,* edited by John H. Marks and Robert McClive Good, 21–42. Guilford, CT: Four Quarters, 1987.

Frymer-Kensky, Tikva. "Atrahasis Epic and Its Significance for Our Understanding of Genesis 1–9." *Biblical Archaeologist* 40/4 (December 1977): 147–55.

———. *In the Wake of the Goddesses: Women, Culture, and the Biblical Transformation of Pagan Myth.* 1st ed. New York: Fawcett Columbine, 1993.

Fuchs-Kreimer, Nancy. "Sibling Rivals." *Reconstructionist* 59/2 (September 1994): 49–52.

George, A. R. *The Babylonian Gilgamesh Epic: Introduction, Critical Edition and Cuneiform Texts.* 2 vols. Oxford: Oxford University Press, 2003.

———. *The Epic of Gilgamesh: The Babylonian Epic Poem and Other Texts in Akkadian and Sumerian.* New York: Penguin Books, 2003.

Gilboa, R. "Who 'Fell Down' to Our Earth? A Different Light on Genesis 6:1–4." *Biblische Notizen* 111 (January 2002): 66–75.

Gillmayr-Bucher, Susanne. "'She Came to Test Him with Hard Questions': Foreign Women and Their View on Israel." *Biblical Interpretation* 15/2 (January 2007): 135–50.

Goodman, Martin, Geurt Hendrik van Kooten, and J. van Ruiten. *Abraham, the Nations, and the Hagarites: Jewish, Christian, and Islamic Perspectives on Kinship with Abraham.* Leiden: Brill, 2010.

Grabbe, Lester L. "The Parables of Enoch in Second Temple Jewish Society." In *Enoch and the Messiah Son of Man: Revisiting the Book of Parables,* edited by Gabriele Boccaccini, 386–402. Grand Rapids: Eerdmans, 2007.

Graver, Margaret. "Dog-Helen and Homeric Insult." *Classical Antiquity* 14/1 (April 1995): 41–61.

Graves-Brown, Carolyn. *Dancing for Hathor: Women in Ancient Egypt.* New York: Continuum, 2010.

Bibliography

Greenstein, Edward L. "The God of Israel and the Gods of Canaan: How Different Were They?" In *Proceedings of the Twelfth World Congress of Jewish Studies, Jerusalem, July 29-August 5, 1997, Division A*, edited by R. Margolin, 47-57. Jerusalem: World Union of Jewish Studies, 1999.

Greig, A. J. "Genesis 6:1-4: The Female and the Fall." *Michigan Quarterly Review* 26/3 (June 1987): 483-96.

Halpern-Amaru, Betsy. *The Empowerment of Women in the Book of Jubilees*. Leiden: Brill, 1999.

Hanson, K. C. "The Herodians and Mediterranean Kinship, 2 Pts." *Biblical Theology Bulletin* 19/3 (July 1989): 75-84.

Hanson, K. C., and Douglas E. Oakman. *Palestine in the Time of Jesus: Social Structures and Social Conflicts*. 2nd ed. Minneapolis: Fortress, 2008.

Harrison, Jane E. "Pandora's Box." *The Journal of Hellenic Studies* 20 (1900): 99-114.

Hawkins, Peter S. "God's Trophy Whore." In *From the Margins 1: Women of the Hebrew Bible and their Afterlives*, edited by Peter S. Hawkins and Lesleigh Cushing Stahlberg, 52-70. Sheffield, UK: Sheffield Phoenix, 2009.

Hawley, Richard, and Barbara Levick. *Women in Antiquity: New Assessments*. International Conference on Women in the Ancient World. New York: Routledge, 1995.

Heil, John Paul. "Jesus with the Wild Animals in Mark 1:13." *Catholic Biblical Quarterly* 68/1 (January 2006): 63-78.

Heliso, Desta. "Enoch as the Son of Man: Contextual and Christological Considerations." *Svensk Missionstidskrift* 98/2 (January 2010): 141-55.

Hesiod. *Theogony; Works and Days; Testimonia*. Edited and translated by Glenn W. Most. Loeb Classical Library 57. Cambridge, MA: Harvard University Press, 2006.

Hess, Richard S. "Lamech in the Genealogies of Genesis." *Bulletin for Biblical Research* 1 (January 1991): 21-25.

Hess, Richard S., and David Toshio Tsumura, eds. *"I Studied Inscriptions from Before the Flood": Ancient Near Eastern, Literary, and Linguistic Approaches to Genesis 1-11*. Sources for Biblical and Theological Study 4. Winona Lake, IN: Eisenbrauns, 1994.

Higgins, Jean M. "Myth of Eve: The Temptress." *Journal of the American Academy of Religion* 44/4 (December 1976): 639-47.

Hoffmann, Geneviève. "Pandora, La Jarre Et l'Espoir." *Études Rurales* 97/98 (January-June 1985): 119-32.

Hollis, Susan Tower. "Goddesses and Sovereignty in Ancient Egypt." In *Goddesses Who Rule*, edited by Elisabeth Benard and Beverly Moon, 215-32. Oxford; New York: Oxford University Press, 2000.

Horsley, Richard A., and Neil Asher Silberman. *The Message and the Kingdom: How Jesus and Paul Ignited a Revolution and Transformed the Ancient World*. New York: Putnam, 1997.

Huggins, Ronald V. "Noah and the Giants: A Response to John C. Reeves." *Journal of Biblical Literature* 114/1 (March 1995): 103-10.

Hurwit, Jeffrey M. "Beautiful Evil: Pandora and the Athena Parthenos." *American Journal of Archaeology* 99/2 (April 1995): 171-86.

Hutchison, John C. "Women, Gentiles, and the Messianic Mission in Matthew's Genealogy." *Bibliotheca Sacra* 158/630 (April 2001): 152-64.

Ilan, Tal. "'Man Born of Woman . . .' (Job 14:1): The Phenomenon of Men Bearing Metronymes at the Time of Jesus." *Novum Testamentum* 34/1 (January 1992): 23-45.
Irvin, Dorothy. *Mytharion: The Comparison of Tales from the Old Testament and the Ancient Near East*. Kevelaer, Ger.: Neukirchener, 1978.
Janzen, J. G. "Hagar in Paul's Eyes and in the Eyes of Yahweh (Genesis 16): A Study in Horizons." *Horizons in Biblical Theology* 13/1 (June 1991): 1-22.
Jarrell, R. H. "The Birth Narrative as Female Counterpart to Covenant." *Journal for the Study of the Old Testament* 26/3 (March 2002): 3-18.
———. "Gospel of Thomas 61 and 62 as a Single Logion: A Textual and Thematic Reevaluation." Paper presented at the annual meeting of the Society of Biblical Literature, Boston, Massachusetts, November 22-26, 1999.
Jay, Nancy B. *Throughout Your Generations Forever: Sacrifice, Religion, and Paternity*. Chicago: University of Chicago Press, 1992.
Johnston, Gordon H. "Genesis 1 and Ancient Egyptian Creation Myths." *Bibliotheca Sacra* 165/658 (April-June 2008): 178-94.
Jongsma-Tieleman, P. "The Creation of Eve and the Ambivalence between the Sexes." In *The Creation of Man and Woman: Interpretations of the Biblical Narratives in Jewish and Christian Traditions*, edited by Gerard P. Luttikhuizen, 172-86. Leiden: Brill, 2000.
Kahl, Brigitte. "And She Called His Name Seth . . . (Gen 4:25): The Birth of Critical Knowledge and the Unread End of Eve's Story." *Union Seminary Quarterly Review* 53/1-2 (January 1999): 19-28.
Kitchen, K. A. *On the Reliability of the Old Testament*. Grand Rapids: Eerdmans, 2003.
Kittel, Gerhard, and Gerhard Friedrich, eds. *Theological Dictionary of the New Testament*. Translated and edited by Geoffrey William Bromiley. 10 vols. Grand Rapids: Eerdmans, 1964-1976.
Klein, Jacob, and Yitzhak Sefati, eds. *An Experienced Scribe Who Neglects Nothing: Ancient Near Eastern Studies in Honor of Jacob Klein*. Bethesda, MD: CDL, 2005.
Klein, Ralph W. "Archaic Chronologies and the Textual History of the Old Testament." *Harvard Theological Review* 67/3 (July 1974): 255-63.
Kline, Meredith G. "Divine Kingship and Genesis 6:1-4." *Westminster Theological Journal* 24/2 (May 1962): 187-204.
Klutz, Todd E. "The Value of Being Virginal: Mary and Anna in the Lukan Infancy Prologue." In *Birth of Jesus: Biblical and Theological Reflections*, edited by George J. Brooke, 71-87. Edinburgh: T & T Clark, 2000.
Kooij, Arie van der. "Peshitta Genesis 6: "Sons of God"—Angels Or Judges?" *Journal of Northwest Semitic Languages* 23/1 (January 1997): 43-51.
Kramer, S. N. "A Blood Plague Motif in Sumerian Mythology." *Archiv Orientaini: Journal of the Czechoslovak Oriental Institute, Prague* 17 (1949): 399-405.
Kramer, Samuel Noah. *The Sumerians: Their History, Culture, and Character*. Chicago: University of Chicago Press, 1963.
Kuhn, Karl A. "The Point of the Step-Parallelism in Luke 1-2." *New Testament Studies* 47/1 (January 2001): 38-49.
Kvam, Kristen E., Linda S. Schearing, and Valarie H. Ziegler. *Eve and Adam: Jewish, Christian, and Muslim Readings on Genesis and Gender*. Bloomington, IN: Indiana University Press, 1999.

Bibliography

Kvanvig, Helge S. *Primeval History: Babylonian, Biblical, and Enochic: An Intertextual Reading*. Supplements to the Journal for the Study of Judaism 149. Leiden: Brill, 2011.

Lachs, Samuel T. "Pandora-Eve Motif in Rabbinic Literature." *Harvard Theological Review* 67/3 (July 1974): 341–45.

Lambert, W. G., A. R. Millard, and Miguel Civil. *Atra-Hasis: The Babylonian Story of the Flood*. Oxford: Clarendon, 1969.

Landry, David T. "Narrative Logic in the Annunciation to Mary (Luke 1:26–38)." *Journal of Biblical Literature* 114/1 (March 1995): 65–79.

Leach, Edmund Ronald. *The Essential Edmund Leach*. Edited by Stephen Hugh-Jones and James Laidlaw. 2 vols. New Haven, CT: Yale University Press, 2000.

Leick, Gwendolyn. *Sex and Eroticism in Mesopotamian Literature*. London: Routledge, 2003.

Lesko, Barbara S., ed. *Women's Earliest Records: From Ancient Egypt and Western Asia: Proceedings of the Conference on Women in the Ancient Near East, Brown University, Providence, Rhode Island, November 5–7, 1987*. Brown Judaic Studies 166. Atlanta: Scholars Press, 1989.

Levenson, Jon Douglas. *The Death and Resurrection of the Beloved Son: The Transformation of Child Sacrifice in Judaism and Christianity*. New Haven, CT: Yale University Press, 1993.

Lincoln, Bruce. *Discourse and the Construction of Society: Comparative Studies of Myth, Ritual, and Classification*. New York: Oxford University Press, 1989.

Loader, William R. G. "The Beginnings of Sexuality in Genesis LXX and Jubilees." In *Septuaginta—Texte, Kontexte, Lebenswelten*, edited by Martin Karrer and Wolfgang Kraus, 300–312. Tübingen: Mohr Siebeck, 2008.

———. *The Dead Sea Scrolls on Sexuality: Attitudes Towards Sexuality in Sectarian and Related Literature at Qumran*. Grand Rapids Eerdmans, 2009.

———. *Enoch, Levi, and Jubilees on Sexuality: Attitudes Towards Sexuality in the Early Enoch Literature, the Aramaic Levi Document, and the Book of Jubilees*. Grand Rapids: Eerdmans, 2007.

Lockwood, Peter F. "Rahab: Multi-Faceted Heroine of the Book of Joshua." *Lutheran Theological Journal* 44/1 (May 2010): 39–50.

Long, Asphodel P. "Asherah, the Tree of Life and the Menorah: Continuity of a Goddess Symbol in Judaism?" In *Patriarchs, Prophets and Other Villains*, edited by Lisa Isherwood, 1–21. London: Equinox, 2007.

Loraux, Nicole. *The Children of Athena: Athenian Ideas about Citizenship and the Division between the Sexes*. Translated by Caroline Levine. Princeton, NJ: Princeton University Press, 1993.

Lyons, Deborah J. *Gender and Immortality: Heroines in Ancient Greek Myth and Cult*. Princeton, NJ: Princeton University Press, 1997.

Malina, Bruce J., and Richard L. Rohrbaugh. *Social-Science Commentary on the Synoptic Gospels*. 2nd ed. Minneapolis: Fortress, 2003.

Marks, Richard Gordon. "Dangerous Hero: Rabbinic Attitudes Toward Legendary Warriors." *Hebrew Union College Annual* 54 (January 1983): 181–94.

Marquardt, Patricia A. "Hesiod's Ambiguous View of Woman." *Classical Philology* 77/4 (October 1982): 283–91.

Marrs, Rick R. "The Sons of God (Genesis 6:1–4)." *Restoration Quarterly* 23/4 (January 1980): 218–24.

Matlock, R. B. "The Birth of Jesus and Why Paul was in Favour of it." In *Birth of Jesus: Biblical and Theological Reflections*, edited by George J. Brooke, 47–57. Edinburgh: T & T Clark, 2000.
Mayer, Kenneth. "Helen and the ΛΙΟΣΒΟΥΛΗ." *The American Journal of Philology* 117/1 (Spring 1996): 1–15.
Meier, Samuel A. "Linguistic Clues on the Date and Canaanite Origin of Genesis 2:23-24." *Catholic Biblical Quarterly* 53/1 (January 1991): 18–24.
Meltzer, Edmund S. "Queens, Goddesses and Other Women of Ancient Egypt." *Journal of the American Oriental Society* 110/3 (July–September 1990): 503–9.
Melvin, David P. "Divine Mediation and the Rise of Civilization in Mesopotamian Literature and in Genesis 1–11." *Journal of Hebrew Scriptures* 10 (2010): 1–15.
Milgrom, Jacob. "Sex and Wisdom: What the Garden of Eden Story is Saying." *Bible Review* 10/6 (December 1994): 21, 52.
Miller, J. M. "Descendants of Cain: Notes on Genesis 4." *Zeitschrift Für Die Alttestamentliche Wissenschaft* 86/2 (1974): 164–74.
Miller, Patrick D. "Yeled in the Song of Lamech." *Journal of Biblical Literature* 85/4 (December 1966): 477–78.
Miller, Troy A. "Surrogate, Slave and Deviant? The Figure of Hagar in Jewish Tradition and Paul (Galatians 4.21–31)." In *Early Christian Literature and Intertextuality: Volume 2, Exegetical Studies*, edited by Craig A. Evans and H. Daniel Zacharias, 138–54. London: T & T Clark, 2009.
Mitchell, Stephen, ed. and trans. *Gilgamesh: A New English Version*. New York: Free Press, 2004.
Moberly, R. W. L. "Did the Serpent Get it Right?" *Journal of Theological Studies* 39/1 (April 1988): 1–27.
Mobley, Gregory. "The Wild Man in the Bible and the Ancient Near East." *Journal of Biblical Literature* 116/2 (June 1997): 217–33.
Moore, Steven. *The Novel: An Alternative History: Beginnings to 1600*. New York: Continuum, 2010.
Mysliwiec, Karol. *Eros on the Nile*. Ithaca, NY: Cornell University Press, 2004.
Narrowe, Morton H. "Another Look at the Tree of Good and Evil." *Jewish Bible Quarterly* 26/3 (July 1998): 184–88.
Newman, Robert C. "The Ancient Exegesis of Genesis 6:2,4." *Grace Theological Journal* 5/1 (March 1984): 13–36.
Nickelsburg, George W. E. "Patriarchs Who Worry about Their Wives: A Haggadic Tendency in the Genesis Apocryphon." In *George W. E. Nickelsburg in Perspective: An Ongoing Dialogue of Learning, Volume 1*, edited by Jacob Neusner and Alan Jeffery Avery-Peck, 177–99. Leiden: Brill, 2003.
Nickelsburg, George W. E., and James C. VanderKam, eds. and trans. *1 Enoch: A New Translation, Based on the Hermeneia Commentary*. Minneapolis: Fortress, 2004.
Nielsen, Kirsten. *Satan the Prodigal Son? A Family Problem in the Bible*. Biblical Seminar 50. Sheffield, UK: Sheffield Academic Press, 1998.
Nissinen, Martti, and Risto Uro. *Sacred Marriages: The Divine-Human Sexual Metaphor from Sumer to Early Christianity*. Winona Lake, IN: Eisenbrauns, 2008.
Noort, Edward. "Created in the Image of the Son: Ishmael and Hagar." In *Abraham, the Nations, and the Hagarites*, edited by Martin Goodman et al., 33–44. Leiden: Brill, 2010.

Bibliography

O'Brien, Joan. "Nammu, Mami, Eve and Pandora: 'What's in a Name?'" *The Classical Journal* 79/1 (October–November 1983): 35–45.

Olson, Daniel C. "'Enoch and the Son of Man' Revisited: Further Reflections on the Text and Translation of 1 Enoch 70.1–2." *Journal for the Study of the Pseudepigrapha* 18/3 (March 2009): 233–40.

Onstine, Suzanne. "Gender and the Religion of Ancient Egypt." *Religion Compass* 4/1 (January 2010): 1–11.

Owen, Paul, and David Shepherd. "Speaking Up for Qumran, Dalman and the Son of Man: Was Bar Enasha a Common Term for 'Man' in the Time of Jesus?" *Journal for the Study of the New Testament* 81 (March 2001): 81–122.

Page, Hugh Rowland. *The Myth of Cosmic Rebellion: A Study of Its Reflexes in Ugaritic and Biblical Literature*. Supplements to Vetus Testamentum 65. Leiden: Brill, 1996.

Pantel, Pauline Schmitt, ed. *A History of Women in the West, Volume 1: From Ancient Goddesses to Christian Saints*. Translated by Arthur Goldhammer. Cambridge, MA: Harvard University Press, 1992.

Parry, Donald W., and Emanuel Tov, eds. *The Dead Sea Scrolls Reader*. 2 vols. Leiden: Brill, 2004–2005.

Peerbolte, L. J. L. "Man, Woman, and the Angels in 1 Cor 11:2–16." In *The Creation of Man and Woman: Interpretations of the Biblical Narratives in Jewish and Christian Traditions*, edited by Gerard P. Luttikhuizen, 76–92. Leiden: Brill, 2000.

Penglase, Charles. *Greek Myths and Mesopotamia: Parallels and Influence in the Homeric Hymns and Hesiod*. New York: Routledge, 1994.

Peters, Dorothy M. *Noah Traditions in the Dead Sea Scrolls: Conversations and Controversies of Antiquity*. Early Judaism and its Literature 26. Atlanta: SBL, 2008.

Phipps, William E. "Eve and Pandora Contrasted." *Theology Today* 45/1 (April 1988): 34–48.

Pinch, Geraldine. *Egyptian Mythology: A Guide to the Gods, Goddesses, and Traditions of Ancient Egypt*. Oxford: Oxford University Press, 2004.

Poulssen, N. "Time and Place in Genesis 5." In *Crises and Perspectives: Studies in Ancient Near Eastern Polytheism, Biblical Theology, Palestinian Archaeology, and Intertestamental Literature: Papers Read at the Joint British-Dutch Old Testament Conference, Held at Cambridge, U.K., 1985*, edited by Johannes Cornelis de Moor, 21–33. Leiden: Brill, 1986.

Rashi [Perush Rashi `al ha-Torah]. *Rashi `al Ha-Torah: The Torah: With Rashi's Commentary Translated, Annonated, and Elucidated*. The Sapirstein ed. Edited by Yisrael Isser Zvi Herczeg et al. Artscroll Series. Brooklyn: Mesorah, 1995–1997.

Reeder, Ellen D. *Pandora: Women in Classical Greece*. Baltimore: Trustees of the Walters Art Gallery, Princeton, NJ, 1995.

Reeves, John C. "Utnapishtim in the Book of Giants." *Journal of Biblical Literature* 112/1 (Spring 1993): 110–15.

Reinhartz, Adele. "Samson's Mother: An Unnamed Protagonist." *Journal for the Study of the Old Testament* 55 (September 1992): 25–37.

Rendsburg, Gary A. "The Biblical Flood Story in the Light of the Gilgameš Flood Account." In *Gilgameš and the World of Assyria*, edited by Joseph Azize and Noel Weeks, 115–27. Leuven: Peeters, 2007.

Riesenfeld, Harald. "The Misinterpreted Mediator in Gal 3:19–20." In *New Testament Age: Essays in Honor of Bo Reicke*, edited by W. C. Weinrich, 405–12. Macon, GA: Mercer University Press, 1984.

Robinson, Bernard P. "Rahab of Canaan—and Israel." *SJOT* 23/2 (January 2009): 257–73.
Rook, John. "The Names of the Wives from Adam to Abraham in the Book of Jubilees." *Journal for the Study of the Pseudepigrapha* 7 (October 1990): 105–17.
Rothstein, David. "Text and Context: Domestic Harmony and the Depiction of Hagar in Jubilees." *Journal for the Study of the Pseudepigrapha* 17/4 (June 2008): 243–64.
Ruiten, J. van. "Hagar in the Book of Jubilees." In *Abraham, the Nations, and the Hagarites*, edited by Martin Goodman et al., 117–38. Leiden: Brill, 2010.
———. "The Interpretation of Genesis 6:1–12 in Jubilees 5:1–19." In *Studies in the Book of Jubilees*, edited by Matthias Albani et al., 59–75. Tübingen: Mohr, 1997.
Sakenfeld, Katharine Doob. "Deborah, Jael, and Sisera's Mother: Reading the Scriptures in Cross-Cultural Context." In *Women, Gender, and Christian Community*, edited by Jane Dempsey Douglass and James F. Kay, 13–22. Louisville: Westminster, 1997.
Savran, George W. "Beastly Speech: Intertextuality, Balaam's Ass and the Garden of Eden." *Journal for the Study of the Old Testament* 64 (December 1994): 33–55.
Sawicki, Marianne. *Crossing Galilee: Architectures of Contact in the Occupied Land of Jesus*. Harrisburg, PA: Trinity, 2000.
Schaberg, Jane. *The Illegitimacy of Jesus: A Feminist Theological Interpretation of the Infancy Narratives*. San Francisco: Harper & Row, 1987.
Schiffman, Lawrence H., Emanuel Tov, James C. VanderKam, and Galen Marquis, eds. *The Dead Sea Scrolls Fifty Years After Their Discovery: Proceedings of the Jerusalem Congress, July 20–25, 1997*. Jerusalem: Israel Exploration Society, 2000.
Selvidge, Marla J. Schierling. "Mark 5:25–34 and Leviticus 15:19–20: A Reaction to Restrictive Purity Regulations." *Journal of Biblical Literature* 103/4 (December 1984): 619–23.
Sherwood, Aaron. "A Leader's Misleading and a Prostitute's Profession: A Re-Examination of Joshua 2." *Journal for the Study of the Old Testament* 31/1 (September 2006): 43–61.
Shields, Martin A. "To Seek but Not to Find: Old Meanings for Qohelet and Gilgameš." In *Gilgameš and the World of Assyria*, edited by Joseph Azize and Noel Weeks, 129–46. Leuven: Peeters, 2007.
Simoons-Vermeer, Ruth E. "The Mesopotamian Floodstories: A Comparison and Interpretation." *Numen* 21/1 (April 1974): 17–34.
Sissa, Giulia. *Greek Virginity*. Translated by Arthur Goldhammer. Revealing Antiquity 3. Cambridge, MA: Harvard University Press, 1990.
Smith, Mark S., and Simon B. Parker. *Ugaritic Narrative Poetry*. Writings from the Ancient World 9. Atlanta: Scholars Press, 1997.
Stanton, R. T. "Asking Questions of the Divine Announcements in the Flood Stories from Ancient Mesopotamia and Israel." In *Gilgameš and the World of Assyria*, edited by Joseph Azize and Noel Weeks, 147–72. Leuven: Peeters, 2007.
Stefaniw, Blossom. "Becoming Men, Staying Women: Gender Ambivalence in Christian Apocryphal Texts and Contexts." *Feminist Theology* 18/3 (May 2010): 341–55.
Steinkeller, Piotr. "On Rulers, Priests and Sacred Marriage: Tracing the Evolution of Early Sumerian Kingship." In *Priests and Officials in the Ancient Near East*, edited by Kazuko Watanabe, 103–37. Heidelberg, Ger.: Carl Winter, 1999.
Stone, Michael E., and Theodore A. Bergren, eds. *Biblical Figures Outside the Bible*. Harrisburg, PA: Trinity, 1998.

Bibliography

Stordalen, T. *Echoes of Eden: Genesis 2–3 and Symbolism of the Eden Garden in Biblical Hebrew Literature.* Contributions to Biblical Exegesis and Theology 25. Leuven: Peeters, 2000.

Stuckenbruck, Loren T. "Why Should Women Cover Their Heads Because of Angels? (1 Corinthians 11:10)." *Stone-Campbell Journal* 4/2 (September 2001): 205–34.

Sweet, Ronald F. G. "A New Look at the 'Sacred Marriage' in Ancient Mesopotamia." In *Corolla Torontonensis: Studies in Honour of Ronald Morton Smith,* edited by Emmet Robbins and Stella Sandahl, 85–104. Toronto: TSAR, 1994.

Tawil, Hayim. "Azazel, the Prince of the Steppe: A Comparative Study." *Zeitschrift Für Die Alttestamentliche Wissenschaft* 92/1 (1980): 43–59.

Taylor, John H. *Death and the Afterlife in Ancient Egypt.* Chicago: University of Chicago Press, 2001.

Teubal, Savina J. *Hagar the Egyptian: The Lost Tradition of the Matriarchs.* San Francisco: Harper & Row, 1990.

Thompson, James W. "The Epistle to the Hebrews and the Pauline Legacy." *Restoration Quarterly* 47/4 (January 2005): 197–206.

Toorn, K. van der, and Sara J. Denning-Bolle. *From Her Cradle to Her Grave: The Role of Religion in the Life of the Israelite and the Babylonian Woman.* Biblical Seminar 23. Sheffield, UK: JSOT, 1994.

Townsend, P. W. "Eve's Answer to the Serpent: An Alternative Paradigm for Sin and Some Implications in Theology." *Calvin Theological Journal* 33/2 (November 1998): 399–420.

Van Seters, John. *In Search of History: Historiography in the Ancient World and the Origins of Biblical History.* New Haven, CT: Yale University Press, 1983.

———. "The Primeval Histories of Greece and Israel Compared." *Zeitschrift Für Die Alttestamentliche Wissenschaft* 100/1 (1988): 1–22.

———. *Prologue to History: The Yahwist as Historian in Genesis.* 1st ed. Louisville: Westminster, 1992.

VanderKam, James C. *The Book of Jubilees.* Guides to Apocrypha and Pseudepigrapha 9. Sheffield, UK: Sheffield Academic, 2001.

———. "Recent Scholarship on the Book of Jubilees." *Currents in Biblical Research* 6/3 (June 2008): 405–31.

VanGemeren, Willem A. "The Sons of God in Genesis 6:1–4 (An Example of Evangelical Demythologization)." *Westminster Theological Journal* 43/2 (March 1981): 320–48.

Vawter, Bruce Francis. "Ezekiel and John." *Catholic Biblical Quarterly* 26/4 (October 1964): 450–58.

Veenker, Ronald A. "Forbidden Fruit: Ancient Near Eastern Sexual Metaphors." *Hebrew Union College Annual* 70–71 (1999–2000): 57–73.

Vermìs, Géza. "The Son of Man Debate Revisited (1960–2010)." *Journal of Jewish Studies* 61/2 (September 2010): 193–206.

Volk, Konrad. *Inanna und Sukaletuda: Zur Historisch-Politischen Deutung Eines Sumerischen Litaraturwerkes.* Translated by Fenna Wachter. Santag 3. Wiesbaden, Ger.: Harrasowitz, 1995.

Walck, Leslie W. "The Son of Man in the Parables of Enoch and the Gospels." In *Enoch and the Messiah Son of Man: Revisiting the Book of Parables,* edited by Gabriele Boccaccini, 299–337. Grand Rapids: Eerdmans, 2007.

Walls, Neal H. *Desire, Discord, and Death: Approaches to Ancient Near Eastern Myth.* American School of Oriental Research 8. Boston: ASOR, 2001.

Walsh, Jerome T. "Genesis 2:4b—3:24: A Synchronic Approach." *Journal of Biblical Literature* 96/2 (June 1977): 161–77.
Watson, Paul. "The Tree of Life." *Restoration Quarterly* 23/4 (January 1980): 232–38.
Westermann, Claus. *Genesis 1–11: A Commentary*. Minneapolis: Augsburg, 1984.
Whitaker, Richard E. *The Eerdmans Analytical Concordance to the Revised Standard Version of the Bible*. Grand Rapids: Eerdmans, 1988.
White, Hugh C. "Direct and Third Person Discourse in the Narrative of the 'Fall.'" *Semeia* 18 (January 1980): 91–106.
Wiggermann, F. A. M. "Some Demons of Time and Their Function in Mesopotamian Iconography." In *Welt Der Götterbilder*, edited by Brigitte Groneberg and Hermann Spieckermann, 102–16. Berlin: Walter de Gruyter, 2007.
Wilson, Brittany E. "Pugnacious Precursors and the Bearer of Peace: Jael, Judith, and Mary in Luke 1:42." *Catholic Biblical Quarterly* 68/3 (July 2006): 436–56.
Witherington, Ben. "The Influence of Galatians on Hebrews." *New Testament Studies* 37/1 (January 1991): 146–52.
Worden, T. "The Literary Influence of the Ugaritic Fertility Myth on the Old Testament." *Vetus Testamentum* 3/3 (July 1953): 273–97.
Wright, Archie T. "Some Observations of Philo's De Gigantibus and Evil Spirits in Second Temple Judaism." *Journal for the Study of Judaism in the Persian, Hellenistic and Roman Period* 36/4 (January 2005): 471–88.
Young, Ian. "Textual Stability in Gilgamesh and the Dead Sea Scrolls." In *Gilgameš and the World of Assyria*, edited by Joseph Azize and Noel Weeks, 173–84. Leuven: Peeters, 2007.

Index

Abrahamic covenant, 106, 109
Abusch, Tzvi, 26, 27, 33, 34, 37
Ackerman, Susan, 111, 123
Adam
    direct discourse with Yhwh, 64, 65
    mortality of, 63
adoption, theological concept for, 157
afterlife, formation of, for humans, 18
Albright, W.F., 73–74
Alster, Bendt, 4, 13
androgyny, 18
angel of God, 121–22
angels. *See also* sons of God; Watchers
    fallen, 81, 101–2
    identity of, determining, 91
    lawgiving and, 138–39
    moral identities of, 100–102
    in Pauline writings, 136–41
    portrayed as "men," 122–23
Annuis, Lucius, 148
annunciation, 151, 152
Anthesteria, 45
anticipation, 43–44
Apollodorus, 47
Aqhat epic, 16
Asa'el tradition, 98
Ataç, Mehmet-Ali, 24–25, 26, 29, 38
Atrahasis epic, 7, 103

Baal, mortality of, 16–17
Baal/Anat Cycle, 16
Barker, Margaret, 144, 145–46, 158
Bat Enosh
    aligned negatively with other daughters of men, 92

    associated with "daughters of men," 89, 95, 96
    name's meaning, 86–87
    sexual validation of, 92
    speech of, 87–89
beloved son motif, 111–12, 128
binary pairings, in creation myths, 4–6
Birth of the Gracious Gods, The, 16
birth narratives, biblical, 106–13, 145, 150
    expanding to include son of man concepts, 123
    as female counterpart to covenant, 107
    importance in, of firstborn's connection to the mother, 112–13
    intersecting themes in, of women, sexual awareness, and transmission of knowledge, 117
    in Luke, 151
    prefigured, in Cain's birth, 109–10
blood, in Egyptian creation stories, 22–23
blood plagues, 8–9
Book of Giants, 99–100
"Book of Parables," 164
Book of Watchers, 101
Brown, Raymond, 144, 145, 151–52, 156

Calef, Susan, 139–40, 142
calling, naming and, 108
character development, 4
Charlesworth, James, 49–50, 57, 71–72, 73, 169–72

189

Fallen Angels and Fallen Women

Chialà, Sabino, 130–34
child sacrifice, 111–12
Christianity, importance to, of Jesus' sexuality and procreative capacity, 173
chthonic myth, 5
civilization, source of, 60
combat, in creation myths, 5
Contendings of Horus and Seth, The, 24
cosmogamy, 13
covenant, androcentric, 108–9
creation myths
  Egyptian, 17–18, 22–23
  Sumerian, 4–7
creator, becoming binary, 4–6

Dalley, Stephanie, 32–33
DAM.DINGIR priestesses, 11
Daniel, as son of man, 133–34
daughter of man, 1, 131, 142
Daughter of Man, 86–87, 89
daughters, significant mythological role of, 22n90
daughters of Eve, 104
daughters of men, 82, 83, 86, 103, 104
  connected to Eve, 84–85
  goodness of, 97
Day of Atonement ritual, linked with Son of Man mythology, 166
death
  linked to fertility, 17
  Sumerian vexation with, 16
  Ugaritic focus on, 16–17
defloration, 8, 9
De Gigantibus (Philo), 139
deities
  relations with humans, 4–5
  vanquishing chaos, 5
deity, naming to, by a human, 108
Delaney, Carol, 142
demons, creation of, 6
desire, 84
Destruction of Humanity, The, 22–23
discipleship, 28, 156
Divine Birth Cycle, 19–20
divine-human boundaries
  gendered blurring of, 7

crossing, for sexual purposes, 11–12. See also *Inanna and Sukaletuda*
divine/human sexual relations, in Greek mythology, 38–39
divinity, gendering of, 17–18

eating, as sexual metaphor, 52–53
Egypt
  cosmogonies of, gender ambiguity in, 17–18
  creation stories in, 22
  divine-human sexual relations in mythic literature of, 19
  goddesses in, distinct from human women, 21–22
  ideology of the soul in, 21
  pantheon of, 18
  royal propaganda myths in, 19–20
Eilberg-Schwartz, Howard, 173
EN, office of, in Ur III dynasty, 11–12
Enhueduana, 11–12
Enkidu
  blessing Shamhat, 32–33
  cursing Shamhat for gift of sexual awareness, 31–32
  death of, 33
  encounter with Shamhat, compared with Gilgamesh-Shiduri encounter, 35–38
  Shamhat's taming of, 26–30
Enki and Ninhursaga, 5, 9
Enlil and Ninlil, 9
"Enlil and the Pickaxe," 44
Enoch, birth of, significance of, 93
Enoch literature, 86. See also *1 Enoch*
Epic of Gilgamesh, 4, 7, 14, 24–38, 105
  compared with Genesis, 60–62
  connecting themes of wisdom, sexuality, and death, 25, 27–28, 31, 37
  emphasizing love and sex as ways to knowledge, 267
  homoerotic encounters in, 24–25
  influence of, 23
  literary development of, 26
  parallels in, to Pandora's adornment scene, 44–45

sex and love in, 9
Son of Man and, 167–68
Erichthonius, 47
eucharistic language, 29
Eve (the woman). *See also* woman, the
  agent separating humans from gods, 78
  as mother of all living, 49, 51, 62, 79–80
  bringing shame and guilt, 58
  close association of, with Yhwh, 109–10
  connected to sons of God and daughters of men, 84
  created as Adam's twin, 77–78
  direct discourse with the serpent and Yhwh, 64–66, 68–69
  gaining sexual awareness, 84
  Manoah's wife's connection to, 121, 128
  mortality of, 63
  Paul's association of, with demonic angels and lawgiving, 138
  receiving knowledge of the prohibition from Adam, 66–67
  relationship to myth and theology of other cultures, 75
  relationship to the Tree of Life, 70
  symmetry of, with Pandora, 77
Exodus, book of, 9
Ezekiel
  Jesus compared to, 164–65
  as son of man, 131, 133

Fable, in Lincoln's taxonomy, 2
fallen angels, 1
false hope, 43
1 *Enoch*, 82–83, 97, 134
Fitzmyer, Joseph A., 86–87
flood, 81–82
  ancient narratives of, 102
  cause of, 91, 100, 127, 139
  linked with Lot's daughters, 163
  reasons for, 127
  related to evil's origin, 103–4
  story of
Foster, Benjamin, 26, 28, 30, 32–33
fruit, as sexual metaphor, 52–53

Gabriel, significance of, in Jesus' birth narrative, 151, 155
gardens, as sexual metaphor, 53
garments, significance of, in creation stories, 58
gazing, 37
gender
  defining, in honor/shame complex, 142–43
  divine-human boundaries and, 1–2
  human struggle between, 10
Genesis
  compared with Epic of Gilgamesh, 49, 55–58, 60–62
  dissociating the woman's role, 75
  Pandora myth and, 49, 75–80
  second creation story in, 49, 50–51, 58–60
  synchronic approach to, 64
George, A.R., 32
gibborim, Samson's similarity to, 127–28
Gilgamesh, 5
  divine/human ratio of, 14n53
  encounter of, with Shiduri, 35–38
  on Enkidu's death, 33–35, 37
goddesses, offspring of, from human fathers, 15
gods
  creation of, 12
  fatherhood of, 11
  sexual reproductive behavior of, 6
Greek mythology
  divine/human sexual relations in, 38–39
  misogyny in, 39
  preserving distance between gods and mortals, 38–39
  as bisexual polytheistic system, 38

Hagar, 135–36, 150
  status of, 108
  theophany of, 107, 108
  Yhwh's contract with, 106–8
handmaid, status of, 107
Harrison, Jane, 45

191

Fallen Angels and Fallen Women

Hatshepsut, recasting earlier birth narratives, 19–21
Haupt, P., 73
Heliopolian myth cycle, 17–18
Herodotus, 12
Hesiod, 39–44, 45, 78
hierogamy, 13
History, in Lincoln's taxonomy, 2
Holy Spirit, role of, in conception of the promised son, 154
Homer, 46
honor/shame code, 139, 142–43
hope, 43
human-divine intercourse, sanctioned, 106
humans
  immortality of, 6
  involvement of, in sexual life of the gods, 2
  mimicking godlike sexuality, 6
  minor role of, in creation myths, 7
  no interactions with gods, in Ugarit myths, 15–16
  struggle between genders, 10

Iliad (Homer), 46
immortality
  diminishment of, 6, 47, 49, 84
  loss of, associated with sexuality and female sexual awareness, 6, 17, 23, 43, 62, 92
  promise of, 2
Inanna/Ishtar, 10, 32, 34
Inanna's Descent to the Netherworld, 4, 44
Inanna and Sukaletuda, 7–10, 14, 22
infancy narrative, in Mark's Gospel, 158–59
infertility, death equated with, 17
intermarriage, to foreign women, 109
Ishtar's Descent to the Netherworld, 44
Israel, angelic mythology of, 23

Jay, Nancy, 108
Jesus
  baptism of, 161
  as binder of angels, 161, 166
  birth of, 141, 144–45
  combining roles of New Serpent and New Adam, 172–73
  compared to God's avenging angel, 161
  compared to Noah, 163
  compared to Samson, 130, 164
  destined for sacrifice, 166
  distinguished from descendants of fallen angels, 60
  Ezekiel compared to, 164–65
  female followers of, virginal status of, 156–57
  future female followers of, new paradigm for, 172
  miracle stories of, 159
  status of, as divine son, 158
  taking scapegoat ritual to logical conclusion, 165–66
  virginal conception of, 151–54
Jewish War (Josephus), 147–48
John the Baptist, 168–69
Josephus, 133, 147–48
Jubilees, 86, 89–90, 93–94, 138
  angelic beings in, moral stance of, 101
  focus in, on shame, 96
  purpose of, 109
  sons of God in, descent of, 95
  women's significance in, 94
Judaism, pre-Christian, nonmonotheistic, 158

ka, 21
Kahl, Brigitte, 110
Kirta epic, 16
knowledge of good and evil, as sexual euphemism, 52–54
Kramer, Samuel Noah, 8–9

Leach, Edmund, 1n1
Legend, in Lincoln's taxonomy, 2
Leick, Gwendolyn, 3
Levenson, Jon, 111–12, 114, 115, 123, 129, 135–36, 157, 166
Life of Adam and Eve, 76
Lincoln, Bruce, 2–3
Lot, 132–33
Lugalbanda, 5, 13–14

Lugalbanda and Enmerkar, 13
Lugalbanda in Hurrumkura, 13

maid-servant, significance of term, 107
Manoah, wife of, 111, 119–22, 123, 125–27, 128
marriage, in creation myths, 5
Mary (mother of Jesus), 107–8
  asceticism of, 147
  dissociated from sexually active mythological ancestors, 155
  final mythological daughter of man, 142
  foreshadowing Jesus' life and death, 155
  in Luke's Gospel, 143, 148–58
  in Matthew's Gospel, 143–45
  not receiving wisdom, 152
  pregnancy of, 145
  role of, in the unfolding revelation, 152–53
  silence after Jesus' birth, in Luke's account, 156
  social-science view of, 147
  virgin status of, 146–47
Mary Magdalene, as the new Eve, 173
MEs, in Sumerian myth, 7n24, 10
Milgrom, Jacob, 52, 72
monotheistic religions, creation in, 152
mortality. *See also* immortality
  linked with evil, 43
  theme of, in Genesis, 83
Myth, in Lincoln's taxonomy, 2–3
myths
  defining, 2–3
  origin. *See* creation myths
  sexual aspects of, 2

naming, act of, 108
Neils, Jenifer, 40, 43
Noah
  birth of, 98–99
  connected to Adam, 94
  Jesus compared to, 163
  paternity of, 87–90, 99–102, 128, 129
  salvific qualities of, 104–5
  significance of name, 104
  as son of man, 103, 104
Noahic covenant, 129

Osiris
  incorporation into, 18–19, 21
  transformation into, 23
overshadowing, as type of salvific activity, 154

painful birth curse, 158
Pandora, 98
  agent separating humans from gods, 78
  as antithesis of wisdom, 76
  creation of, 76–77
  garments of, 79–80
  as a maiden, 77
  symmetry of, with Eve, 77
Pandora myth, 39–44
  connected to Erichthonius, 47
  and Genesis, 75–76
  connected to wisdom and knowledge, 45–46
  similar to Sumerian myths, 44–46
paronomasia, 132
paternity, Jewish conception of, disrupted, 157
Paul
  angelology of, 136–41
  writings of, developing the son of man motif, 134–41
Pausanias, 47
Penglase, Charles, 44, 45
Philo, 76, 80, 81, 135, 138–39
Pongratz-Leisten, Beate, 13
power, legitimization of, 20
primogeniture, law of, 112–13
Prodigal Son, parable of, 162
promised son
  birth of, concept transformed, 146
  and evidence of God's favor, 129–30
  substitution ritual for, 129
Pseudo-Philo, 81

Quaestiones et Solutiones in Genesin (Philo), 139

193

Quod Deus immutabilis sit (Philo), 139

Rahab, 131–33
rape, 119–20, 148
Ras Shamra, texts of, 15n56
Rashi, 110
rebirth, 18–19
righteous remnant, 104–5
rulers, human, holding divine titles, 20

sacred marriage, 10, 12–13
sacrifice, 111–13, 123, 129
salvation, 141, 170–72
Samson
    bridging birth narrative genre and son of man ideology, 117–19, 123–30
    linking Noah and Jesus, 130
    named by woman, 125
    parallels of, with Jesus, 130, 164
    paternity of, 128–29
    similarity of, to the *gibborim*, 127–28
Sawicki, Marianne, 147
scapegoat ritual, 166–67
Sepphoris, 147–48
serpent
    discourse with Eve, 66, 68–69
    discourse with Yhwh, 66, 68–69
    having the power of speech, 71
    referring to the deity, 72
    supernatural knowledge of, 72
    using Yhwh's words, 67–69, 71–72
    wisdom of, 71
    Shiduri associated with, 73–74
sex
    as aspect of myths, 2
    productive and nonproductive, 6, 9
    unproductive, 6, 9, 26
sexual awakening, 84
    sin of, Noah attempting to mitigate, 94
    wisdom and life linked with, 74
    women's procreative ability linked to, 110
sexual congress, related to godlike states, 56–57
sexual intercourse, 1

sexuality
    human, value of, 17
    human mortality and, 6, 16–17, 23
    linked with wisdom and death, 52–53
sexual reproduction, focus of Sumerian creation myths, 4
shame, 8. *See also* honor/shame code
    preceding experience of sexuality, 95–96
Shamhat, 24–37
    agency of, 27, 28–30
    bringing enlightenment, 58
    defended after Enkidu's curse, 31–32
    offered divine status, 33
    significance of name, 25
    as wisdom figure, 30, 33
Shiduri, 34–38
    associated with serpents, 73–74
    as goddess, 73
Simkins, Ronald, 139
son of God, 141
Son of God, Jesus acknowledged as, 160
son of man
    characteristics of, 102–3, 105–6
    Daniel as, 133–34
    development of title, underlying structure of, 130
    exaltation and sacrifice of, 111
    Ezekiel as, 131, 133
    ideology of, linked with birth narrative genre, 117–19
    in John's Gospel, 169–73
    in Luke's Gospel, 161–62
    linguistic significance of, 131
    in Mark's Gospel, 158–61
    Noah as, 128
    ongoing relationship of, with Yhwh, 113
    in Pauline writings, 134–41
    representing a particular function, 131
    salvific role of, 134
    Samson as, 128
Son of Man
    coming of, 146

criteria for, 157
death of, expected, 164
development of concept, 130, 136–37
and the Epic of Gilgamesh, 167–68
eschatology and, 163
expected death of, 164
in Mark's Gospel, evolution of term, 161
mythology of, and the birth narrative, 114
physical characteristics of, 103
requirements for, 117
sons of Elohim, 158
sons of God, 88, 98
  actions of, linked to Eve, 83–84
  descent of, 95
  interpretation of phrase, 80–82
  role of, similar to the woman/Eve's, 84
  sexual aggression of, 132
sons of heaven, 97–98
sons of men, wine and, 130
Sophia, 29
soul, Egyptian ideology of, 21
Stuckenbruck, Loren T., 101, 139n73
Sumer
  creation myths in, 4–7
  erotic elements in myths of, 3
  literary mythologies of, 2
  myth of Pandora and, 44–46
  pantheon of, 11–12
  stories of, corresponding to history, 3
  women's temple/palace role in, 33
  writings of 3–4, 14, 15, 44–46

Targumim, 81
theodicy, 82–83, 166
theogamy, 13
Theogony (Hesiod), 39, 41–46, 78, 79, 80
time, resulting from reproductive act, 5–6
transversal, 5
Tree of Life, 63–64
  eating from, 69–72

Tree of the Knowledge of Good and Evil
  location of, 63–64
  relation of, to Adam and Eve's mortality, 63. *See also* immortality
  significance of, 51–52

Ugarit
  cosmogonies of, 15
  myths of, 15–16
  pantheon of, 15, 16
Ur III dynasty, 11
Utnapishtim, 35, 99, 102, 105

van Seters, John, 19
Varus, 147–48
Veenker, Ronald A., 72
veiling, linked with procreation, 139–40
Vespasian, 148

Watchers, 87, 88, 98
  descent of, 93
  myth of, 82
  polluting the daughters of men, 89
  tradition of, Philo's knowledge of, 139
wilderness themes, 168
wine, associated with sons of men, 130
wisdom
  attainment of, 2
  connected to human sexuality and mortality, 23, 31
Wisdom, 29
Woman, as title, 55
woman, first, primeval story of, 78
woman, the. *See also* Eve
  choosing wisdom over immortality, 70
  combining Shamhat and Shiduri, 74
  mythological antecedents of, 74
  referring to the deity, 72
womb
  imagery of, in myth of Pandora, 41, 43, 45–46
  opened to Yhwh, 111

women
- associated with creation, 152
- bodies of, male authority over, 143
- in Matthew's genealogy, 144
- procreative ability of, linked to sexual awakening, 110
- reputation of, dependent upon the patriarch, 143
- sexuality of, linked with lack of morality, 104
- sexual/procreative roles of, and the honor/shame complex, 142–43
- significance of, in *Jubilees*, 94
- theological status of, raising, 107
- veiling of, linked with procreation, 139–40

Works and Days (Hesiod), 39–43, 44, 46

Yhwh
- messengers of, linked with the sons of God, 108
- wombs opened to, 111

www.ingramcontent.com/pod-product-compliance
Lightning Source LLC
Chambersburg PA
CBHW062038220426
43662CB00010B/1549